SURVIVING RACE, ETHNICITY, AND NATIONALITY
(2005)

SURVIVING RACE, ETHNICITY, AND NATIONALITY

A Challenge for the Twenty-first Century

JORGE J. E. GRACIA

ROWMAN & LITTLEFIELD PUBLISHERS, INC.
Lanham • Boulder • New York • Toronto • Oxford

ROWMAN & LITTLEFIELD PUBLISHERS, INC.

Published in the United States of America
by Rowman & Littlefield Publishers, Inc.
A wholly owned subsidiary of The Rowman & Littlefield Publishing Group, Inc.
4501 Forbes Boulevard, Suite 200, Lanham, Maryland 20706
www.rowmanlittlefield.com

PO Box 317, Oxford, OX2 9RU, UK

British Library Cataloguing in Publication Information Available

Library of Congress Cataloging-in-Publication Data
Gracia, Jorge J. E.
  Surviving race, ethnicity, and nationality : a challenge for the twenty-first century / Jorge J. E. Gracia.
      p. cm.
  Includes bibliographical references and indexes.
  ISBN 0-7425-5016-8 (cloth : alk. paper)—ISBN 0-7425-5017-6 (pbk. : alk. paper)
  1. Philosophy and social sciences. 2. Sociology. 3. Racism—Philosophy 4. Ethnicity—Philosophy. 5. Citizenship—Philosophy. I. Title.

  B63.G73 2005
  305.8'001—dc22   2005012199

Printed in the United States of America

∞™ The paper used in this publication meets the minimum requirements of
American National Standard for Information Sciences—Permanence of Paper for
Printed Library Materials, ANSI/NISO Z39.48-1992.

For Sofia Grace and Eva Lucia

[T]here are four or five species or races of men in particular whose difference is so remarkable that it may be properly made use of as the foundation for a new division of the earth.

—François Bernier

There are no races. There are only a number of variations in man, in the details of habits and customs . . . which do not change that which is identical and essential. . . .

—José Martí

It is by uttering the same cry, pronouncing the same word, or performing the same gesture . . . that [persons] become and feel themselves in unison.

—Émile Durkheim

[E]thnic trash always becomes fanatical standard bearers of counter revolution. . . .

—Friedrich Engels

[A citizen] lives only for his fatherland. . . . [T]he moment he has no fatherland, he is no more.

—Jean-Jacques Rousseau

[P]atriotism, founded upon a common national history and land occupation, becomes . . . a veritable stumbling-block and impediment.

—Jane Addams

CONTENTS

PREFACE

R ace, ethnicity, and nationality pose one of the greatest challenges to the survival of humankind in the twenty-first century, for they touch the very core of the social fabric, personal identity, and individuality; they influence how we think of others and ourselves; they play a role in our morality and political behavior; and they affect our everyday existence in significant ways. Indeed, they seem to affect most things we do and think, from the most mundane ways in which we behave to the most dear beliefs we hold about ourselves and others. As Linda Alcoff has so aptly noted about race in particular, "race, or racialised identities, have as much political, sociological and economic salience as they ever had" (Alcoff 1999, 31).

Race, ethnicity, and nationality have been, and still are, the sources of satisfying pride and enduring joys. Who is not proud of the achievements of members of his or her own race, ethnic group, or nation? Who fails to find satisfaction and pleasure in a history shared, the experiences of the community, and the beliefs that tie us together? But they are also sources of horrendous crimes and injustice. Human history is filled with examples of heinous racial, ethnic, and national abuses. Attempts have been repeatedly made to annihilate entire groups of people because of their race, ethnicity, or nationality. Genocide is a commonplace in the human story, and the growth of civilization and technological advancement do not seem to make a difference, as the twentieth century so well illustrates. When it comes to racism, ethnicism, and nationalism, the only difference between peoples seems to be the effectiveness with which they have been able to dominate, oppress, or even wipe out entire populations. At bottom, there is not much difference between Germany and Nigeria, Yugoslavia and Indonesia, Northern Ireland and Iraq, Cambodia and ancient Rome, or Spain and Brazil. Indeed, the methods of extermination and abuse become more efficient and sophisticated with so-called progress, and the process of globalization, instead of stopping these abuses, seems to be contributing to their effective implementation.

Racial, ethnic, and national conflicts are ubiquitous today. One need only pick up the newspaper to see evidence of this in every continent. Consider the situation in the former Yugoslavia, in which for a while there appeared to be no end to bloodshed between Croats, Bosnians, Serbs, and Kosovo Albanians. In southern Mexico, the remnants of the Maya are engaged in a struggle for survival against the general mestizo, dominant population; in Africa, the confrontations between Tutsi and Hutu reveal the degree to which group resentment can lead to genocide and attempts to eliminate entire segments of a population; in Asia, there is endemic strife between Hindus and Muslims, and Tamils and Sinhalese; and in the Middle East, there have been violent clashes between Arab Iraqis and Persian Iranians, and the struggle between Israelis and Palestinians seems to defy solution. Some of the most recent and repulsive cases of group conflict that have shaken the world community occurred in East Timor, Pakistan, and India. In the first, a dominant group, backed by the power of the government, proceeded to vandalize and terrorize an entire population. In Pakistan, Muslim zealots slaughtered a community of Christians while they worshiped in a church. And in India, a mob of Muslims set on fire a train crowded with Hindus, including women and children, and this in turn set off a Hindu reaction that left dead close to one thousand Muslims. Some of these conflicts involve religion, but religion is often integral to ethnicity and nationality, and ethnicity and nationality are themselves, as Anthony Smith has pointed out, frequently mixed (Smith 1991, 6).[1]

The mentioned conflicts have been violent, and they have occurred mainly in underdeveloped and undemocratic regimes, but there are also lower levels of group conflict or potential conflict in developed and democratic nations.[2] When European democracies and the United States consider the massacres that have happened elsewhere in the world, they often congratulate themselves for the relative peace in which they currently live. Yet there have been violent confrontations with, and abuses committed against, certain groups of people in these parts of the world, and there is the potential for even greater social disruption. Do we have to remind ourselves of the long list of abuses "Blacks" have suffered in the United States, and of the discrimination against them that continues to play a role in segments of American society to this day?[3] Do we need to remind ourselves of the race riots, not so distant in the past, the burnings of "Black" churches in the South, and the continued economic deprivation of "Blacks," Puerto Ricans, and Native Americans? Some of these perhaps cannot be classified as conflicts strictly speaking, but they certainly qualify as oppression, abuse, and injustice. Consider the imprisonment of American citizens of Japanese ancestry during World War II. And what do we make of the recent ethnic and racial confrontations in England, France, Germany, and other Western European democracies?

Abuse and oppression based on race have been particularly pernicious insofar as they are connected to slavery and all the foul consequences of that most inhuman institution. Whereas ethnic groups and nations have been oppressed and dominated, and sometimes even exterminated, they have seldom been regarded as nonhuman. But some races have denied humanity to other races. Posing the very question of whether certain races are human, holding discussions about it, and offering arguments for and against contrary positions is in some ways so preposterous that it shakes the very foundations of one's faith in human rationality. Consider the notorious disputation between Juan Ginés de Sepúlveda and Bartolomé de Las Casas in Seville in 1550, in which the latter had to answer the former's charges against the very humanity of Amerindians (Las Casas 1992).[4]

Perhaps even more pernicious than open conflict and discrimination is neglect. Often, the problem faced by racial and ethnic groups is not that they are engaged in open conflict with other groups or are subject to clear oppression, abuse, and discrimination at the hands of those groups, but rather that they are ignored, treated as nonexistent entities whose legitimate complaints do not merit attention. As a consequence, their needs are not met by the societies of which they are part and they remain at a disadvantage. The invisibility of "Blacks," Hispanics, and Native Americans in some dimensions of the social life in the United States and elsewhere, for example, has been well documented by Robert Bernasconi, Frantz Fanon, and others (Bernasconi 2001a; Fanon 2001, 284–99, 184–201; Gracia 2000b, 159–88).

But, of course, matters are even more confused and worse when one keeps in mind that the lines between race and ethnicity have never been clearly drawn. Indeed, Jews have routinely been regarded as a race by certain groups, such as the Nazis, and Hispanics are frequently classified as "non-White" by bureaucrats, institutions, the media, and even academics in many parts of the world (see Stepan 1982, 41–43; Banton 1977, 63–88; 1987b, 56–59). Even to this day, some scientists speak of Jews or subgroups of Jews (Sephardic, Ashkenazi, Cichin, and Ethiopian) as micro races (see Garn 1993, 852). And Leopold Senghor openly defended an ethnic conception of "negritude" (Senghor 1961, 1211). Racial and ethnic abuse and discrimination cannot be easily isolated, and authors as diverse as Alain Locke, W. E. B. Du Bois, and Linda Alcoff have argued for a racial understanding of ethnicity or an ethnic understanding of race (Locke 1924; Senghor 2001; Du Bois 1897; Alcoff 2000a; see also sources cited in notes to the section "Blurring the Distinctions between Race, Ethnicity, and Nationality," chapter 2).

With respect to nations and their conflicts, very little needs to be said. The history of humanity seems to be an endless series of violent acts perpetrated by some nations against others. Wars are frequent, and tyrants with imperialistic ambitions are, to this day, glorified even in countries that pride themselves on their humanity. A brief visit to *Les Invalides* in Paris proves the point. How can we explain that France, a self-proclaimed civilized nation, has erected such a shrine to someone whose legacy was unequivocally one of imperialism, destruction, and death?

The lines between racial, ethnic, and national conflicts are not sharp. Often, national confrontations amount to racial or ethnic ones. When nations become identified with ethnic groups, then national struggles become ethnic, or vice versa. And the same occurs with races (Hudson 1996; Du Bois 1897). The internment of Japanese Americans in the United States during World War II can only be explained based on the confusion between nationality on the one hand and ethnicity or race on the other, for although some of the Japanese Americans in question were born in the United States and others had become American citizens, nonetheless they all were treated as foreign nationals because they shared with the Japanese their ethnicity and race. History, even recent history, is full of similar occurrences.

Moreover, there is a personal dimension to these issues. The confusions that surround the concepts of race, ethnicity, and nationality extend to the way individual persons think of themselves. Conflicting positions are evident quite often. Consider a person who has all the external marks of a "Black" and yet denies he is one, thinking himself rather as a Latino. Is there a conflict between being "Black" and being Latino? Are these categories of the same sort? And, for that matter, is there a conflict in being Latino and Puerto Rican, or Hispanic and Jewish when Jewish is not taken as a religious designation? Some think so, whereas others disagree, although most of the time these agreements and disagreements are based on gut feelings or folk psychology rather than well-developed views of race and ethnicity. Consider also the Oreo phenomenon. Some "Blacks" think of other "Blacks" as Oreos, by which they mean that they are "Black" on the outside but "White" on the inside. And what does this mean but that they are "Black" in appearance but "White" in the way they think and behave?

What does it entail for the conception of race and ethnicity? These confusions exacerbate the social conflicts that arise from racial, ethnic, and national denominations.

Unfortunately, the future does not bring a promise of better times and looks quite bleak.[5] Still, we need to do what we can to survive, and if we are going to do so at all, or at least to live together with a modicum of harmony, peace, and comfort, it is clear that we must attempt to understand and come to terms with race, ethnicity, and nationality. In order to prevent the conflicts and help ameliorate the injustices and oppression to which these social phenomena seem to give rise, we must find ways to deal with them effectively. This is the challenge that race, ethnicity, and nationality pose for us in the twenty-first century. But this requires in turn that we understand them clearly; we need to develop adequate theoretical conceptions of race, ethnicity, and nationality, and of their relations, if we are ever going to solve the practical problems they pose in the world today.

Some scientists, humanists, and social activists of various sorts have grasped this with clarity, but all too frequently they have come up merely with tired platitudes about the need to become blind to racial, ethnic, and national distinctions. Others have tried to address these issues by claiming that race, ethnicity, and nationality are mere human inventions created by interested segments of humankind for purposes of survival or exploitation. Alarmed by the use of these notions for the justification of countless crimes and abuses, and armed with recent scientific research particularly in the case of race, they have argued not just that these notions are fictions, but also that they are incoherent and must be abandoned altogether.[6]

Prima facie, these approaches appear to have considerable sense and value, but they often make some of the same conceptual mistakes that give rise to the positions they oppose. Because of this, they can turn out to be not only counterproductive, but also downright dangerous. Rejection requires understanding, so understanding race, ethnicity, and nationality is a required first step toward the solution to the problems for which they are thought to be responsible. Besides, the case against these continues to be opposed by others. Some still argue that there is something to the reality of race, ethnicity, and nationality, and many, although agreeing that these concepts do not refer to realities in the world, point out that merely rejecting them will not eliminate their palpable consequences.[7]

But, we may ask, from which perspective should we try to approach them? All too frequently, the way of doing it has been disciplinary. Considering their social and political implications, it is anthropologists, sociologists, and political scientists in particular who have paid attention to them, although we also find studies developed from the perspective of linguistics, biology, archaeology, history, geography, cultural studies, literary criticism, and psychology, among others.[8] Yet many of these studies suffer from the same malady. They are undertaken from disciplinary perspectives that are by themselves too narrow for the appreciation of the depth and breadth of the issues involved. Each discipline looks at human experience from a certain angle, applies to it a certain methodology, and uses a specialized vocabulary (cf. Cavalli-Sforza et al. 1994, x). To be sure, both the angle and the methodology help bring out aspects that otherwise might not be noticed, but at the same time they exclude something else: for the psychologist, it is phenomena that cannot be effectively translated into psychological categories; for the sociologist, facts that do not have an immediate expression in social reality; for the literary critic, experiences that have not been documented in literature; and so on.

The weakness of the exclusively disciplinary approach has not been overlooked. Indeed, the call for interdisciplinary vantage points is heard frequently these days. We are told that in the understanding of race, ethnicity, and nationality, we need to take into account observations from many different disciplines because the phenomena under investigation have different and multifaceted dimensions and affect more than one aspect of human experience (for race in particular, see Cavalli-Sforza et al. 1994, ix, 372–73). Indeed, David Mason has noted that, in the United States especially, there has been a concerted effort to use an interdisciplinary approach (Mason 1999, 13).

Combinations of two or more disciplines have been attempted, giving rise sometimes to entire new subdisciplines (e.g., social psychology) and sometimes to entire new fields (e.g., American, ethnic, cultural, and racial studies). All these new branches of learning have the same aim: to make up for the shortcomings of the insularity of particular disciplines. Nonetheless, often these interdisciplinary approaches end up being either disciplinary, unrigorous, or both. In some cases, one of the disciplines that enters into the mix dominates those that are supposed to be its partners. At other times, the result lacks proper unity and method and yields no more than personal and subjective musings disguised as serious research. Indeed, many publications about race and ethnicity in particular are in the form of autobiographical testimonies and personal anecdotes. Obviously, these have an important function in the discourse on these topics, for they dramatize a situation that otherwise might appear abstract and removed. However, the theoretical contribution of these narratives is limited. More than this needs to be done to make sense of race, ethnicity, and nationality. Recording abuses is one thing; understanding the causes of the abuses and providing a conceptual framework that could be used to mount preventive measures is another.

Clearly, a holistic approach is desirable, but this approach cannot be just a disorderly mixture of diverse approaches. And even if it were, there would still be important questions and problems, perhaps the most important ones, that would fall outside the disciplines that have been most often used, particularly scientific ones. To recall a well-known statement of Wittgenstein: "We feel that even if *all possible* scientific questions be answered, the problems of life have still not been touched at all" (Wittgenstein 1981, sec. 6.52; 187). That science is not enough should be obvious insofar as it aims to describe rather than prescribe, and when it comes to race, ethnicity, and nationality, we need more than mere description; we need guidance for our actions. As Weber put it, "it can never be the task of an empirical science to provide binding norms and ideals from which directives for immediate practical activity can be derived" (Weber 1969, 52). So where can we turn to attempt the laborious and difficult task of understanding race, ethnicity, and nationality?

Some may feel satisfied with the spiritual guidance provided by religion. And, indeed, religion supplies something important not available in science, namely, principles of action. However, religion is no solution to the problem for at least three reasons. First, the record of religion is very poor when it comes to group conflict. Just consider the abuses that Muslims, Hindus, Buddhists, and Christians of almost every denomination, to name just some of the main world religions, have perpetrated against each other. If the record of these major religions is so dismal, there is little hope that others will be any better on this account. Second, religion is frequently tied to nationality and ethnicity. Hispanics are predominantly Roman Catholic, and certain nations are officially linked to particular religions. Consider that a former president of Argentina, while in office, described the nation as "Christian, European, and White." And in most predominantly Muslim countries, Islam is regarded as essentially tied to the state. Religion cannot, then, be taken as a neutral ground on which to base an understanding of race, ethnicity, and nationality. Finally, religion is fundamentally a matter of belief, not rational understanding, even if some religions make room for rational understanding. This means that a reasoned response to the issues raised by race, ethnicity, and nationality cannot be based on religious principles, even if some religions propose principles that are indeed reasonable and in accordance with reason. So where can we turn?

One possibility is philosophy. Unlike other disciplines, which are narrower in scope and have developed specialized methodologies, philosophy aims to be comprehensive and lacks a single set of methodological norms. Philosophy tries to produce a comprehensive view that integrates all the knowledge we have, whereas other disciplines attempt to be less inclusive insofar as they are circumscribed by their methodological boundaries and limited subject matter. Another difference between philosophy and other disciplines is that philosophy raises certain questions that are outside the province of all other disciplines. And still a third is that philosophy functions as a watchdog of other branches of human learning. All three differences give philosophy an advantage in the inquiry with which we are concerned here.

Philosophy is essentially interdisciplinary insofar as its task consists of putting together as complete a picture of the world as possible, based on our overall experience of it, and lacks a specific methodology. Although not all philosophers have thought so, philosophy's history vouches for its breadth. Philosophy is comprehensive in a way no other discipline is. Psychology looks at the mind, sociology at social phenomena, mathematics at numbers, physics at the physical world, anatomy at the body, botany at plants, astronomy at the heavenly bodies, literary criticism at literature, and so on. But philosophy tries to integrate the conclusions of all these into an overall conceptual framework that makes sense, is faithful to our experience, has support in sound arguments and evidence, and satisfies our various needs.

Moreover, some branches of philosophy—such as metaphysics, epistemology, logic, ethics, and politics—provide analyses not available in any other discipline, even though these analyses are essential for developing human knowledge and carrying out human action. In metaphysics, philosophy is able to relate the categories studied in more specific sciences to the most general categories about which humans can think. Epistemology establishes the conditions of knowledge and scrutinizes the adequacy of procedures to acquire it. Logic develops and monitors criteria of valid and adequate reasoning and is, therefore, at the heart of any disciplinary enterprise. And ethics and politics analyze the requirements of a sound individual and state morality and, therefore, supply the prescriptions for human action missing in other humanities, in science, and in the arts.

Finally, philosophy functions as a critic of other disciplines, imposing on them the requirement that they meet the most general criteria of understanding. This is a task resulting from both its comprehensive reach and the areas of inquiry that are uniquely philosophical. By addressing issues that have to do with the overall requirements of understanding and the very foundations of knowledge, philosophy stands guard over other disciplines.

And philosophy not only sits in judgment over them, but also relates their claims and methods, seeking to integrate all we know into a coherent conceptual schema.

In spite of the advantages that philosophy would seem to bring to the study of race, ethnicity, and nationality, however, there has been some resistance both by philosophers and nonphilosophers to make room for it in their discussions of these topics. Some of it is active hostility, and some merely neglect. Within philosophy, we find both among members of the two main philosophical traditions of the past one hundred years—the so-called Continental and Analytic. Analysts often reject or disparage the philosophical investigation of race and ethnicity, in particular because they find most of the existing treatments of these topics to be ideological, confused, or "soft" for their tastes. In some cases, they dismiss them as mere political propaganda or unintelligible gibberish, concluding that race and ethnicity are the province of science, not philosophy.

The case with Continental philosophers is somewhat different, for in principle one would expect them to be sympathetic to these topics insofar as these authors make a point of their strong interest in the social realm. Nonetheless, some of them have tended to neglect these topics until very recently, although the source of their attitude is not, like that of analysts, generally based on objections to the approach that has been used to deal with them, but rather is to be found in their own methodology. It is part of most Continental philosophers' method to proceed through the analysis of past philosophical texts, but texts concerned with race and ethnicity in particular are relatively scarce in the history of philosophy. Moreover, most of the comparatively few available turn out to be rather embarrassing. If we consider what past philosophers have said about all three of the notions that concern us, we find that they often reveal very limited and distorted understandings of them, and often contain statements that are not just factually wrong but also clearly dictated by bias. Consider the following text from Hegel, who by all accounts is one of the great philosophers of all times and is particularly revered by members of the Continental tradition:

> Negroes are to be regarded as a race of children who remain immersed in their state of uninterested *naïveté*. . . . [T]hey do not show any inherent striving for culture. . . . [T]hey do not attain to the feeling of human personality, their mentality is quite dormant, remaining sunk within itself and making no progress. . . . [By contrast,] in Europe . . . there prevails this infinite thirst for knowledge which is alien to other races. (Hegel 2000, 40–43)

This and similar passages, which are not hard to find in Hegel's writings, were written at the beginning of the nineteenth century and the end of the so-called Age of Enlightenment. One cannot but wonder, if this was light, what was obscurity at the time? Although there is plenty that can be praised about this age, there seems to have been little clarity about race and ethnicity in particular in it.

But it is not some of the heroes of the Continental tradition alone who show this obtuseness. Consider the outrageous statements by Hume, generally thought to be one of the greatest of all British philosophers:

> I am apt to suspect the negroes to be naturally inferior to the whites. There scarcely ever was a civilized nation of that complexion, nor even any individual eminent either in action or speculation. No ingenious manufacturers amongst them, no arts, no sciences. On the other hand, the most rude and barbarous of the whites, such as the ancient GERMANS, the present TARTARS, have still something eminent about them. . . . Such a uniform and constant difference could not happen, in so many countries and ages, if nature had not made an original distinction between these breeds of men. (Hume 1987, n208)

Some may want to claim that charity demands that we make excuses for Hegel and Hume when it comes to race in particular. After all, these statements were made a couple of hundred years ago, at a time when awareness of race was very limited. But this will not do; time does not rescue philosophy from the charge of stupidity. Recall that the mighty Heidegger, one of our contemporaries and regarded today as a philosophical Olympian by a large segment of the philosophical community not only in Europe and the United States, but also in non-Western countries such as Japan and Korea, had what can be characterized—even in charitable terms—as a rather ambiguous attitude toward the Nazis. What excuse can be found for him?

A list of outrageous statements about race, ethnicity, and even nationality by famous philosophers is not difficult to compile. The examples are not isolated, and the existence of similar statements is not consigned to certain philosophical traditions. Pronouncements of the sort can be easily found among philosophers respected within every philosophical school. Consider Aristotle, who viewed anyone who was not Greek as a barbarian and slave by nature. Or take a less negative, but still distorted and biased view, such as that of Suárez, who thought that, although "Blacks" are fully human, it is still better to be "White." From the very beginning of philosophy until the present, there seems to have been a steady stream of philosophers whose views about race, ethnicity, and nationality can only be described in the most negative terms. No wonder some current philosophers avoid dealing with these topics!

The objections that nonphilosophers voice against philosophical discussions of these notions are both similar and different from those voiced by some present-day philosophers. Nonphilosophers share with these a general distaste for what past philosophers have said about these topics, but some of them also reject these statements because they think of them as primarily *a priori* and speculative, the result of armchair musings, without any grounding in empirical data. For all their knowledge and claims to the contrary—they claim—most philosophers seem to be oblivious to facts and experience, so why should anyone pay attention to what they say? Moreover, they argue that philosophers notoriously tend to ignore the urgency of social problems. Although a few of them have cried for active social involvement—let's not forget Marx, Mill, and Dewey—most are content to watch events go by, playing the role of detached observers. They usually agree with Hegel's view that the owl of Minerva flies only at dusk. And, finally, philosophy seems to be stuck. Whereas other disciplines show progress, philosophers appear to be concerned with the same set of unresolved old questions; they are the curmudgeons of the intellectual community, hopeless conservatives for whom change is anathema. Why turn to philosophy, then, if what we need is advancement?

The reason is that, in spite of all that has been said, philosophers do have something especial to contribute to the understanding of race, ethnicity, and nationality. Certainly, we should ignore their opinions if they are erroneous or dictated by wrong assumptions, biased principles, or perverse motives. If the views of Hegel and Aristotle are wrong, we should not hesitate to reject them, and to do so openly. But it is not particular philosophers and their opinions and writings that can contribute to the discussion of race, ethnicity, and nationality, but rather the discipline of philosophy itself. This contribution stems from the three differences mentioned earlier that distinguish philosophy from other disciplines: the holistic approach possible in philosophy; the fact that this discipline covers certain areas essential to understanding not covered by any other enterprise of learning; and the critical attitude that philosophy can apply to all human investigations.

Philosophy can "put it all together," as the cliché goes, by taking from other disciplines what they offer, by critically analyzing this information, and by supplementing it with the analyses that it uniquely can provide. Logic can help us to clarify the various conceptual issues raised by the notions of race, ethnicity, and nationality, and to identify hidden assumptions used in discourse about them and judge the validity of the arguments offered for various views; epistemology can aid us in determining the conditions of knowledge and how to acquire it; metaphysics can relate the categories that correspond to these notions to more general categories, thus making clear how they stand with respect to them and to each other; and ethics and politics can provide the framework of a personal and public morality that takes race, ethnicity, and nationality into account and serves to direct human action.

Moreover, if the task of philosophy is to put together the information that other human pursuits and experiences yield, it cannot be convincingly argued that the discipline is oblivious to empirical data. Philosophy begins where other fields of human learning end, but that does not mean that the philosopher forgets the accomplishments of these fields. On the contrary, these accomplishments constitute the very bases of philosophical reflection. Consider recent discussions in the philosophy of mind, for example, where philosophers rely heavily on the empirical research and theories of neurobiologists and other scientists. And the same can be said about the biology of race or the sociology of ethnicity.

The difficulty of finding sensible philosophical texts in the history of philosophy about the topics that concern us here should not stand in the way of this project, either, for contrary to what some think today, philosophy is not just about texts; philosophy is about the world and the human experience of it. The task of philosophers is not merely to comment on what others have said, but also to move beyond these statements in order to formulate new and adequate views. If philosophers who form part of the philosophical canon in the West have not contributed enough to the discussion of race and ethnicity in particular, this should be taken as an opportunity to extend the discipline beyond its present boundaries, rather than as a handicap in the investigation. The need is certainly there, present in our everyday lives. Let philosophers rise to the challenge, unburdened by narrow conceptions of their enterprise as dogmatized within particular philosophical traditions. Of course, I am not advocating that we forget texts, or traditional philosophical problems; rather, I am advocating that we do not become slaves of the past. The only value the study of the past has, other than the satisfaction of mere curiosity, is that it can help us avoid its mistakes.

The response to the difficulty involving progress is that philosophy does not experience this in the same way empirical disciplines do; but this does not mean that there are no advances in philosophy. The progress of philosophy is measured differently precisely because the daunting aim of the discipline is the critical integration of all human knowledge. Philosophy makes progress in at least three important ways. First, it does so by raising new issues. In many ways the history of philosophy can be seen not as the discovery of new facts, but as the formulation of new issues posed by the new conditions in which humans find themselves as a result of historical and scientific developments. Hegel was right when he claimed that self-consciousness reaches its highest level in philosophy. The second way in which philosophy makes progress is by helping us realize the complexity of the issues that humans encounter in the understanding of themselves and their circumstances. The human grasp of new issues and problems begins usually in a simple-minded way, assuming easy solutions and clear boundaries, but with time and reflection this naive picture becomes increasingly complex. Finally, philosophy advances in a third way, by distinguishing the various issues that confront humans with greater clarity and by explaining how they, and their possible solutions, are related.

When philosophy turns to race, ethnicity, and nationality, however, it finds not only a very large and complex set of issues that go beyond the ethical, political, and practical matters to which some reference has already been made, but also a different set of questions that have been ignored altogether or that, if not ignored, have elicited contrary answers that often lead to puzzling dilemmas. Consider, for example, the cluster of problems related to identity: the contested issue whether in fact there are such things as racial, ethnic, and national identities; the question of what these identities consist of, if indeed there are such things; the matter of accounting for these identities throughout time and history; and the question of the relation between them. Racial, ethnic, and national groups seem to endure through time, and yet when one tries to pin down something specific that ensures such endurance, it is difficult, if not impossible, to point to anything.

The task ahead of the philosopher with respect to race, ethnicity, and nationality, then, is not just fraught with difficulties but entails much more than what could be undertaken in a book of this size. Even before the many specific issues that this task entails are addressed, however, one needs to be clear about what race, ethnicity, and nationality are. For this reason, what I do here can be taken only as a beginning of what needs to be done. My aim is to lay down some of the foundations of a philosophical analysis of them. I put a heavy emphasis on clarity because many discussions of these notions, both in philosophy and outside of it, suffer from confusions, sometimes elementary, whose clarification is essential for advance. By clarity I mean the distinction of different, even if related issues, and the precise understanding of key concepts. This entails a variety of procedures: considering ordinary usage, introducing logical distinctions, illustrating pertinent principles with cases and examples, making references to historical events, and so on. This does not entail that I have shied away from substantive claims; it only means that, even if the more substantive theses of the book are found wanting, the clarificatory function of the analyses should nonetheless prove useful. In neither case do I mean for them to be taken as definitive, however. The issues I raise are too complex for anyone to claim to have settled them once and for all times.

To my knowledge, there is no extended and systematic philosophical discussion of race, ethnicity, and nationality by any one author in any one place (from a sociological perspective, however, see the discussions of these notions by Omi and Winant 1994, 9–24, 36–47; Eriksen 1997, 33–35; and Balibar and Wallerstein 1988; and from the point of view of political science, see Guibernau 1996). Moreover, although there are many treatments of race and nationality, relatively less attention has been paid to ethnicity by philosophers. The reasons for this situation are not difficult to surmise, particularly in the United States. American philosophers have given considerable attention to race for at least two reasons: first, because of the egregious abuses that "Blacks" have suffered, and still suffer, because of their race, and in particular those associated with slavery; second, because "Blacks" have constituted the largest minority in the country for a very long time. Nationality has also been a subject of frequent discussion for at least two reasons: first, a long-standing tradition that goes back to the formation of European modern nations a few centuries back; second, the need of a relatively new nation to carve out a place for itself in the world.

Reasons that American philosophers have not paid the same kind of attention to ethnicity may be that until recently the presence of ethnic groups has been felt mostly regionally (e.g., Scandinavians in the upper Midwest), the numbers of any one ethnic group have been relatively small (e.g., Asians), many were subgroups within an overall dominant Germanic or Anglo-Saxon ethnic group (e.g., Swedes), and members of these groups have tended to assimilate fairly quickly (e.g., Germans). However, this situation has dramatically changed in the past few years because of Hispanics, for this ethnic group does not fit these models. Hispanics are found in every state of the nation; in some states they already constitute more than 30 percent of the population, and in the country at large they have already surpassed "Blacks" as the largest minority group; they are not ethnically a subgroup of any dominant group in the country (or even related to them); and they tend to resist assimilation.

This poses an enormous challenge for the United States and has emphasized the need to discuss not only the situation of Hispanics, but also issues of ethnicity in general. Naturally, this leads in turn to race and nationality. But the situation in the rest of the world is not so different. The pressures on nations that think of themselves as ethnically or racially homogeneous is enormous. The several million non-German ethnic minorities who live in Germany pose an extraordinary challenge to a nation that, to this day, believes itself not to be "a classic community of immigration," a code expression for "an ethnically and racially homogeneous nation" (Cohen 2001, 9). And the story is not very different in France and England. Even Spain, with its evident ethnic diversity—Spanish people are regarded by some as the mestizos of Western Europe—is being challenged by the pressures of an ethnically and racially different immigration.

The process of globalization is irreversible, and it carries with it the movement of peoples. An ethnically and racially homogeneous nation has probably never existed, but its myth has been kept alive because of the relatively small numbers of diverse peoples in some nations. Now, however, the reality of ethnic and racial diversity is too obvious, and the pressures it creates too strong, to be ignored.

The issues involved in race, ethnicity, and nationality are frequently entangled with many other matters, such as those concerned with gender, sexuality, religion, and politics.[9] To try to sort out these relations in this book would be impossible. An adequate treatment of them would require much more space than I have available here, so I refer to these topics only in passing (for the connection to gender in particular, see Bhavnani 1994; Butler 1990; Heckman 1994; and Segal 1990). This should not be construed as entailing that I do not think these issues are pertinent or important. Indeed, some argue that the discussion of gender is essential for the understanding of particular races and ethnicities, although others disagree (see, e.g., Wasserstrom 2001; Thomas 2001b). All these discussions and issues are related to the topics discussed in this book, but my immediate concerns here are more general. Finally, I should make clear that I do not address issues involving particular races, ethnicities, or nationalities, but rather more general questions concerned with race, ethnicity, and nationality as such.

Even leaving out questions of the relation of these issues to other matters, the questions and problems that could be raised about race, ethnicity, and nationality themselves are just too many to be dealt with in a single volume. Necessarily, then, I have omitted the discussion of some issues that are not just interesting, but even central to the understanding of race, ethnicity, and nationality. Two examples, which can be framed in terms of two questions, should make this clear: Are there duties that members of racial, ethnic, or national groups have just in virtue of being members of those groups? Are there rights that members of these groups have just in virtue of their membership in the groups? The importance of these controversial questions for contemporary society can hardly be underestimated, but I am forced to ignore them at this time (for discussions of these issues in the context of particular groups, see Du Bois 1897; Gutmann 1996; Appiah 1996, 92; Hall 2000, 168–81; Allen 2000, 182–205; Young 2000, 147–66; Zaibert and Millán-Zaibert 2000, 167–80; Pogge 2000, 181–200; Gracia 2000a, 201–21; Corlett 2000, 223–34; De Greiff 2000, 235–52; Walzer 1970, 46–73; Wasserstrom 2001).

I have tried to be as responsive as possible to the sensibilities of the various racial, ethnic, and national groups I mention in the book, but I have not sacrificed what I consider to be truths to it. Political correctness has not played a role in my choice of point of view, my criticism of various positions, or my selection of words. Unfortunately, there is an increasing tendency in contemporary American society to sacrifice truth and clarity to perceived sensibilities, and the results are deplorable. My aim is neither to offend nor to placate, but rather to understand.

The main thesis I defend is that race, ethnicity, and nationality are distinct and coherent concepts necessary in order to understand society. This goes against many mainstream discussions of these notions that argue that they are incoherent and therefore should be abandoned. Accordingly, I reject racial and ethnic notions of nations, ethnic notions of race, and racial notions of ethnicity. It is also a commonplace nowadays to argue that these notions are so closely tied that they cannot be clearly separated, even logically. Specifically, I argue against Anthony Appiah's rejection of race as both a reality and a coherent concept, and in support of a notion of racial identity, presented in *Color Conscious* (Princeton, 1996). Instead, I propose a social view of race conceived in terms of descent and genetically transmittable physical features, which I call the Genetic Common-Bundle View. I also reject Angelo Corlett's descent view of ethnicity presented in *Race, Racism, and Reparations* (Ithaca, 2003) and instead defend a position, inspired by Du Bois, that I call the Familial-Historical View. My Political View of nationality, whose roots go back to the French Enlightenment, is presented as an alternative to David Miller's conception based on territoriality, a history, and a common public culture, formulated in *On Nationality* (Oxford, 1995).

Much has been written about race, ethnicity, and nationality as social constructs, and in particular against a biological conception of race. I do not see my task here as disputing these views, insofar as I find them to be fun-

damentally correct. But no one to my knowledge has articulated a systematic model of the social concepts of race, ethnicity, and nationality, taken together, that could be used as a starting point of the discussion of other ethical and political issues of concern in the twenty-first century. This is what
I see as the main task of this book, although I have stayed away from ethical and political issues here, owing both to considerations of economy and
to the desire not to get entangled in matters that require greater attention
than I can give them at this time. It should be clear, however, that part of
the motivation for the book are precisely ethical and political concerns. It
should also be clear that the view I present is prescriptive in the same way
that a scientific theory is: it is intended to be used because it claims to have
advantages over other theories. Finally, the model I present differs in substantial ways from other recent attempts at clarifying the notions of race,
ethnicity, and nationality, as will become clear in the chapters that follow.

The discussion is divided into six chapters. Because the case against
race, ethnicity, and nationality has been forcefully articulated recently, and
may in fact be the most popular position today among those who discuss
them, the first chapter identifies and summarizes the general arguments that
have been proposed in support of this position. The second chapter lays
down the conceptual foundation of the notions of race, ethnicity, and nationality that I propose to defend in the book. This should make clear to
the reader my assumptions and approach. The three chapters that follow
present the substantive views about these three notions. Finally, the sixth
chapter compares the views of race, ethnicity, and nationality presented in
the previous three, summarizing the main theses of the book.

In the composition of this book, I have sometimes relied on previously
published materials or views. The view of ethnicity presented in chapter 3
is related to that originally sketched in chapters 2 and 3 of *Hispanic/Latino
Identity: A Philosophical Perspective* (2000b). In addition, I have used materials
from "Response to My Critics: *Tahafut Al-Tahafut*," *Philosophy and Social
Criticism* (2001); "The Nature of Ethnicity with Special Reference to His-
panic/Latino Identity," *Public Affairs Quarterly* (1999b); "Hispanic/Latino
Identity: Homogeneity and Stereotypes," *Ventana Abierta* (2000c); and "Language Priority in the Education of Children," *Journal of Social Philosophy*
(2004). In some cases, I have reproduced sections of these discussions, although I have always introduced modifications that change the original
texts in substantial ways. I am grateful to the editors of the journals and
presses that published the mentioned articles and books for their permission
to include these materials here.

I also need to acknowledge that I have profited much from the advice of many friends and colleagues in the preparation of this book. In particular I would like to thank Daniel Novotny, who was my assistant during part of the time when I was writing the book and raised some probing questions; the student members of a seminar I taught on the topic of the book, who posed interesting questions throughout the seminar; Rudolph Luethe and Svetozar Stojanović, who made presentations to the mentioned seminar and brought to bear a European perspective; Mercedes Torrevejano, who attended the seminar and introduced a firsthand knowledge of the situation in the Iberian peninsula; Gregory Reichberg, who planted the idea of writing this book in my mind in the first place and also made suggestions concerning the preface and chapter 5; Susana Nuccetelli, who raised some general questions; Jorge García, who used several chapters in a seminar he taught; Linda Alcoff, who commented on several chapters; J. Angelo Corlett, who offered comments in light of his book on race and reparations; Leo Zaibert, who approached the manuscript from a legal and political perspective; Eduardo Mendieta, who was a source of detailed criticisms, on the preface and chapter 1 in particular; Rosemary Geisdorfer Feal, who made a happy suggestion concerning the title; Leigh Duffy, who helped with the bibliography; and Paul Symington, who compiled the index.

Finally, let me end these initial remarks with a personal note. As some of those who will read this book know, my philosophical work to this day has not primarily been concerned with issues of race and nationality, although I have done substantial work on ethnicity, particularly Hispanic or Latino ethnicity. I was trained as a historian, and my philosophical contributions have hovered around topics in metaphysics (individuality, categories, and the nature of metaphysics) and hermeneutics (philosophical historiography and textual interpretation). Yet, as a Cuban, Latino, Hispanic, and naturalized American and Canadian, I have been progressively drawn into issues related to ethnicity, race, and nationality. My work in the history of philosophy and metaphysics in particular has provided me with a perspective on these matters that tends to be different from the standard approach of American philosophers who work on these issues. In thinking about these topics for several years, I have especially profited from the work of Linda Alcoff, Anthony Appiah, Bernard Boxill, Angelo Corlett, Lucius Outlaw, David Miller, and Naomi Zack, but most of all from that of W. E. B. Du Bois, whose pioneering view on race I consider an inspiration for my position concerning both ethnicity and race. In this book, I criticize some of the ideas of these authors, but this should not obscure my debt to them. Without their groundbreaking contributions to the field, this book would have been impossible.

NOTES

1. For recent discussions of the changing character of conflicts, see Kaldor (1999) and Keen (1998).

2. For ethnic conflict in the United States, see Dinnerstein and Reimers (1975, 56–72); for conflict in the world at large, see Gurr (1993), Horowitz (1985), Montville (1990), Brown (1997), McGarry and O'Leary (1993), and O'Leary and McGarry (1995). The literature on racial conflicts is very extensive, but see, for example, Cashmore and Troyna (1990). There is little need to give sources for national conflicts insofar as a state of war between nations seems endemic to our species. Gleditsch et al. (2002) have compiled figures on various kinds and levels of conflicts.

3. Throughout this book, I place racial designations within quotation marks to indicate that, although I am using them, I am not necessarily endorsing them. More on this in chapter 4.

4. I am using the noun "Amerindian" to refer to peoples of pre-Columbian origin and the corresponding adjective for anything related to them. In the U.S. context, I use instead "Native American."

5. Some argue, however, that the level of conflict worldwide has decreased since the end of the Cold War (see Gleditsch et al. 2002; Mueller 1989, 2001; Gurr 2000; Gurr et al. 2000). But these studies were done before recent developments in the Middle East.

6. In favor of the elimination of racial concepts or language from our discourse are, for example, Montagu (1941, 1945), Appiah (1996), Herder (2000, 23–26), and Malcomson (2000).

7. In favor of preserving racial notions are, for example, Alcoff (2001, 267–83) and Outlaw (1996). Some, such as Boas (2000) and Du Bois (1897), endorse a provisional use of racial classifications. And Hirschfeld (1996) argues that the concept of race is good for thinking but bad for acting. Scientists also fall on opposite sides of this debate. Among opponents of racial designations are Cavalli-Sforza et al. (1994) and Lewontin (1972, 1998); among supporters are Garn (1993) and Nei and Roychoudhury (1974). This situation is mirrored in the literature on ethnicity and to some extent in that on nationality. For ethnicity, see the discussion in the context of Hispanics in Gracia (2000b, 1–26). References to the social science literature will be provided as we go along.

8. Even in the social sciences in general or in some particular ones, however, some claim that race especially has not been a top priority. See Omi and Winant (1994, 9) and Taylor (1999, 122). For a survey of the situation in different disciplines, see Bulmer and Solomos (1999).

9. Politics in particular is seldom far from discussions of these topics (Mason 1999, 13, 18–19; Baker 1998, 208–28).

1

AGAINST RACE, ETHNICITY, AND NATIONALITY

One of the most popular views among intellectuals these days is that grouping persons by race, ethnicity, or nationality is unintelligible, inaccurate, nefarious, or all three, and therefore should not be done. Although the motivation behind this view is usually related to the social conflicts and abuses alluded to in the preface, in fact many different reasons are given for it. When examined closely, however, it becomes clear that these reasons tend to fall into five main classes: epistemic, factual, moral, political, and pragmatic. The first argues that there are no clear and effective criteria that can be used to distinguish races, ethnic groups, and nations; the second, that there is no fact of the matter to race, ethnicity, and nationality; the third, that the use of these categories is morally objectionable; the fourth, that their application works against the polity; and the fifth, that there are some clear benefits in the elimination of racial, ethnic, and national divisions.

These arguments have taken many forms and have been presented by many authors, often from different philosophical traditions. To do justice even to their most important formulations would require more space than I have here and would bog down the discussion. For these reasons, I have chosen instead to discuss general formulations of them that attempt to capture the salient features of the arguments regardless of origin or philosophical context. However, in some cases I have made references to the most prominent proponents of these views and their particular arguments. Let me begin with the political argument because it is perhaps the one that has attracted most attention recently.

1

THE POLITICAL ARGUMENT

The general thrust of this argument consists in pointing out that it is politically harmful to use racial, ethnic, or national names, to think in terms of the notions to which these point, or to allow racial, ethnic, or national groups to develop and grow. To talk about, say, "Blacks" or "Whites," to think in terms of "Blacks" or "Whites," or to allow persons to group themselves as "Black" or "White" has serious negative consequences for the body politic.

The specific details of the political arguments against race and ethnicity on one hand and nationality on the other tend to be different, however. Against the first two, the argument has often been framed in terms of what Iris Young has called the "politics of difference" (Young, I. M., 1995, 155–76; 1990; see also Minow 1990; Connolly 1991). This expression has become a commonplace in the pertinent literature in the United States.[1] It refers to attempts at making room in American society for groups who do not fit the prevailing Anglo-American view of the nation. Those who oppose these efforts see them as threatening. The politics of difference is perceived as a destabilizing factor that can adversely affect the country and bring down its democratic way of life. Groups that engage in it presumably undermine the principles on which American democracy is founded when they assert their identity over those of others, and particularly over that of Anglo-Americans. Some critics go so far as to portray some of these groups as trying to take over the country in order to impose their particular culture and language on it (Butler 1986). As a result, we see more frequent calls to make English the official language of the United States and to stop immigration from non-European nations, where the population does not fit within the racial and ethnic parameters that are taken to characterize the dominant group of American citizens. The same argument can be applied in other nations, regardless of racial or ethnic character. Indeed, one finds echoes of it in political speeches in places as distant and different as Japan, Norway, Zimbabwe, and Saudi Arabia.

David Miller has eloquently described the case made by those who support the politics of difference:

> Group identity, whether sexual, cultural, or ethnic, should not merely be expressed in private settings, but should be carried into the arena of politics—that is, one should participate politically *as* a gay, a religious fundamentalist, or a black—and political institutions should operate in such a way as to respect these group differences. On the one hand, they must val-

idate group identities by ensuring that the various groups are represented in politics *as* groups; on the other hand, they must ensure that the policies that emerge show equal respect for the values and cultural demands of each group—there should, if necessary, be subsidies for the activities that each group regards as central to its identity; educational materials must avoid discriminatory judgments which imply that one cultural norm might be superior to another; and so forth. (Miller 1995, 132)[2]

In short, the body politic should not be conceived as an association of individual persons, but rather as a conglomerate of different groups each of which has its own identity, be it racial, ethnic, religious, sexual, or what have you. From this it follows that the body politic should ensure that these group identities are respected and preserved. Politics, then, should be guided by the differences that separate these groups, so that no group is given any advantages over others and, as Young (2001) has argued, the social structures that favor one group over another are dismantled.

The emphasis on group identity in this view makes groups, rather than individual persons, the basic components of the body politic, and this poses, according to opponents, especial dangers to it. The theoretical argument against the politics of difference has been taken up by various ideological traditions, from Marxist to Liberal. Consider Jean Bethke Elshtain's formulation of it:

> To the extent that citizens begin to retribalize into ethnic or other "fixed identity" groups, democracy falters. Any possibility for human dialogue, for democratic communication and commonality, vanishes as so much froth on the polluted sea of phony equality. Difference becomes more and more exclusivist. If you are black and I am white, by definition I do not and cannot, in principle, "get it." There is no way that we can negotiate the space between our given differences. We are just stuck with them, stuck in what political thinkers used to call "ascriptive characteristics"—things we cannot change about ourselves. Mired in the cement of our own identities, we need never deal with one another. Not really. One of us will win and one of us will lose the cultural war or the political struggle. That's what it's all about: power of the most reductive, impositional sort. (Elshtein 1995, 74)[3]

The argument here is that the politics of difference, the assertion of racial and ethnic identity in the body politic, undermines democracy and leads to a system in which power ultimately determines justice, for this position translates not only in the tolerance for different social phenomena, whether cultural or behavioral, that these groups see as essential to them, but also in their active preservation and encouragement as groups. The resources of a nation, then, are used for those purposes, provided the various groups have sufficient political clout to ensure they get the means to support their activities. This has an adverse impact on other groups, ultimately creating a situation in which power determines outcome.

Although this position applies to groups identified in terms of sexual orientation and religion as well as many others, I am only concerned here with ethnicity and race. In these more restricted terms, the argument in favor of the politics of difference is that the state should play an active role in the preservation and encouragement of elements and behavior identified with particular ethnic groups or races. If Latin American music is essential to the identity of Latinos, then the United States should support it. And if hunting sea lions is part of what it means to be an Eskimo, the government of Canada should make sure this is possible and encourage it.

So much, then, for the political argument against ethnicity and race. The argument against nationality is usually of a different sort and proposed by internationalists of various stripes. Their view is that nations as they have thus far existed, and particularly after the rise of European powers in the sixteenth century, are not only a perishing breed, but also a breed that should perish. The world is increasingly smaller, and the relations between different peoples are becoming increasingly closer. As Archibugi and Midgley have argued, globalization requires the development of a new political reality (Archibugi et al. 1998; Midgley 1999). The concept of a nation as a sovereign political entity is as dated in the contemporary world as the concept of the Greek *polis*. Nations stand in the way of progress, and the artificial boundaries they establish among peoples interfere with the effective functioning of human societies. The future of the world depends on the integration of humanity into an overall, comprehensive political system, and the division of the world into separate political units only serves to prevent this achievement.

The survival of humanity is contingent on the eradication of conflicts that could escalate and produce a human holocaust, but wars are waged by nations and result from conflicts between nations. Only by doing away with nations can humanity ever hope to survive. Indeed, as Marx and Engels proposed and some other supporters of this view echo, the issue that confronts humanity does not concern nations, but economic classes. And the proletariat, the core of the revolution, has no nationality, race, or ethnicity. National divisions are merely temporary stages on the way to a world in which everyone is a citizen, and often they are used by tyrants to separate people and create prejudice and antagonism (Marx and Engels 1968; 1975, vol. 22, 608; 1976, 49; Marx 1978, 78).

THE MORAL ARGUMENT

Like the political argument, the moral argument used against racial or ethnic classifications often differs from that used against nationality and has also been presented in various ways. The former can take several particular forms, but in general it proceeds from the premise that both using racial or ethnic names and concepts and allowing racial or ethnic groups to develop—and even worse, to promote their development—is harmful to some persons within or without the groups and, therefore, immoral. At least six versions of the argument are commonly found in the literature.

The first begins by noting that racial and ethnic names generally have negative connotations. Consider the case of "Irish," for example. This term, when used ethnically, is associated with negative qualities: drunkenness, quarrelsomeness, low class, lack of education, and so on. In the case of "Hispanic," other qualities are involved, such as laziness, drug abuse, drug dealing, and poor linguistic skills. The cases of "Black" and "Oriental" are similar: "Black" connotes poverty, low intelligence, and laziness, and "Oriental" is taken to imply shiftiness, cowardice, and lack of cleanliness, among other things. The use of racial and ethnic names and the categories to which they refer create a hostile atmosphere for members of these groups and often lead to discrimination, placing obstacles in their proper integration in society. For this reason, these categories, and the use of the terms with which we refer to them, should be eliminated from discourse.[4] Least of all should society condone or promote the formation of groups of people along these lines.

A second version argues that racial and ethnic classifications must be abandoned because they unfairly privilege some groups over others. To talk about "Whites" and "Blacks" results in discrimination against the latter and serves to establish the dominance of the former over them. Racial notions are used to separate and, once separation is accomplished, to order in accordance with a hierarchy of privilege and value. And the same can be said about ethnic notions. To say that someone is Latino is to put the person on a lower level of a hierarchy of social status and value, and the same applies to "Black" and some other racial classifications (see Hernández and Torres-Saillant 1992, 1–7; Gracia 2000b, 15–17).

This leads to a third version of the moral argument. As Wilkins and Gutmann have argued, the use of racial and ethnic classifications perpetuates the situation of inferiority and domination in which certain groups find themselves (Wilkins 1993; Gutmann 1996, 162ff.). Certain racial and ethnic groups are considered inferior, and their identification as such ensures the continuation of their disadvantaged position in society. When we use terms such as "Black" or "Hispanic" in a country such as the United States, where the powerful elite belongs to the group of "Whites" and Anglos, or a term such as "Indian" in Peru, where "Whites" are the dominant group, this places members of the subordinate groups at a disadvantage. This disadvantageous position tends to continue unless extraordinary efforts are made to change it. But, of course, extraordinary efforts are not easily made insofar as they do not favor the interests of the dominant group, so the result is the perpetuation of the status quo, as many sociologists have shown (see Cafferty and McCready 1985, 253; Giménez 1989, 558–62; Hernández and Torres-Saillant 1992; Mason 1999, 19).

A fourth version of the argument, powerfully articulated by Suzanne Oboler, objects to the use of racial and ethnic classifications because they wrongly contribute to the homogenization of the groups to which they refer, ignoring both differences between subgroups within the groups and individual peculiarities, thus causing harm to them (Oboler 1995, xvii). Consider, for example, the case of "Black" or "Hispanic." Both of these terms are used to refer to very large groups of people composed of many different subgroups and individual persons. These subgroups and individuals have never in fact constituted single homogeneous groups—so the argument goes—which means that there is no justification for lumping them together into the same homogenizing category. What do all "Blacks," or all Hispanics, have in common but a name? What does a Bantu share with a Mandinga, and an American "Black" with a Cuban "Black"? The individual members of these groups are also very different. José is different from María and Mobutu from Mfume, and their differences are significant. José is Venezuelan, "Black," tall, and principled, whereas María is Cuban, "White," short, and unprincipled. Mobutu is thin, agile, strong, short, and deliberate, whereas Mfume is fat, slow, weak, tall, and impulsive. These differences matter and resist attempts at lumping these individual persons together. The lumping is contrived, and its bases are secondary and insignificant. In short, the classification of people along racial or ethnic lines should be avoided.

In a fifth version of the moral argument, Frantz Fanon (2001) points out that racial and ethnic names are usually imposed on certain groups by other groups, and not by themselves, therefore reflecting the arbitrary exercise of power of some over others (see also Guibernau 1996, 87). Naming is an exercise of power that goes beyond language, extending to knowledge and value; to name is to direct us to know and evaluate the named thing in accordance with the parameters used by the one who names it. God is supposed to have given dominion over creation to Adam, who exercised it by giving names to things and thus classifying them in accordance with a hierarchy of value. Who invented the name "Black"? The origin of the term is in the Spanish *negro*, which was the term used by Spaniards to refer to the slaves they brought from Africa. Who invented the name "Latin American"? As I point out elsewhere, some French European whose aims were imperial and colonial (Gracia 2000b, 19–20). The racial and ethnic terms of particular groups are often created by members of other groups for the purpose of dominating and exploiting them, and result in their oppression. It is unfair, then, to continue to use the names whose origins go back to oppression and abuse. Omi and Winant argue, for example, that the very notion of race is the result of a project whose aim is the hegemony of one group over others (Omi and Winant 1994, 56; see also Cox 1970; Montagu 1945).

A sixth version of the moral argument against race and ethnicity is based on the continuous damage that racial and ethnic divisions cause on members of racial or ethnic groups. Indeed, Greeley and Wasserstrom note that the history of humankind is full of examples that demonstrate how such divisions have been most pernicious, being the causes of wars, destruction, and bitter conflicts (Greeley 1974, 29; Wasserstrom 2001). Many of the examples mentioned in the preface can be used here, so no further elaboration is needed. In short, it is morally unjustifiable to continue to classify people along racial or ethnic lines insofar as doing so causes harm to innocent people.

The moral argument against nationality can also take many forms. Some of these mirror closely the arguments already given against race and ethnicity. Indeed, just like these—so the argument might go—certain national classifications serve to place some people below others and to identify certain persons with undesirable features. Because these arguments were discussed in the context of race and ethnicity, there is no need to dwell on them again, but there are at least three versions of the moral argument that are particular to nationality and therefore need to be mentioned.

The first claims that the breakdown of humans into nations serves the aims of dominant elites who, by controlling the power structures in nations, are able to exploit certain members of the populations for their own benefit. As Hintzen has noted, nationalism is often used to hide domestic racial capitalism (Hintzen 2002, 493). The myth of nationality, just like the myth of religion, serves to keep people under a yoke. Nations are inventions of the few to take advantage of the many. And, indeed, we could ask, for example, how many children of the ruling classes—the senators, governors, presidents, owners of large fortunes, and even members of the military establishment—have actually fought in the wars in which the United States has been involved in the past fifty years? Did Bill Clinton or George W. Bush serve in Vietnam? Wars tend to be fought by the poor, the disadvantaged, and the marginal, including ethnic and racial minorities.

A second version of the moral argument against nations points out that even the limited sovereignty accorded to nations in our times allows horrendous crimes to go unpunished. Sovereignty stops nations from interfering in the internal affairs of other nations, precluding the effective opposition to abuses occurring within those nations. National sovereignty prevented interference with Stalin's purges, the abuses of Mao's Cultural Revolution, Franco's tyranny, and the Taliban's massacre of non-Islamic communities in Afghanistan, and currently allows the oppression of women in Saudi Arabia and Brazil. Dictators and tyrants profit from the institution of nationhood, for through it they are able to exploit and oppress large portions of humanity for their personal benefit. By controlling the means of communication and taking advantage of a misplaced sense of patriotism, they maintain themselves and their supporters in a style of grand living at the expense of others. Think of Trujillo, Saddam Hussein, and Castro. The argument, then, points out the need to do away with the myth of nationality and to recognize that all humans are equal and deserve an inter-national, rather than a national, government.

The third version of the argument objects to nationalities because the recognition of national obligations conflicts with universal duties. If I have special obligations to my fellow citizens, these can interfere with my duties to human beings who are not my fellow citizens. In *concreto*, one could argue, for example, that the duty of Americans to provide a safe environment for each other forces Americans to provide an unsafe environment for, and even perhaps to kill, those who appear to be the cause of unsafety in the United States. Indeed, Miller has brought attention to the fact that the conflict between these duties seems to be the foundation for the dialectic of war (Miller 1998, 660). For this reason, contrary to the view of MacIntyre (1995), who emphasizes questions of personal identity—whether ethnic or national—in matters of morality, Kedourie (1961) argues that these matters need to be kept separate. The next step, of course, is to advocate the elimination of the source of these moral conflicts, namely nations.

THE FACTUAL ARGUMENT

The third kind of objection argues against the use of racial, ethnic, or national terms and categories because in some cases the connotations of the pertinent terms are (1) too narrow, excluding some necessary elements; (2) skewed, giving unwarranted attention to some elements over others; or (3) inaccurate insofar as they do not correspond to anything real outside the mind. In short, these terms do not name realities and therefore are misleading.

The factual argument in the case of race has been powerfully articulated in the literature and supported with scientific evidence: race is not a biological reality, that is, a fact that exists independently of human thought. Rather, race is a social construction and not a characteristic of anything in the world (Appiah 1985, 23ff.; 1990a, 496–97; Carter 2000, 157; Omi and Winant 1994, 56ff.; Davis 1991, 7; Zack 2002, 106ff.).[5] It is in fact a meaningless and groundless concept, a remnant of archaic science, as Zack has argued (Zack 2001; the roots of this argument go back to Montagu 1941, 243). "Black" and "White" do not exist, except as terms that refer to fictional concepts invented by humans; they belong with such concepts as unicorn and centaur.

The main problem with racial taxonomies, as Zack points out, is that they lack an objective basis, which is a reason why they have proven extraordinarily unstable in the hands of taxonomists and often reflect personal preferences rather than facts. In Zack's own words: "'Race' means a biological taxonomy or set of physical categories that can be used consistently and informatively to describe, explain, and make predictions about groups of human beings and individual members of these groups" (Zack 2002, 1). The problem is that there is no evidence to back this notion up: "the crux of the matter [is this]: *It is the taxonomy of human races that science fails to support, not any one or even many of the hereditary traits that society deems racial*" (Zack 2002, xi).

And scientists agree: science has failed thus far to establish a consensus on the notion of race. Until precise genetic studies became possible in the past quarter of a century, the data on which to base racial classifications were too inaccurate and unstable to support any clear conclusions, although conclusions were nonetheless drawn. Skin pigmentation, cranial configuration, and even blood profiles, among others, proved unreliable. Indeed, recent, more accurate, genetic studies have not supported racial classifications.[6]

Zack points out that "there have been four bases for ideas of physical race in common sense: geographical origins of ancestors; phenotypes or physical appearance of individuals; hereditary traits of individuals; [and] genealogy" (Zack 2002, 26). But all four fail the scientific test. Here are some of the reasons that she and others have cited.

First, the genetic differences between races, say "Blacks" and "Whites," are minuscule if compared with what they have in common. As genetic scientists such as Nei and Roychoudhury have demonstrated, the bases for racial distinctions are flimsy, insofar as there can be greater genetic difference between two individual human beings presumably belonging to the same race than between two races (Nei and Roychoudhury 1982; 1972; 1974; see also Lewontin 1972; Hoffman 1994, 4; van den Berghe 2001, 103; Zack 2002).

Second, science has shown that either single genes or the various forms they can take (known as alleles) are present in all populations. This means that, as Cavalli-Sforza has pointed out, "No single gene [or allele] is sufficient for classifying human populations into systematic categories," let alone racial ones (Cavalli-Sforza et al. 1994, 19; see also van den Berghe 2001, 103; Zack 2002).

Third, various scientific studies have shown that there is no strict correlation between the directly observable traits of a person, known as *phenotypes*, such as skin color and hair texture, and genetic specifications inherited from parents, known as *genotypes* (Cavalli-Sforza et al. 1994, 6–7; Nei and Roychoudhury 1982; Lewontin 1998; Zack 2002, ch. 5). The reason is that some phenotypes are the result of very complex genetic relationships and also involve environmental factors (King 1981, 20–21, 28–29, 33–34; Cavalli-Sforza et al. 1994, 4–5, 7, 17–18; Lewontin 1998; Zack 2002, especially ch. 5).

Fourth, particular phenotypes can be the result of different gene combinations and do not adhere to stable racial boundaries, or as Zack has stated, are not orderly (Zack 2002, 43). Again, this is in part due to environmental factors, for as King and van den Berghe have argued, phenotypes are the result of the interaction between a genetic program and the environment (King 1981, 50–51, 59–60; van den Berghe 2001, 103).

Finally, there is the reason already noted by Darwin, that so-called races "graduate into each other"; there are no strict boundaries between what are regarded as different racial groups, but rather a gradation from one to the others (Cavalli-Sforza et al. 1994, 17–19; van den Berghe 2001, 103). The concept of race lacks sufficient foundation in fact; races do not actually exist.

To this scientific case against the taxonomy of races, some other scientists and philosophers add that racial categories arbitrarily put unwarranted emphasis on certain features of people, neglecting others, and for this reason constitute misleading descriptions of reality. Why should skin color, for example, be given the important place it is given in most racial classifications? As Senghor (2001) questions, why should cultural characteristics or mental abilities be subordinated to skin color, for example?

Moreover, racial categories and labels homogenize. They make us think of all members of a race as being the same or very similar. Yet it is clear that racial groups are very diverse not just because of the differences among their individual members, but also because they contain what appear to be many subracial groups.[7] This means, of course, that the use of general racial terms and categories present an inaccurate picture of the way things are.

The case of ethnicity is similar to that of race. Consider Hispanics. Alcoff (2005) has argued that the use of "Hispanic" to describe members of the Latin American community in Latin America, or the Latino community in the United States, inaccurately privileges the Spanish, Iberian, and European component of these communities, leaving out, sometimes altogether, significant elements of it.[8] "Hispanic" means somehow derivatively Spanish or Iberian, and therefore European, giving prominence to this cultural element in contrast to the Amerindian and African elements that are integral parts of the community. Labels and names appear to establish priorities and send messages, and if "Hispanic" does in fact privilege the Spanish, Iberian, or European elements to the detriment, or exclusion, of Amerindian and African elements in this community, it is certainly inaccurate and thus unacceptable. If the term can be understood only in this way, it should be dropped in favor of some other, more accurate term.

Ethnic terms and categories, like racial ones, also homogenize the groups to which they refer—so it is argued—ignoring both differences between subgroups within the groups and also individual idiosyncracies (Lentz 1995, 305). Consider, for example, the case of "Native American" or "Indian." Both of these terms are used to refer to a very large group of people, namely, the peoples who lived in the Americas before the encounter between them and Europeans in the fifteenth century. But, as I have argued elsewhere, these people were never one people; they were rather a collection of widely different groups with different cultures, languages, religions, and even genetic makeups (Gracia 2000b, 97–100).[9] Senecas and Seminoles are not culturally or historically the same. So what do they have in common? Merely a name artificially imposed on them. Moreover, as individuals, the members of these groups are also very different, and yet the common ethnic name and category tends to make us think of them as the same.

One of the problems that is frequently noted with thinking in ethnic terms is that it is distorted insofar as ethnic notions are based on stereotypes. Humans need to generalize. Indeed, all we do when we think is either generalize or apply a generalization to a particular case, for generalizations are of the essence of all knowledge. There is not one single, well-formed sentence in any language that does not contain a general term. We cannot think without them. So it is impossible to ask us not to generalize. But stereotypes are not mere generalizations; they are *hasty* generalizations, and they are about people. This makes them potentially dangerous because, when they do not correspond to a reality—and they seldom do—they can have harmful consequences. Consider that federal funds in the United States are appropriated on the basis of bureaucratic classifications, and often these classifications are indeed hasty generalizations, or are based on hasty generalizations, that is, on stereotypes about certain groups of people, such as African Americans, Hispanics, Asian Americans, women, the elderly, gays, and so on, that sometimes affect them negatively.

The moral of the story is that ethnic labels and classifications do not entail much that is generally associated with them, and therefore they fail to satisfy the stereotype, for the groups to which they refer are not in fact homogeneous. This, so the argument goes, can be easily documented with ethnic groups, such as Hispanics or Latinos, as Oboler (1995) has claimed. In short, there are no facts that support the use of ethnic names and categories.

When the factual approach is applied to nationalities, these also appear to be artificial and changing and, therefore, more a matter of perception and perspective than of facts, as Renan (1996) indicates. What are nations but contrived entities whose boundaries are the result of historical contingent events and therefore subject to change? Consider the case of the Spanish nation. In comparison with some other nations in Europe, the Spanish nation has been quite stable, because of its geographical location largely in the Iberian peninsula. Countries such as Germany, Poland, Italy, and Austria, by contrast, have experienced drastic changes in boundaries, and therefore population, frequently and recently. And these changes have affected these nations and the national identity of the peoples who compose them. Some people who are currently Italian were Austrian earlier in this century, and some people who were German earlier are today Poles by nationality. The situation with Spain, however, has been different, but even in this case there have been changes in national membership. Not too long ago, the inhabitants of both a part of southwestern France and Gibraltar were Spanish, but now they are not.

If nations are artificial creations established on the basis of historically contingent events, they cannot be considered facts or at least unchangeable facts. They are rather arti-facts, that is, facts that are by-products of human art and that are therefore subject to human manipulation. So, although we may recognize the existence of nations, we should also realize that their existence is contingent. This by itself is not an argument against nations and nationality, but it opens the way for their elimination on other grounds. This argument prepares the way for the political and moral arguments against nationality considered earlier. And, indeed, some argue that nations are on their way to disappearance.[10]

Another factual argument against nationality is that the concept of a nation as generally accepted has ceased to reflect a reality (Miller 1995, 155ff. discusses a version of this view). Insofar as all states are officially nations, Hobsbawm has claimed that it makes no sense to refer to nations independently of states (Hobsbawm 1997, 69–79). So why talk about nations at all?

THE EPISTEMIC ARGUMENT

The epistemic objection makes a case against the use of racial, ethnic, or national terms and categories based on the lack of clear and unchanging criteria for distinguishing races, ethnic groups, or nations, arguing that, even if there are such things, we have no effective means of knowing them with clarity or certainty. The case with race is most dramatic because until recently it was thought that race could be easily ascertained. But the facts suggest otherwise, for the criteria used to determine race vary from individual to individual, group to group, context to context, place to place, country to country, and time to time. Consider the following example. In Cuba, being "Black" (i.e., *negro*) entails that one appears as if one has no mixture with the "White" (i.e., *blanco*) race. A person who looks to be mixed is not *negro* but *mulato*, that is, a mixture of *negro* and *blanco*. But in the United States, the situation is quite different, for to be "Black" requires only that one have some "Black" blood, that is, that one have a "Black" ancestor. This is known as the One-Drop Rule: one drop of "Black" blood is sufficient to make a person "Black." In Cuba, of course, persons of mixed "Black" and "White" ancestry are supposed to be mulattoes, as long as they appear to be mixed, and therefore neither "Black" nor "White." If they do not appear to be mixed, then they are considered "White" or "Black," depending on where the appearance lies. So the question is, who is right? Epistemically, we have a serious conflict, for what is known as a "Black" in Cuba is also a "Black" in the United States, but what is known as a "Black" in the United States is sometimes considered a mulatto, and even in some cases a "White," in Cuba.[11] Differing epistemic racial criteria preclude agreement as to who qualifies as a member of a race and provides the grounds for Hanchard's argument that racial categories are subjective and depend on particular attitudes (Hanchard 1994, 165–85).[12] Indeed, Carter argues that the very viability of sociology as a discipline requires the abandonment of the concept of race (Carter 2000, 157).

The epistemic difficulties posed by the instability of racial criteria are not restricted to the variability of these criteria. There is also the problem of the accessibility of the evidence used to satisfy the criteria. In Cuba, a mulatto is supposed to be a mixture of "Black" and "White," but we may ask how one is supposed to tell that someone is mixed. Through a blood test, DNA analysis, or some such procedure? Obviously not! The category *mulato* was developed before any of these tests were available and still today is used without reference to them. The judgment that someone is a *mulato* is generally made in terms of visual inspection, as it is also done with "Blacks" or "Whites." Because of this, a *negro* in Cuba can never be considered "White," insofar as he cannot change appearance: skin color, many features, and hair texture. To be considered "White" would require drastic changes that are, at least currently, impossible. However, a "Black" and "White" racially mixed person can be considered "White" if he or she does not have the physically perceptual features associated with "Blacks." "White" nose, lips, hair, and skin color may be sufficient to have someone qualify as "White," even if he or she has a "Black" grandmother in the closet. This is why a popular saying in Cuba asks: Where is your grandmother? It is assumed that many, and perhaps even most, "Whites" have in fact a racially mixed ancestry.

The epistemic situation with "Blacks" in the United States is similar to that of *mulatos* in Cuba, for one drop of "Black" blood surely does very little to make a person qualify as "Black." Just as in Cuba many racially mixed persons eventually join the "White" population, in the United States many "Blacks" do so as well. For how can we possibly tell if a person had a "Black" ancestor twenty generations removed? We would have to carry out some scientific analysis that accurately reveals a race line. The problem is that it is not at all clear that such an analysis is possible, and even if it is possible, it is never in fact carried out. The knowledge we have of someone's race in the United States is not determined by any kind of scientific analysis, but rather by simple inspection, and this is deceptive and imprecise when it comes to the application of the One-Drop Rule.

Here again we have serious epistemic questions that remain unresolved. We act as if we could be certain who is, and who is not, "Black" in the United States, but we cannot be sure of this knowledge on the bases that are regularly used to do so. Du Bois himself pointed out that mixing of "Blacks" with other races is so widespread that it is impossible to discern "a Negro race" (Du Bois 1968, 16). And various studies have demonstrated that American "Blacks" have a substantial "White" component and some "Whites" have a "Black" component (Hudson 1996; Shreve 1994, 58).

Clearly—so this argument goes—the criteria of races we use are ineffective, even when they are not in conflict. In some cases, we use color; in others, it is lineage; and in still others it is culture. "Indian" is a racial term associated with physical appearance in the United States, but in many places in Bolivia and Peru, it refers to culture (see Banton 1983, 23, about the cases of Mexico and Guatemala). To be an Indian in the latter two countries indicates merely that one has not adopted the ways of Europeans.

The criteria for ethnicity are epistemically even more controversial than those for race, for they are more clearly contextual. Indeed, this is one of the major problems that some authors raise with affirmative action for ethnic groups in the United States. They point out that criteria of membership in these are imprecise and changing and therefore cannot function effectively. Consider the case of Hispanics (Zaibert and Millán-Zaibert 2000, 167–79). What is it that we can use to identify them? That they speak Spanish? No, for obviously many persons regarded as Hispanic do not speak Spanish at all or speak Spanish only as a second language. Food? Again this does not work, for there is no food that is common to all Hispanics; Cubans and Mexicans eat very differently. Music? Not possible for similar reasons: Argentinians have little liking for *jarabe tapatío*. Religion? Hispanics belong to all sorts of religions, from Roman Catholic to Jewish and Islamic to Voodoo. Race? Well, as we have seen, race is controversial, but even if it were not, Hispanics come in what count as all kinds of racial varieties. So where are the criteria, or where is even one criterion, that we can use everywhere to identify Hispanics? And what I have said about Hispanics can be said, *mutatis mutandis*, about many other ethnic groups.

The epistemic problems in the case of nationality are less clear, but still present. Although there are often clear criteria of citizenship for certain countries, there do not seem to be clear criteria for nationality that apply and are used across the board, and this puts in doubt the possibility of establishing judgments about national identity on firm grounds. In some countries, nationality is determined by blood relation, what is known as the law of blood (*jus sanguinis*). In others, it is birthplace, that is the law of the land (*jus solis*). And in still others it is established by a combination of both. But most countries allow a process whereby persons can be naturalized if they fulfill certain requirements that do not have to do with blood or land. This means, of course, that there is considerable latitude as to what determines nationality and, therefore, one cannot count on applying a single criterion or set of criteria of nationality everywhere.

In short, it should be clear that there are epistemic questions that need satisfactory answers before we can claim that the notions of race, ethnicity, and nationality are viable. Moreover, these questions, and the difficulties one encounters in answering them, can form the basis of arguments against the use of racial, ethnic, or national names and categories.

THE PRAGMATIC ARGUMENT

Finally, one can argue against race, ethnicity, and nationality in pragmatic terms. One can say something like this: Let us be practical. It is clear that the division of humans into racial, ethnic, and national groups has not worked well and that the elimination of these classifications and the corresponding groups through assimilation benefits the people in question, for in places where assimilation has taken place, the less developed groups improve and the degree of conflict in the community decreases (see, e.g., Lissak's thesis about Jane Addams; Lissak 1989). In short, because assimilation works and segregation does not, we should do all we can to implement assimilation. Mill puts it eloquently:

> Experience proves it is possible for one nationality to merge and be absorbed in another: and when it was originally an inferior and more backward portion of the human race the absorption is greatly to its advantage. Nobody can suppose that it is more beneficial to be Breton, or a Basque of French Navarre, to be brought into the current of the ideas and feelings of a highly civilized and cultivated people—to be a member of the French nationality, admitted on equal terms to all the privileges of French citizenship— . . . than to sulk on his own rocks, the half-savage relic of past times, revolving in his own little mental orbit, without participation or interest in the general movement of the world. The same remark applies to the Welshman or the Scottish Highlander as members of the British nation. (Mill 1972, 395)

Here we have a pragmatic approach favored by a well-known exponent of liberalism: absorption of the inferior by the superior raises the inferior to the level of the superior. But we also get a similar posture from some Marxists, as Engels makes clear when he writes:

> There is no country in Europe which does not have in some corner or other one or several fragments of peoples, the remnants of a former population that was suppressed and held in bondage by the nation which later became the main vehicle for historical development. These relics of nations, mercilessly trampled down by the passage of history, as Hegel

expressed it, this ethnic trash always becomes fanatical standard bearers of counterrevolution and remain so until their complete extirpation or loss of their national character, just as their whole existence in general is itself a protest against a great historical revolution. Such in Scotland are the Gaels. . . . Such in France are the Bretons. . . . Such in Spain are the Basques. (Engels 1952)

Both Mill and Engels are thinking of nations broadly, including in them what some would today call ethnic groups. Neither speaks of race, but race has been thought of in similar terms. In the early histories of Argentina and Cuba, for example, when the populations of these countries had a large proportion of "Blacks" (in both) and Amerindians (in Argentina), the founding fathers of the nations argued for the assimilation of these groups into the European population, to raise them to a proper level of development and purge them of elements they thought counterproductive. Indeed, they implemented a policy of European immigration to whitewash the non-"White" elements in the populations of these countries. The message behind these procedures is clear: let us assimilate and homogenize, for this is what works.[13] The continued use of racial and ethnic categories, then, should be eliminated, for they stand in the way of assimilation and advancement.

There is finally an important consideration against the category of nationality that needs to be pointed out. This is that, as Guibernau has indicated, with the increase in globalization, the problems that humans confront are global in character and cannot be solved at the local level (Guibernau 1996, 129). Some of these problems have to do with the nuclear threat, ecology, and the distribution of food: nuclear detonations affect everyone in the global *barrio*; ecological disasters have consequences everywhere in the globe; and the problem of hunger cannot be addressed in the countries where it occurs for they lack the means to feed their people. The national structure, then, is inadequate to deal with the challenges facing humanity and, therefore, according to this point of view, should be abandoned for more efficient and global structures.

THE PERSISTENCE AND INFLUENCE OF RACE, ETHNICITY, AND NATIONALITY

From everything that we have seen thus far in this chapter, one can easily be led to conclude that it is a serious mistake to continue to talk about race, ethnicity, and nationality. There are political, moral, factual, epistemic, and pragmatic reasons that militate against the use of these categories and the concepts and terms that accompany them. Indeed, even mentioning them might be counterproductive, although one could argue that mentioning them should be allowed if the mention has as its purpose their elimination or the elimination of the foul consequences of their use (for the issue of use versus mention of racial terms, see Zack 2002, 80). Yet further reflection suggests that this inference is too hasty. The following points, recognized by a variety of authors, are worthy of attention.

First, as Charles Mills (1998) points out, race, ethnicity, and nationality have influenced, and still influence, the course of human history in significant ways and have substantially affected the lives of individual persons. Can we deny the existence of segregation and discrimination based on them? Can we ignore that these categories have been, and still are, the causes of wars and genocide? Is it possible to brush aside their influence in even the most common and ordinary ways in which we function? Don't I have a special relation to black beans and rice because I am ethnically Cuban? Doesn't O. J. Simpson have a greater probability of suffering from sickle-cell anemia than President Bush because he is "Black"? Did not my college friend go to Vietnam because he was an American national, and did I not go because I was a Cuban national residing in Canada? Surely the answers to these questions are affirmative, and because they are so, it becomes very difficult to argue that we can do away with race, ethnicity, and nationality.[14] If they have such a significant impact on human history as a whole, and on the lives of individual persons, how can we dispense with race, ethnicity, and nationality?

The second point that requires attention is that, as Du Bois argued, the understanding of the past, and even the present, is unintelligible without reference to race, ethnicity, and nationality (Du Bois 1897, 7; see also Corlett 2003, chs. 1–4; Miller 1995, chs. 1 and 2). How can we make any sense of racial, ethnic, and national discrimination without reference to these categories? How can we understand the nature of racism, ethnicism, and nationalism without them? And how can we understand racial, ethnic, and national conflicts in their absence?

These considerations lead to a third point that may be characterized as moral. The future is built on the past, and charting a course for the future that is different from the past requires understanding the past. So, if we wish to eliminate from the future the ills we associate with racism, ethnicism, and nationalism, we need to talk about race, ethnicity, and nationality, and this entails both linguistic terms to designate them and concepts through which we can grasp them. Refusing to accept the presence of race in our experience in particular, and even to talk about it, only serves to exacerbate racism and ignores that the notions of race, just as those of ethnicity and nationality, can be used to correct social ills, provide meaning, and develop a beneficial sense of identity in people, as Alcoff and Young have eloquently pointed out (Alcoff 1999, 32; Young 2001, 392ff.; see also Mosley 1997). Indeed, as Corlett (2003) has forcefully argued, justice requires it.

Nor should we forget that, although there is much controversy about, and certainly serious difficulties with, racial, ethnic, and national boundaries, some scientists still favor the use of these divisions because of what they see as significant differences among human populations. Indeed, even concerning the most controversial of these, that is, racial ones, some scientists claim there is evidence of significant biological and genetic differences among different populations based on evolutionary processes.[15] And in fields such as medicine, racial and ethnic labels are frequently used. Recently, I received the results of some blood tests, and one of them was divided in racial categories: the normal range for "Blacks" was given as different from that of "Whites."[16] Indeed, some scientists argue that it is unlikely that some of these differences will disappear in the foreseeable future, even in the face of much mixing all over the world (Garn 1993, 853; see also Patterson 2000, 15).

Finally, there is a logical point to be made. Even an argument against race, ethnicity, and nationality requires both that we employ terms to refer to them and that we use concepts to grasp them. So, again, we cannot dispense with these terms and concepts altogether. Of course, this does not mean that the concepts of race, ethnicity, and nationality need be coherent or that the terms we use do in fact refer to real things, properties, or relations. To reject that square-circles exist I need to have a term ("square-circle") to refer to them and a concept (a geometrical figure with the properties of a square and a circle) through which I can think about them. But I do not need to think that square-circles exist or that the concept of a square-circle is consistent. Indeed, I do not precisely because the properties of a square and those of a circle are incompatible. The case against race, ethnicity, and nationality, however, covers the whole spectrum, from those who at one extreme want to eliminate the terminology altogether, to those who at the other extreme consider them indispensible taxonomical concepts that correspond to real things in the world.

CONCLUSION

It looks as if, contrary to the view supported by the arguments presented earlier in the chapter, we cannot, or even should not, do away with the language and concepts of race, ethnicity, and nationality. As Try Duster has recently stated about race: "It's there. It's often buried. But I assure you, it's alive" (quoted in Stolberg 2001, section 4, 3). But this creates a gigantic paradox that has been the subject of relentless reflection in recent years. On the one hand, this language and these concepts appear inadequate, and their use is objectionable on various grounds; on the other, we need them to make sense of the past and to chart a better future devoid of the abuses resulting from their use. So what do we do? The only procedure that makes sense is to turn to race, ethnicity, and nationality and explore whether there is any way of understanding them that can help us decide whether to keep them in, or permanently banish them from, our thought and discourse. The answer will depend on whether we can articulate coherent notions that capture the fundamental elements of those concepts, while avoiding the obvious mistakes of such views as the biological conception of race prevalent in the nineteenth century.

We must ask ourselves, then: What is race? What is ethnicity? and What is nationality? Tentative answers to these questions are contained in chapters 3, 4, and 5, respectively. Before we turn to them, however, we need to be clear about what we are asking and the conditions that a good answer would have to satisfy, and this requires that we do away with some conceptual confusions that might cloud the discussion. I turn next, then, to certain sources of obscurity whose clarification can help lay the foundations of subsequent analyses.

NOTES

1. Other expressions, such as "identity politics," are also in use (Guibernau 1996, 143; Young 2001).

2. For another important statement, see Young (2001) and (1990).

3. For another argument in this direction, see Schlesinger (1998).

4. For the discussion of arguments of this sort, see Giménez (1989, 557–71) and Gracia (2000b, 21–26).

5. Among scientists, Lewontin (1972, 1998) and Cavalli-Sforza et al. (1994, 19–20) have proposed versions of this argument. For an accessible, nontechnical account, see Malcomson (2000).

6. For a short history of the science of race, see Cavalli-Sforza et al. (1994, 16–20).

7. Studies show that Caucasoids are extremely heterogeneous genetically, and even races that display less heterogeneity, such as Negroids, present many variations (Nei and Roychoudhury 1982, 36–38, 19–22).

8. See my response in Gracia (2005).

9. As evidence of the extraordinary linguistic variety among Amerindians, consider that there are six different phyla of Amerindian languages, each consisting of several to many different families, in North America alone (Nei and Roychoudhury 1982, 24–25). And the situation in South America is much more complicated.

10. This point is often made by some Marxists, internationalists, and globalists, and it is found in Marx and Engels themselves (Marx and Engels 1968, 55).

11. Banton compares the views of racial variation in Brazil, the United States, and the Caribbean (Banton 1987b, 17ff.).

12. But Gil-White has objected that Hanchard's conclusion is premature, based only on the cases of Brazil and the United States (Gil-White 2001a).

13. The same attitude to homogenize and assimilate is common elsewhere and in recent years has been aggressively pursued in Arab countries, Ethiopia, Ceylon, and many other places. See Guibernau (1996, 125).

14. Among those who answer them affirmatively or provide materials for an affirmative answer are Alcoff (2001); Gooding-Williams (2001b); Fanon (2001); Bernasconi (2001a); Donald and Rattansi (1992); Boxill (2001a); and Levin (1997).

15. Even concerning the most controversial features—such as skin pigmentation, facial structure, and hair texture—some scientists propose that they came about by strong processes of natural selection through a small number of gene substitutions and therefore that they are significant. See, for example, Nei (1978) and his other authored or coauthored articles listed in the bibliography. Also see van den Berghe (2001). For a defense of a biological conception of race, see M. G. Smith (1986) and Olson (2001). Boxill (2001a) makes a case against the philosophical arguments given against the view that biological races do not exist.

16. For a discussion of the issues in medicine and race, see Zack (2002, 100–102).

2

CONCEPTUAL FOUNDATIONS

To answer the questions What is race? What is ethnicity? and What is nationality? is by no means easy. Some of the difficulties involved have to do with the objects of the questions themselves, but some arise from at least four other sources: (1) a certain ambiguity present in the questions; (2) confusions between different approaches one may adopt when pursuing answers; (3) the kinds of evidence provided in support of answers; and (4) a general tendency to blur the distinctions between race, ethnicity, and nationality. Some of this needs to be cleared up before we can make any serious headway in our inquiry.

AMBIGUITY IN THE QUESTIONS

The questions What is race? What is ethnicity? and What is nationality? have the same form: "What is X?" But questions with this form may be intended to ask a variety of things, as is clear from the many correct answers that one can give to them: a woman, a mother, substance, a quality, a relation, a thought, a quantity, a point of view, a place, the time at which I have to leave, a source of trouble, a Catholic, a democrat, a Cuban, a dumbbell, a letter, an idiot, the place he bought, the Democratic Party, a criminal, a philosopher, a good sister, a priest, a discipline of learning, a look, a government official, a value, universal, individual, stupid, strict, a policeman, a category, a piece of wood, a color, a text, the color of the paper, and so on. How I interpret the question depends very much on what "X" stands for and the circumstances surrounding it. If "X" stands for a cat, then it makes no sense to interpret the question as asking for religious affiliation; and if the question is asked in a political strategy session, it probably means that the correct answer has to do with political affiliation rather than gender or religion. In short, as Aristotle (*Topics* 103b25) noted, a question of this form can be intended to ask for quite different things, depending on a variety of factors.

In order to be clear as to how to understand a question with this form, then, we must first ask whether it makes any difference if, instead of asking What is X? one were to ask What is *an* X? The answer is affirmative, for although "What is X?" can be taken in various ways, the question "What is an X?" always concerns a kind. If I ask "What is a human being?" the answer sought is probably something such as "a rational animal." And if I ask "What is a boat?" the answer will probably have to do with the kind of thing a boat is. Indeed, "What is an X?" seems elliptical for "What particular kind is X?"

If instead of an indefinite article we introduce a definite article into the question, to read "What is *the* X?" then the description of X becomes definite, and therefore, the object of inquiry is a particular thing. "What is the woman?" is short for "What is the woman who came to visit?" And the answer might be: "A democrat." "What is the cat that spilt the milk?" requires an answer such as: "Nutty." Still, the answers to these questions could be kind answers, although they could also be descriptive in some other ways. "What is the X?" can be answered by: "The kind we have been talking about." But there are differences between "What is the X?" and "What is X?" insofar as the latter is generic, whereas the former is specific. "What is X?" when it is a question about a kind, is always a question about a general kind; "What is the X?" is a question about an instance of a kind, even if the instance is itself a kind.

If we apply these observations to race, for example, we end up with three different questions, each of which displays in turn some degree of ambiguity: What is race? What is a race? and What is the race? In the last question, "the race" is elliptical for a definite description that refers to a particular race, such as "the race that originates in the Caucasus." Insofar as this book is not concerned with particular races, ethnicities, or nationalities, we need not be concerned with this kind of question and its answer. The other two questions are more pertinent. The second is less ambiguous than the first insofar as it asks for a kind. "What is a race?" seems to be asking for the particular kind that race is. But the first is very broad and could be interpreted in many different ways, two of which in particular are important for us to consider here. One interprets the question as asking for a definition; another, for a metaphysical categorization. Note that what will be said here about race also applies to ethnicity and nationality.

Definition

A definition is a sentence in which the *definiens* (defining expression) is supposed to identify the conditions that the referent of the *definiendum* (expression to be defined) satisfies. "A triangle is a geometrical figure with three angles" is a definition of a triangle, because the *definiens* (i.e., a geometrical figure with three angles) is supposed to identify the conditions that are satisfied by the *definiendum* (i.e., a triangle). There are, of course, many kinds of definitions: functional, ostensive, stipulative, by genus and difference, and so on (Robinson 1954). For present purposes, however, it is enough that we understand a definition in a general way, as an attempt to make clear necessary and sufficient conditions. But, one may ask: Necessary and sufficient conditions of what?

Here we have to remind ourselves that we can be speaking of knowledge, language, or being. Definitions are frequently divided into real and nominal. Real definitions identify necessary and sufficient conditions of being, as when I define humans as rational animals. Nominal definitions identify conditions of linguistic usage, as when I define "human" as a term to be predicated only of subject terms of which also "rational" and "animal" are predicated. A real definition of *race, ethnicity*, or *nationality*, then, will consist of a sentence in which the predicate is supposed to express the necessary and sufficient conditions that race, ethnicity, or nationality must satisfy, whereas a nominal definition will aim to identify the conditions of the proper use of the terms "race," "ethnicity," and "nationality."

To real and nominal definitions, one may want to add epistemic ones. The function of these is to establish criteria that can be used by a knower to distinguish the kind in question. Thus, in an epistemic definition, the predicate is supposed to establish the necessary and sufficient conditions that make it possible for a knower to distinguish the kind to which the subject term of the definition refers. When "Humans are rational animals" is taken epistemically, the predicate proposes to establish the conditions I have to know in order to know something as human. More on this later.

A definition—whether real, nominal, or epistemic—of *a* race, *an* ethnos, or *a* nation will aim to identify conditions of a particular race, ethnos, or nation, such as "Black," Hispanic, or American, in contrast with the conditions of race in general, ethnicity in general, or nationality in general. As I said earlier, here I am concerned with the latter, rather than the former.

Metaphysical Categorization

The question "What is X?" may also be interpreted as a request for a metaphysical categorization. This is in many ways like a definition, except that it is more general. The identification of conditions that definitions identify involve categorization, of course. When I say that a triangle is a geometrical figure with three angles, I have in fact categorized triangles as geometrical figures and as geometrical figures that fall into a further category, namely, that of a thing having three angles. So I have made the claim that triangles belong to the category "three-angled geometrical figure." But the categorization in question has been made in terms of categories that are very close—some would claim immediate—to the thing being categorized. I can, of course, also categorize triangles in more general ways. For example, I can say that they are imaginable objects, or that they are physical or nonphysical objects, and so on. When the categorization attempted is in terms of more, or the most, general categories, then it is metaphysical.[1] In such cases, one might try to determine whether triangles are substances or features of substances, mental concepts or entities existing independently of minds, and so on. In the case of race, for example, we would be searching for the general categories under which it can be classified—a group, a relation, a concept, a quality, and so on.

The difference between a definition and a metaphysical categorization is a matter of degree of generality. One is more general than the other, but both are required for a thorough analysis, and therefore for a comprehensive understanding. Moreover, both involve categorization. What is X? then, may be used to ask for a variety of things, two of which are particularly pertinent for our inquiry: a definition and a metaphysical categorization. Both involve categorization, but the second refers to more general categories, whereas the first refers to categories closer to whatever is being categorized.

We should keep in mind, however, that often definitions include references to most general categories for a variety of reasons, two of which stand out: first, the definer desires to give as complete an analysis of the notion in question as possible; second, the immediate category of which the thing being defined as a member is close to a most general category. An example of the first is Boethius's classic definition of person as "an individual substance of a rational nature" (Boethius 1968, III, 85). Normally, one would expect the definition of person to be something less comprehensive, such as "A person is a rational animal." An example of the second is the definition of color as a quality of objects that allows them to affect the way light is reflected by them. Again, normally one would expect something different, which in this case would be less general.

As we shall see later, I combine both definition and metaphysical categorization in the discussions of race, ethnicity, and nationality in subsequent chapters. However, my aim is to provide not strict definitions or metaphysical categorizations, but only approximations sufficient to establish clear distinctions between race, ethnicity, and nationality. We must keep in mind the overall modest goal of the book. Now, for the sake of convenience, henceforth I refer to this combined approach as a metaphysical analysis.

THREE APPROACHES

Apart from the various ways in which the question What is X? may be interpreted, the discussion of its answer is frequently marred by a confusion between three different approaches that one may adopt in trying to answer it. The distinction between these may be illustrated by comparing the following three kinds of questions: (1) What is X? (2) How do I know X? and (3) How do we speak about X? By the first question, we mean to ask something about X itself, considered independent of what we know or say about it. If I ask, for example, What is Hunter? the answer would be something such as a cat, because Hunter is one of my two cats. This approach might be described as *metaphysical* because it is an inquiry into things themselves, whatever they are. By the second question, How do I know X? we mean to ask something about the way in which I know X, so that this has to do with the knowing relation between X and me. Thus, I may ask about how I know Hunter, or how I know that Hunter is a cat. The answer might be that I know Hunter because I perceive it or that I know it is a cat because Hunter has features that characterize cats and only cats. This approach might be described as *epistemological* because it has to do with the knowledge we have or can have.

Finally, by the third question, How do we speak about X? we mean to ask something about the language we use to talk about X. In the example of Hunter, I could have in mind to ask something about the proper name "Hunter" that I use to refer to Hunter, or about the common term "cat" that I also use to talk about Hunter. In this context, what is important is not what Hunter is independently, or what I might think about Hunter, but rather the language I use when I talk about Hunter and how it functions and accomplishes the tasks that it is intended to accomplish, such as cause-effective reference or correct understanding. This approach might be described as *linguistic* because it has to do with language.

The confusion between metaphysics, epistemology, and linguistics is not unusual in philosophy, or peculiar to discussions of race, ethnicity, and nationality. Indeed, it permeates much philosophy today, and examples of it can be found almost in any period of the history of the discipline, particularly in the discussion of fundamental philosophical topics such as universals and individuals. One need only examine the works of Porphyry, Boethius, and Abelard, and in particular their respective discussions of universals, to see how they mixed these approaches in various ways, often unwittingly, but sometimes with what appears to be full awareness (Gracia 2000a). This last point should alert us to the fact that what I have been referring to as "confusions" here are in many cases conscious positions taken by philosophers in answer to problems whose solutions they think requires them. Indeed, the epistemological approach to metaphysical questions became especially popular in early modern philosophy as a result of the belief that it makes no sense to ask questions about what things are in themselves apart from the human mechanisms whereby we know them. Questions about what X is were translated into questions about how I know X. For example, whereas a metaphysical approach to individuation asks *what it is* that makes this 3 x 5 card the individual card *it is*, those who use an epistemological approach would ask rather *how I know* that this 3 x 5 card is the individual card *I think it is*. A question about *individuation* is thus translated into a question about *identification*.[2]

More recently, the belief that all thought and knowledge is mediated through language has prompted many philosophers to abandon the discussion of both metaphysical and epistemological questions independently of language and to frame all philosophical issues previously thought to be metaphysical or epistemological in linguistic terms. Questions about *what X is*, or *how I know it*, have been translated into questions about *how I speak of X* or *how the language I use to speak of X functions*. Going back to the example mentioned earlier, questions about Hunter's individuality or identification are translated into questions about the terms I use to speak of Hunter, namely terms such as "individual," "this," and "Hunter," and how these terms function when I use them. The result is that a great part of the discussion of these issues has been turned over to the philosophy of language or to logic, and the metaphysical and epistemological projects that had preoccupied other philosophers have been changed into the search for a precise logical language.[3]

If we apply what has been said to race, ethnicity, and nationality, it is easy to see how it affects their philosophical discussion and can create confusion. If the metaphysical, epistemological, and linguistic approaches are kept separate, we end up with different questions, for example: (1) What is race? What is ethnicity? What is nationality? (2) How do we know race?

How do we know ethnicity? How do we know nationality? and (3) How does the term "race" function in English? How does the term "ethnicity" function in English? How does the term "nationality" function in English?

Keep in mind that, although the second and third sets of questions clearly point in the direction of epistemology and linguistics (or logic), the import of the first is unclear. Indeed, we saw earlier that, apart from signaling a request for at least two different kinds of categorizations—definitional and metaphysical—the search for a definition can itself be understood in three ways, as involving conditions of being, of knowing, or of speaking. This means that the three approaches of which we have been speaking in this section apply to the first type of question we intend to explore. We need, therefore, to be on our guard both about what we want to accomplish and about what those who have addressed these issues have actually accomplished.

Clearly, both the questions that have been presented and the examples that have been given contain substantial ambiguities. We need to keep in mind the propaedeutic requirement to begin any analysis of race, ethnicity, or nationality by conceptually distinguishing the three different kinds of questions to which I have referred and the three approaches one may adopt even with respect to the first question. To assume, as many philosophers do, that these questions or approaches are indistinguishable because the answers to the questions are interdependent, or that the impossibility of answering one of the questions immediately justifies its collapse into the others, are serious mistakes. Logically, both the questions and the approaches are distinguishable, and this distinction should not be disregarded unless one can muster convincing reasons for doing so.

The moves that are usually made to disqualify some of these questions are quite unwarranted. I may not be able to answer the question of *whether there are* intelligent beings in the rest of the universe because I lack the empirical techniques to do so, but that does not mean that the question should be considered illegitimate—indeed, even the members of the Vienna Circle and their followers granted this—or that it should be regarded as the same question as *whether I am able to know that there are* intelligent beings in the universe besides humans (Ayer 1936, 38). It appears essential that both questions be distinguished, particularly in a case when, in principle, it may be possible to find answers to both, even though in practice it is not presently possible to answer one of them. Likewise, it would be absurd to argue that the question of whether the universe has a beginning in time is nonsensical, or is identical to the question of whether we can know that the universe has a beginning in time, because we cannot at present have an answer to it, or even because, as Kant argued, it is unanswerable (Kant 1963, 396ff.).

Making the distinction is helpful even to those who believe that the answer to the question is impossible for humans. We need, then, to keep in mind the differences between these questions and what they tell us about different approaches to race, ethnicity, and nationality. It will not do to confuse questions about race with questions about how we know race, and likewise with ethnicity and nationality. Moreover, it is methodologically unsound to reduce some of these questions, and the approaches they reveal, to others without proper argumentation and evidence. Until such time as a sound argument is made that shows the need to collapse some of these approaches or to disregard some in favor of others, it is better to keep them separate. In this way at least, we can ascertain the force of the claims being made and the value of arguments proposed for them.

In short, the proper understanding of race, ethnicity, and nationality requires us to make sure that we do not carelessly confuse the metaphysical, epistemological, and linguistic approaches to them. Consider, for example, the case of a national group such as Americans. One thing is to ask about the necessary and sufficient conditions that make someone American; another is to ask about the necessary and sufficient conditions of knowing that someone is American; and still another is to ask about the necessary and sufficient conditions of the effective use of the term "American." The answer to the first could very well be that the necessary and sufficient conditions of being American is to have American citizenship; one must be an American citizen to qualify as American. The answer to the second, however, could be something such as having a birth certificate or a certificate of naturalization. And the answer to the third would involve making clear the rules under which the term "American" can be and is effectively used. Clearly the answers to these questions are quite different insofar as citizenship is a feature of persons, a birth certificate is a document, and a rule is a norm of behavior. It is essential, then, to be clear as to what is being sought, and this applies not just to nationality, but also to race and ethnicity.

In the discussion of race, ethnicity, and nationality in chapters 3, 4, and 5, I shall show how some proposed views about these phenomena fail to preserve the distinctions between them. This weakens the positions and undermines the validity of the arguments used to support them.

THREE KINDS OF EVIDENCE

A third source of confusion found in discussions of race, ethnicity, and nationality feeds from the first two, but is of a different kind. Here the confusion is not with respect to the nature of the questions asked or the approaches used in answering them, but rather with the kinds of factors presented in the arguments employed to defend particular views.[4] These factors can be of three sorts. First are what might be called facts. A fact is a state of affairs that is independent of what humans think, although human thoughts themselves are also facts. *That* the Earth is round is a fact, and *that* I perceive it as flat, when I am standing on it, is another. Second, what is adduced as evidence may consist of human views. For example, when some persons think that the Earth is round, *what* they think is a view about the shape of the Earth, and when some think the Earth is flat, *what* they think is another view. Of course, *that* I think the Earth is round, or flat, is a fact, even though *what* I think about the Earth is a view rather than a fact. Third, factors used as evidence may consist of value judgments about both facts and views. For example, the judgments *that* killing a person is wrong or *that* the view of the Earth as flat is false are both value judgments—the first concerns morality and the second truth.

Arguments are constructed on the bases of these three different kinds of evidence. Someone may argue, for example, that because the Earth is round, its center is equidistant from all points on its periphery. Or someone may argue that because some person or persons think the Earth is flat, the Earth is indeed flat. Or still, someone may argue that because he dislikes broccoli, broccoli is not good. In the first, a fact is established on the basis of another fact; in the second, a fact is established on the basis of a view; and in the third, a fact is established on the basis of a value judgment. These examples should make my point clear to some extent, but examples concerning race, ethnicity, and nationality would even be more helpful. Here are some.

One may argue that races do not exist (fact) because there is evidence that the notion of race is merely a social construction without grounds in the makeup of human beings (fact). This argument is common in the literature, and many of the arguments given in chapter 1 based on scientific evidence fall into this category. Or one may argue that ethnicity has to do with descent (fact) because that is what some people believe it is (view). This argument has been proposed by anthropologists such as Gil-White, who argues that descent is a necessary and sufficient condition of ethnicity because an ethnic group he studied regards it as such. Or finally, one may argue that there are no real distinctions among nations (fact) because accepting national distinctions results in the oppression of people and this is bad (value judgment). Some of the pragmatic arguments against nationality we saw in chapter 1 take this direction.

Note, then, that the fundamental issue in all these cases is the kind of evidence used in argumentation. In one case this evidence consists of facts, in another of views, and in still another of value judgments. The aim of the arguments themselves and the claims that they are geared to establish, however, can vary. Facts may be used by some to establish other facts, people's views, or even value judgments. Likewise, people's views may be used by some to establish facts, people's views, or value judgments. And value judgments may also be used by some to establish facts, people's views, or other value judgments.

The problem with some of these moves is that they are illegitimate. For example, people's views cannot establish facts—other than those concerning the view in question—even if in certain circumstances they may help to make us know about them. My view of the shape of the Earth cannot be used to establish the shape of the Earth, even though a small child might learn about the shape of the Earth from my view about it. This is the basis of all education. Likewise, value judgments cannot legitimately be used to establish facts. Differences in intelligence cannot be denied because such differences may be used discriminatorily against certain persons.

Unfortunately, some of the illegitimate moves mentioned are frequently found in the literature on race, ethnicity, and nationality. Often, people's views about these in general, or about their particular race, ethnicity, and nationality, are taken as determinant of facts about these. Indeed, it is quite fashionable to say that these are matters of individual choice or social preference. To be "Black" is just a matter of self-identification with other "Blacks"; to be Hispanic is just a matter of self-identification with other Hispanics; and to be Cuban has to do with self-identification with other Cubans. Racial, ethnic, and national membership are determined by personal choice, self-identification, or group identification, that is, the views that people have, rather than by factors independent, or at least partially independent, of what anyone may think. Likewise, racial, ethnic, and national differences are denied, without regard for the facts, on the basis that, were such differences to be accepted, they could or would have negative consequences for certain people.[5] Thus value judgments are used to reject views without a proper examination of facts. Finally, facts themselves are used to ignore moral issues. The fact that certain groups score lower than others on certain tests is used to conclude that these groups should not have the same rights as others. Most of these moves are unwarranted and lead to confusion and obfuscation rather than clarity and enlightenment. And it is important to contrast these illegitimate moves with legitimate ones made by authors such as Appiah and Zack against the biological conception of race (fact), on the basis of scientific evidence (fact) against it.

BLURRING THE DISTINCTIONS BETWEEN
RACE, ETHNICITY, AND NATIONALITY

A fourth source of confusion in discussions of race, ethnicity, and nationality has to do with the boundaries between them. Race, ethnicity, and nationality are so confused and mixed in the popular mind that it is not easy
to distinguish them (Sollors 2002, 98; Cohen 1999a, 1–3; Takaki 1982, 13).
Almost no day goes by in which I do not run into statements by members
of the press, politicians, and ordinary people that confuse them. The confusion in government agencies is notorious and is most clear in the way questions about race, ethnicity, and nationality are asked in official documents
such as the Census, where, for example, the category "White," which is
racial, has been opposed to Hispanic, which is ethnic, and to Mexican,
which is national (although the last one can also be ethnic; Mattson 1992).
Garn has noted that these confusions go deep into history and are part of
the unfortunate fabric of racial, ethnic, and national thinking going back
several centuries (Garn 1993, 844). The Nazis spoke of Germans and Jews
as both races and nations, and even Du Bois talks of Negroes as a nation (Du
Bois 1897, 8; see also Gobineau 2000, 45; Darwin 1874, 190; Galton 2000;
and Voltaire 1965, 9).[6] And some anthropologists, such as Gil-White (1999;
2001b), argue that it is part of our evolved linguistic mechanism to think of
ethnicity in terms of descent, as we think of species.

Among academics who discuss these categories there are explicit attempts to blur the distinction between them (cf. Mason 1999, 21; Wallman
1978; 1986). Indeed, Omi and Winant (1994) argue, quite effectively, that
race has generally been studied under three paradigms: ethnicity, class, and
nation (see also the definition of "ethnic group" in Dinnerstein and
Reimers 1975, xiii, note). In particular, the attempts to eliminate the distinction between race and ethnicity come from two sides: on the side of race
insofar as it is seen as including ethnic elements and therefore as fundamentally ethnic,[7] and on the side of ethnicity insofar as this is taken to be
so permeated with racial elements that it cannot be clearly separated from
these (Gordon 1995, particularly 119, 130–31; Alcoff 2000a; Goldberg 1993,
who introduces the term "ethnorace"). The first might be described as trying to substitute the notion of ethnic race for the notions of race and ethnicity. The second might be described as doing the same but with the notion of racial ethnicity.

At least three important arguments can be given in support of the first.
First, one can appeal to history. Historical discussions of race have always included ethnic elements. From the very beginning, racial divisions involved
cultural divisions. Negroes and "Blacks" have always been described as being

different from "Whites" and "Yellows," not only in terms of their physical and genetic characteristics, but also in terms of customs, attitudes, and achievements. Witness the views of such authors as Hegel, Gobineau, Kant, Senghor, Du Bois, and Sartre (Hegel 2000; Gobineau 2000; Kant 1991, 111; Senghor 1961, 1211; Du Bois 1897; Sartre 2001, 125). This reflects the fact—so the argument goes—that the notion of race is inextricably mixed with ethnic elements.

A second argument is factual: the notion of race cannot be separated clearly from the notion of ethnicity because, as Zack and other authors mentioned in chapter 1 argue, the physical phenotypes on which race is based are not easily distinguishable from cultural ones. Most phenotypes in fact are the result of both physical and environmental forces, and racial phenotypes are notoriously so (King 1981, 20–21, 28–29, 33–34; Cavalli-Sforza et al. 1994, 4–5, 7, 17–18; Lewontin 1998). This extends to such obvious ones as the color of one's skin.

The third argument is pragmatic and points out that every time one tries to separate the notion of race from the notion of ethnicity, race gets entangled with ethnicity, so it is counterproductive to keep trying. We need not do more here than refer to the case of the change of name from "Black" to "African American." This example indicates that, as Alcoff points out, in spite of the efforts of "Blacks" to develop a conception of themselves and an identity based on ethnicity, race gets into it (Alcoff 2000a, 36ff.).

The arguments for the substitution of the notion of a racial ethnicity for the notions of ethnos and race follow similar lines. The first argument, formulated by Alcoff and others, points out that historical conceptions of ethnicity have always involved racial elements, such as physical phenotypes and descent (Alcoff 2000a; see also Grosfoguel and Georas 1996). This is evident in that most opinions about peoples and the like involve race.

The second argument points out that the notions of ethnicity cannot be separated from the notion of race because in fact that is how humans think. Gil-White (1999; 2001b) has conducted research that suggests that humans might be hardwired to think of ethnicity as involving the sharing of an essence based on descent. If this is so, then there is very little sense in arguing for a conception of these notions that keeps them separate.

Finally, pragmatically we see that when one tries to separate ethnicity from race, one usually fails, so there is no point in maintaining the effort. Here the case of Hispanics is instructive, for this group is generally regarded as racial, in spite of the efforts of Alcoff (2000a) and others to point out that this is inaccurate in that Hispanics come in all kinds of races. So why maintain a distinction that is generally ignored?

In short, race and ethnicity are regarded, intentionally or unintentionally, as hopelessly intertwined and not capable of distinction apart from each other. The phenomenon of the Oreo, in which one speaks of the same person being "Black" on the outside (i.e., racially) and "White" in the inside (i.e., ethnically), illustrates the difficulties of keeping these two notions separate. Indeed, it looks as if in this case the same terms are used racially and ethnically, and this suggests that in fact what we have are perhaps two sides of the same phenomenon. Race and ethnicity are simply two sides of the same coin. So much for the argument in favor of keeping race and ethnicity together.

But there is another side to this story, supported by at least four arguments. First, the attempts at merging race and ethnicity often undermine their understanding, for in order to construct notions of "ethnic race" or "racial ethnicity," we must first be clear as to the differences between race and ethnicity. Without a determination of these differences, we cannot possibly come up with a clear concept that combines the two. Note that the argument is not that these concepts are not possible. The argument is rather that in order to propose a clear understanding that combines the notions of race and ethnicity, we need first to be clear as to what race and ethnicity are and how they are related to each other. If this is not possible, we must be clear as to why it is so.

But this is not all, for just as there is considerable evidence in ordinary language that suggests that these concepts are mixed in the public mind, there is also plenty of evidence that shows an effort to keep them separate (Takaki 1993, 10; 1982, 29). Consider the whole effort of African Americans to change their name from "Blacks" to "African Americans," and of Jamaicans to emphasize ethnicity rather than race (see Grosfogel and Georas 1996). The very language of an Oreo, which implies "racially 'Black'" but "ethnically 'White,'" and the efforts of Hispanics to keep the two notions separate, indicate the strong sense that they should be kept distinct (Gracia 2000b). This repository of public opinion should not be set aside unless one has some very good reasons to the contrary.

Third, the opinions of some members of the scientific community tend to confirm a distinction between race and ethnicity. The evidence comes from investigations in various sciences, but primarily biology, sociology, and linguistics. Biologists generally agree that, although some of the gross divisions that ordinary folks make concerning race are imprecise and inadequate, there are significant genetic differences, developed in a long process of evolution, that separate various human populations.[8] Moreover, it is quite clear that linguistic differences, which are generally regarded as the

most significant ethnic differences we have, do not correlate with these genetic differences (King 1981; 67–71; Nei and Roychoudhury 1982, 42;
Cavalli-Sforza et al. 1994, 381). And some sociologists accept that societies
divide themselves along what their members believe to be racial and ethnic
lines, but that these are generally separate and separable (cf. McKee 2000,
xv–xvi; Ringer and Lawless 1989, 27; van den Berghe 1967, 910; Smedley
1993, 29–30; Banton 1983, 1–15).

Finally, we could add what might be called a moral or political argument, namely, that the obliteration of the distinction between the notions of
race and ethnicity contributes to their neglect as what Omi and Winant
have called their "autonomous fields of social conflict, political organization,
and cultural/ideological meaning" (Omi and Winant 1994, 48). And this
constitutes, in turn, an obstacle to the correction of ills in social reality that
we need to undertake.

Matters are not very different when it comes to ethnicity and nationality, or race and nationality. In Europe in particular, nations are usually understood in ethnic terms, and even sometimes in racial terms (e.g., Herder
2000, 26; Gobineau 2000, 46; Poliakov 1974). Examples of the former are
clear in the Balkans, but can also be found elsewhere, including Russia,
Spain, and Germany.

THE PLAN

The plan for the remainder of this investigation is to take up race, ethnicity,
and nationality and examine them in depth. In the title of this book, I put
race first because in many ways race is the most controversial topic with
which we shall be dealing. It is also the one that has the most far-reaching
consequences in the sociopolitical structure, and one that has been the
source of much suffering in the world. In the discussion, however, I alter this
order and put ethnicity first, for three reasons: first, ethnicity is less controversial, and there are some aspects of its analysis that should help us with the
understanding of race; second, we can better discuss the recent attempts at
understanding race in terms of ethnicity if we first understand ethnicity; and
third, I have developed a theory of ethnicity elsewhere that I partly use in
the analysis of race (Gracia 2000a).

In the discussion that follows, we need to keep in mind the distinctions
between various questions we can ask about race, ethnicity, and nationality;
the different ways in which the question "What is X?" can be understood;
the three different approaches that can be used to answer it; and three dif-

ferent kinds of evidence that can be brought forth in support of the answers. "What is race, ethnicity, and nationality?" should be taken as asking for a categorization that includes both general metaphysical categories as well as the more specific categories included in definitions. The metaphysical, epistemic, and linguistic approaches used must be kept separate, and in order to prevent fallacious reasonings, we must also be clear as to whether the evidence we use in arguments consists of facts, views, or judgments of value.

The most fundamental task of this book is to come up with effective metaphysical analyses of race, ethnicity, and nationality. So it is appropriate to ask how these are to be taken in relation to Strawson's notorious distinction between descriptive and revisionary metaphysics. Do these analyses express claims about the way we think about the world (conceptual description) or about the ways in which we should think about the world (conceptual revision; Strawson 1959, 9)? Or, adding a third term to Strawson's distinction, do they express claims about the way the world is (real description)? Surely, it should not be the first, both because we can always be wrong about the things about which we think and because there is strong disagreement between the ways people think about race, ethnicity, and nationality. The second faces difficulties insofar as prescription independently of facts makes no sense. And the third is inappropriate if race, ethnicity, and nationality, as many believe, are mere conceptual human constructions without bases in reality.

The answer is that these formulas are intended to be both descriptive and prescriptive, but in different ways.[9] They are intended to be descriptive in that they reflect the most fundamental principles that underlie the ways in which we think about race, ethnicity, and nationality because these ways are based on a common, collective experience of the way the world is. But they are also prescriptive in that they are intended as ways in which it makes sense for us to think about these matters; they are meant to tell us the right way of thinking about these topics precisely because of the way the world is. In this, the enterprise is not very different from that of a physicist or a biologist, even though the objects of investigation may not be of the same sort that concern physicists or biologists. Nor should it be confused with ethical and political discussions in which the implications for individual or collective action are drawn out.

NOTES

1. I defend the view of metaphysics implied by this in Gracia (1999a, 131–58).
2. Wolff is a case in point. See Gracia (1994).

3. This was characterized as "the linguistic turn" in the well-known work of Rorty (1967).

4. These often lead to fallacies, many of which have been indicated in the context of race (Ingle 1978).

5. Boxill (2001a) criticizes this move in the case of race.

6. Apparently, Sir Walter Scott's popular novel *Ivanhoe* (1820) did much to expand the use of "race" in this way because it refers to Norman and Saxon races (Banton 1998, 18).

7. This approach goes back to Du Bois (1897). See also Gilroy (1993); Sartre (2001, 137); Senghor (2001); Fanon (2001, 185). Locke (1924) speaks of "a notion of ethnic race."

8. For the discussion of this view, see Garn (1993); Nei and Roychoudhury (1974); Cavalli-Sforza et al. (1994); Zack (2002, 66–70).

9. I discuss Strawson's distinction and my view of metaphysics in relation to description and prescription in Gracia (1999a, 94–98).

3

ETHNICITY

So what is ethnicity, and are there any answers to the objections against it presented in the opening chapter of this investigation? In a recent book, *Race, Racism, and Reparations*, Angelo Corlett attempts to answer these questions and makes an important distinction between two analyses, one in terms of "public-policy" and another "metaphysical, " which in his opinion do not have to coincide (Corlett 2003, 51). His main concern in the book is with the first, but he does offer some concrete ideas about the second as well.

The primary aim of a public policy analysis of ethnicity is "to accurately classify people into categories of ethnicity for purposes of justice under the law" (Corlett 2003, 46). The main topic of the book is reparations for members of ethnic and racial groups that have suffered discrimination and other social ills as a result of their ethnicity or race. And reparations of this sort require the accurate identification of people along ethnic and racial lines. However, the need to come up with accurate classificatory criteria for ethnic and racial groups is not just a requirement of reparations; it is also necessary to implement other social policies, such as affirmative action. After presenting his view in the context of the Latino ethnic group, Corlett claims that it "serves more than any other philosophical conception of who and what we are as Latinos to assist governments in enacting and administering positive public policies aimed at Latinos" (Corlett 2003, 60). Of course, his point is not intended to apply only to Latinos; it is intended to cover all ethnic groups, although he uses Latinos as what he considers a clear and effective illustration. So what is his view, and is it really effective for the implementation of public policy?

In Corlett's own words, it is that, "for public policy considerations, genealogy ought to be construed as both a necessary and sufficient condition of award or benefit" (Corlett 2003, 51). So if reparations are in order for Latinos, a genetic tie is both necessary and sufficient to carry them out. This is what the government needs to pay attention to. But, of course, there is more to belonging to an ethnic group than genealogy. To be a Latino is more than just having Latino ancestry. And here is where the metaphysical analysis comes in. The result is a graded conception in which to be Latino is a matter of degree and involves various factors. As Corlett puts it:

> *Aside from public policy consideration,* however, factors that would go toward making one more or less a Latino may include the degree to which one knows and respects a Latino language or dialect thereof; possesses and respects a traditional Latino name; engages in and respects Latino culture or parts thereof; accepts and respects himself or herself as a Latino; is accepted and respected as a Latino by other Latinos; and is construed as a Latino by outgroup members. . . . Each of these conditions admits of degrees . . . [but] neither (*sic*) . . . is either necessary or sufficient to make one a Latino. (Corlett 2003, 51)

In short, then, the metaphysical view of Latino consists of a list of conditions (Corlett does not tell us whether the list he provides is intended to be exhaustive), each of which is subject to degree, resulting in one being more or less Latino. The public policy view also is subject to degree, but unlike the metaphysical one, it is presented as a necessary and sufficient condition for the implementation of public policy. Presumably, something similar can be said about other ethnic groups.

The test of the effectiveness of both of these views is whether they can answer the objections considered in the opening chapter of this study. Unfortunately, the answer is negative. The genealogical view can muster some strength in some of the categories identified, such as the factual. And Corlett tries to answer some of the objections in the other categories—the epistemic, moral, political, and pragmatic. But his account is unconvincing insofar as genealogy is as imprecise, in the social context, as most of the other markers used to identify members of ethnic groups. This point has been made before by more than one author (see Gracia 2000b, 2000a; García 2001a).

Consider the following four problems. First, the descent criterion involves either circularity or a reduction to some other factor, for it always must have an origin. Membership in a descent line presupposes the line. The problem arises in that the identity of the line has to be assumed (thus the circularity) or analyzed in terms of nongenetic factors, such as territory, political unit, language, culture, and so on (thus the reduction). If I am Latino because my grandfather was Latino, why was he Latino?

Second, descent appears to be both too narrow and too broad as a criterion of membership in an ethnos such as Latinos. It is too narrow because there are people classified as Latinos who have no genetic link to other Latinos (e.g., children of Welsh immigrants to Argentina who have settled in the United States). And descent is too broad because it would have to include far-removed descendants of Latinos who have not lived in a Latino country, have not associated with other Latinos, and do not share with them any perceptible traits. Indeed, it could apply to humanity as a whole, insofar as all humans seem to be connected by descent. And if so, how could this giant ethnos be divided into other ethne? Consider that the courts have at various times established artificial descent boundaries in the case of "Blacks," for example, great-grandparents, eighth generation, thirty-second generation, and so on. The genealogy criterion needs to be more specific; we must be told where it begins and where it stops. This is why the courts have had to make rules about it. Corlett's criterion of descent, then, taken by itself, is ineffective for the very purpose he has devised for it, namely, as a sufficient condition of being Latino for social policy implementation.

Third, descent is too imprecise a criterion insofar as it is not clear what it involves, for what constitutes descent? A completely unmixed descent or a partially mixed one? If the first, it is doubtful many Latinos would qualify insofar as many Latinos in the United States, for example, have mixed ancestry. If descent is taken to involve only partially mixed ancestry, then having had a single Latino ancestor, one hundred generations removed, would be sufficient to make one qualify.

Fourth, although as we saw earlier, some research indicates that some ethnic groups regard descent as a necessary, and perhaps even as a sufficient, condition of membership in the groups, there are others that do not. Indeed, there are many counterexamples to Corlett's view. One is Jews. One can become Jewish through conversion, but one's children would still be Jewish even if they decided to reject the Jewish religion. Another counterexample is adoptions. An adopted child can join the ethnic group of the adopting parents. But let me cite a particular and very well-known counterexample: Ivo Andric, a Nobel Prize winner who is in fact Croatian by descent, and even Catholic in religion, but considers himself a Serb and is treated as such by both Croatians and Serbs. If Corlett's view is correct, then Croatians and Serbs are mistaken about who qualifies as a Serb, and this seems far-fetched.

In short, descent cannot consistently function as a condition, necessary or sufficient, of ethnicity. It cannot be necessary because people not connected by descent can belong to the same ethnos; and it is not sufficient because there are people connected by descent who belong to different ethnic groups.

So much, then, for Corlett's public policy analysis, but what of his metaphysical one? It is difficult to evaluate this because, as mentioned earlier, he seems to have intended it as an open-ended list of possible conditions. The factors he considers cannot each be taken separately or strictly, and he does not mean to do so, for reasons that are rather obvious. Consider for example, language, a name, culture, self-identification, and outer-group identification.

Language is a frequently proposed justification of ethnic unity. Indeed, speaking Spanish is frequently used as a marker of Hispanics (or Latinos).[1] But this fails as a necessary or a sufficient condition of this ethnicity. Spanish is spoken by many people who are not native speakers of it, and there are people considered Hispanics (or Latinos) for whom it is not their native tongue—such as a third-generation American of Cuban ancestry—or even speak it well. And respect, added by Corlett, does not seem to have much punch to it.

Culture in general appears to be a more promising factor than just language, but it also fails if taken by itself. If culture is understood broadly to include values, attitudes, lifestyles, customs, rituals, music, religion, and language, the cultural conception of ethnicity is widely accepted and is often applied to Latinos, for example.[2] After all, certain cultural practices and traits appear to separate Latinos from other cultures. Latinos seem to share all sorts of cultural characteristics that are idiosyncratic to them and are not found in other ethnic groups. But culture proves inadequate in that it is too vague, and when we try to pin it down in particular cases, we end up by reducing it to other criteria that are also vague or inadequate, as Horowitz has argued (Horowitz 1975, 124; see also Wilkins 1996, 22ff.). Most often it amounts to language, but as we saw, language is hardly an adequate mark of ethnicity.

By outer-group identification, Corlett means that the members of an ethnic group are picked out as members of the group by members of other groups (see also Banton 1967). This condition also fails insofar as the identity of an ethnic group has to precede a public awareness of it. Other groups cannot identify anyone as Latino unless they already understand what it means to be Latino or have some means to separate Latinos from non-Latinos. Moreover, there is often a difference between the publicly identified ethnicity of a person or group and the self-identified ethnicity of the same person or group. This creates difficulties for those who hold that public identification is either a necessary or sufficient condition of ethnicity, for in case of conflict, which identification is correct? This "disconnection" is often ignored in the literature, but Guibernau, among others, has noted it (Guibernau 1997, 3, 8). This does not mean, however, that public identification plays no role in the development and preservation of ethnic groups, for what others think of us does have a role in shaping our identity.

Paula Moya (2001) argues for a stronger version of this position according to which ethnicity requires not just self-identification with a group, but also awareness of belonging to it. Gordon (1964) speaks of a feeling of peoplehood. And sociologists frequently make self-naming, self-definition, and self-awareness necessary conditions of ethnicity (cf. Isaacs 1975, 34–35; Parsons 1975, 56; Horowitz 1975, 113; Hayes-Bautista 1983, 275–76; Aboud 1987, 32; for philosophers, see Bernstein 2001; Outlaw 1996, 7). This position can take various forms. One holds that ethnic self-identification is a sufficient condition for a person to belong to an ethnic group, whereas another holds that it is only a necessary condition. With respect to the group itself, there are also modalities, for one can hold that the self-identification of the members of the group is precisely what constitutes the group as ethnic (a sufficient condition of ethnicity), but one can also hold that the group requires the self-identification of the members with it (a necessary condition), although there are also other required factors.

One cannot deny that there are advantages to the various forms this view takes, for self-identification surely plays a role in the development and strengthening of an ethnic identity by consciously focusing on it. But closer inspection reveals problems similar to those we saw with the previous position. In the first place, there is the logical point, that in order to *identify with* an ethnos I must have previously *identified* the ethnos. Awareness of the ethnic group must precede my identification with it, and this indicates that what ties the group together cannot be the identification of its members with it, but something else. Moreover, most people who belong to ethnic groups do not in fact consciously identify with the groups; indeed, often they have not even thought of the groups. So are we going to eliminate them from membership? Self-identification is certainly a powerful tool of ethnicity, but it is not what accounts for it.

From the foregoing discussion it should be clear that the factors discussed, considered in isolation, cannot account for ethnicity. Of course, in particular contexts, some of these factors do function effectively as necessary and sufficient conditions of ethnicity in certain groups, but they rarely, if ever, do so throughout the existence of the groups in question. More important still, it is clear that there is no uniform factor that functions as such across all ethnic groups. What to do, then?

Most investigators have opted for a combined approach, as Corlett does when he discusses what he calls the metaphysical conception of ethnicity. Mindel, Smith, and Kornberg, for example, combine self-identification and common cultural factors (Mindel et al. 1988, 1; Smith and Kornberg 1969, 342). Weber emphasizes belief in common descent, shared memories, and similarity of physical appearance or of customs (Weber 1978, 1: 389). Smith proposes shared histories and cultures in combination with a territory and self-identification (sometimes described as solidarity; Smith 1997, 27). Isaacs and Horowitz think in terms of birth and both physical and sociocultural factors (Isaacs 1975; Horowitz 1975, 113). And Brown has provided a very elaborate set of criteria for group ethnicity, including: (1) having a name for itself; (2) belief in a common ancestry; (3) shared historical memories; (4) shared culture; (5) attachment to a territory; and (6) thinking of itself as a group (Brown 1997, 81–82). Clearly, these criteria, except for (4), are psychological and attitudinal and based on the group's self-perception and thus ignore other important factors, such as the perception of the group by others, historical connections, and actual descent ties.

Even the most elaborate and sophisticated attempts at combining various factors in order to account for ethnicity turn out to be inadequate for the two reasons mentioned earlier: first, there seems to be no common constant factor to the ethnicity of a group throughout the group's history (ethnic groups appear to be fluid and changing social realities); second, no factor, or even a kind of factor, accounts for the ethnicity of *all* ethnic groups (ethnicity seems to be a particular, contingent, and contextual phenomenon). So what to do? Clearly we are back where we started.

Let me propose that we attempt a different approach to the categorization of both ethnicity and ethnos. Only if we succeed can we effectively address issues concerned with the formulation and implementation of public policy to which Corlett and others call attention. Going back to the clarifications introduced in chapter 2, let me emphasize that this attempt is metaphysical rather than epistemological or linguistic; it concerns the categorization of ethnicity and ethnos, not the way we know them or speak about them, even if the way we know or speak about them may help our task.

Let's begin by making clear that both ethnicity and ethnos, considered in general, can be words, concepts, or objects about which we speak or think, and it is important to distinguish between these. As words, they are signs composed of sounds, visual designs, or tactile objects conventionally used to understand certain things, that is, whatever "ethnicity" and "ethnos" are used to mean or refer to. Ethnicity and ethnos are also concepts insofar as, when "ethnicity" and "ethnos" are used in discourse, our minds engage in certain acts through which we think about them. Finally, they are also the very objects to which the words refer and about which we think through the corresponding concepts. By "object" here, I mean what we think or talk about, or are supposed to think or talk about, regardless of what that may be. Consider an example: "cat" is, as written on this page, a visual sign that I use to communicate with the readers of this book; the concept "cat" is a mental act through which I think about cats; and *cat* is the object to which the word refers and that I understand via a concept. The object about which I think can be of any sort, of course: it can be mental, like a concept or mental act; it can be physical, like something I touch; and it can be a word I use to communicate with someone else.

Our concern here is not really with the words "ethnicity" and "ethnos" themselves, or even with the concepts knowers may use when they think about ethnicity and ethnos. Rather we are concerned with the objects we think about when we think of ethnicity and ethnos and to which the words "ethnicity" and "ethnos" refer.[3] In other words, we are concerned with what in chapter 2 I called categories, and in particular with the categories ethnicity and ethnos. To ask about the categorization of the words themselves would fall into the philosophy of language, and to ask about the categorization of the concepts would lead us into the philosophy of mind. Neither of these is the subject of our inquiry. We are concerned rather with ethnicity and ethnos *simpliciter*, that is, not considered as this or that in particular, or as related to this or that in particular, but as whatever they may be. And our task is to inquire about the more general categories into which these less general categories of ethnicity and ethnos fall. I begin with ethnos, because ethnicity is the characteristic shared by those things that belong to an ethnos, so ethnicity is in a way derivative from ethnos.

THE FAMILIAL-HISTORICAL VIEW

In thinking about ethnos, I have in mind such groups of people as "Hispanics," "Jews," and "(ethnic) Germans," although I am not concerned with any of these in particular. My task is not to categorize particular ethnic groups, but rather to investigate what an ethnos is.

Needless to say, an ethnos is a group, but groups come in various sorts. First, there are groups of individuals and groups of nonindividuals. For our purposes, it is sufficient to give a few examples of individuals such as: this cat, this pen, Voltaire, the instance of the color red that characterizes that automobile, and the ink smudge on this page.[4] Examples of nonindividuals, usually referred to as "universals" in the philosophical literature, are such things as: cat, pen, human being, red color, and ink smudge. Universals are instantiated in individuals: this or that cat, this or that pen, Peter or Jacinta, this or that red color, and this or that ink smudge are instances of cat, pen, human being, red color, and ink smudge. If individuals and universals are understood in this way, then it seems that there can be groups of both. I can speak of a group of individuals, such as this pen, that pen, the pen you have in your hand, and so on (or even of this pen, that cat, and that ink smudge) and of a group of universals, such as pen, cat, ink smudge, and so on.

The group we are talking about when we speak of a particular ethnos is not a group composed of universals but rather one composed of individuals. When we talk about Hispanics, for example, the object in question is composed of María, Juan, Pedro, Gumerzinda, and so on. But this does not yet tell us all we need to know about an ethnos, for we still need to specify the general kind to which the individual members of the ethnos belong, which is the corresponding universal. There can be groups of many kinds of individuals in which all the individuals belong to the same kind. Apart from the ones already mentioned, we can have groups of stones (composed of this stone, that stone, and so on), molecules (composed of this molecule, that molecule, and so on), pens (composed of this pen, that pen, and so on), and so on. But there can also be groups of individuals belonging to different kinds, such as we mentioned earlier. An ethnos, however, is always composed of the same kind of individuals, and this kind is human (this human, that human, and so on). But even to say this is not sufficiently informative for our purposes in that not every group of individual humans constitutes an ethnos. Consider, for example, a city, a government, a faculty committee, a religious congregation, a football team, and a political party. All these appear to be groups of humans, but none of them is an ethnic group.[5] So what kind of group of humans constitutes an ethnos? This is a way of asking for two things: first, the larger category of group to which ethnic groups belong and, second, the distinctive character of an ethnos within that category that gives it unity.

As an answer to the first question, I propose that ethnic groups belong to the larger kind of group we know as families, for as van den Berghe has argued, kingship plays an important role in ethnicity (van den Berghe 1981, 18ff.). To give credibility to this claim, I need to make sure we understand the term "family" broadly. Families come in at least three pertinent varieties:

nuclear, extended, and—if my proposal is correct—ethnic. (In the next chapter, I add racial families to these.) The nuclear family, a concept of rather recent origin, consists of a father, mother, and their children. An extended family has more members in it than these, including grandparents, nephews, cousins, and in some cases even concubines and servants. Finally, an ethnic family is a still more extended group with some important idiosyncratic characteristics, as we shall see.

Even if one accepts this proposal, a key question that still needs to be answered concerns the source of the unity of an ethnic group as a family. We know what gives unity to various other kinds of groups. For example, the unity of a religious group comes from a set of shared beliefs and practices, and the unity of a committee of faculty comes from the act of the administrator who appointed it for a particular purpose. In both of these cases, the unity of the group derives from some feature shared by the members of the group: for religious groups, it is the belief in certain doctrines or the will to engage in certain activities; for the faculty committee it is the appointment. Now, if an ethnic group, unlike those other groups, is a kind of family, as I have claimed, then its unity must be found in what gives unity to families. Unlike a religious group or a faculty committee, however, a family does not have a single feature, let alone a set of them, that is shared by all its members.

Consider the Gracia family. What is it that makes individual persons members of it? I submit it is a set of unique historical relations of diverse sorts, in which the relations are contingent and do not necessarily apply to all members. My grandmother on my father's side, a member of the Dubié family, became a member of the Gracia family through marriage to my grandfather Gracia. My father Gracia became a member of the Gracia family because he was the issue of my grandmother and grandfather. My wife is a member of the Gracia family because she married me. My cousin Estevan is a member of the Gracia family because he was adopted by one of my uncles. And so on. Some disciples of Wittgenstein might want to say that the only thing that all members of the Gracia family have in common is that they are called Gracia (Bambrough 1960–61, 207–22). But this suggestion does not work, for two reasons: first, there are some members of the Gracia family who are not called Gracia at all, such as my daughters' children; second, it is not sufficiently informative, because the Gracias who call themselves, or are called by others, Gracia, do so because of particular features, although it turns out that these features are not the same for all members of the family, even if they are always the same, at least in principle, for more than one of us. (The fact that there are people named Gracia who are not members of my family is irrelevant, of course—there are several Gracia families, as there are many individual persons called John.)

These features in turn are founded on a variety of relations that are historical and contingent but that nonetheless tie the members of the family, such as marriage, adoption, and births. Indeed, this is the basis of the notion of family resemblance—my nose is like that of my maternal grandfather, my late brother's nose was like that of my father, my eyes are like those of my mother, and so on, so that we all resemble each other in some, but not always in the same, ways. A family resemblance does not entail that all members of a family share the same features, but that everyone of them shares some feature with at least some other member of the family. Of course, the notion of family resemblance does not accommodate adopted members of a family, a clear reason why it is not family resemblance that ties a group of people into a family. The tie is based on certain relations that in turn produce a resemblance in some cases and other kinds of features in others.

This idea can be applied to ethnic groups. The reason why I am, in a certain context, considered Hispanic might be that I speak Spanish and was born in Cuba. The reason Ignazio Angelleli is taken as Hispanic is that he speaks Spanish and lived for a long time in Argentina. The reason for Joan Miró is that he was born in Catalonia and spoke Catalan. The reason my daughters are Hispanic is that they have Hispanic parents, one Argentinian and one Cuban. All these reasons point to historical and contingent features that have nothing to do with the metaphysical categorization of Hispanic, except insofar as they confirm that categorization as familial, relational, and historical.

In short, a family does not get its unity from common features among its members, but rather from the particular historical relations that tie its individual members, which in turn produce features common to some of those members. These relations also ultimately separate one family from another, even though the features they generate also can serve to distinguish members of some families from members of other families in particular contexts. I am not a Gutiérrez both because I am not closely related to any Gutiérrez—although I may be distantly related to some—and because, in context, I share no features that tie members of the Gutiérrez family. Clearly, all human families are related insofar as their members are human beings and either originate from a single set of parents or, if not, have nonetheless mixed throughout history. Yet families are distinct entities based on the concrete historical relations that tie their members, also separating them from the members of other families. And families are distinguishable based on the features that those relations have generated. So, even though members of the Gracia family may be related to all other human beings in some way, they constitute a distinct group of people who are also distinguishable in context. In some cases, the members of the family are distinguishable because of the shape of their noses, in others because of their big eyes, in others because of their last name, in others because they speak Spanish, and so on.

My contention is that the unity of an ethnos is similar to that of a family. For this reason, it must not be understood as involving features common to all the members of the ethnos, but as based on a series of changing relations that tie the members throughout history and generate features common to at least some members of the group in particular contexts. This means that, contrary to what many believe, the unity of an ethnos cannot be always understood in terms of political, territorial, linguistic, cultural, racial, genetic, experiential, or class boundaries, even if in context these tie the members of the ethnos and can be used to identify them as such. Nor is this unity a matter of self-identification or other-group identification.

Consider, for example, the ethnic group we know as Hispanics.[6] The understanding of this group in any of the terms suggested is ineffective, for there is no feature, or set of features, that can be regarded as common, let alone essential, to all Hispanics throughout history.

The basic principle of the Familial-Historical View is that there is no necessarily identifiable feature, or set of features, that is shared by members of an ethnic group throughout its history. This accounts for the lack of agreement among members of ethnic groups, and among those who study them, concerning any particular conditions, or even kinds of conditions, that are necessary and sufficient for ethnicity. Even the most superficial kind of research indicates that different groups and individuals do not agree on any conditions; ethnic groups are not homogeneous. We must, then, abandon the project of trying to conceive all ethnic groups in terms of any empirically discernible features. This means, in turn, that in order to belong to an ethnic group it is not necessary that one share a feature or set of features with other members of the group, which explains why, in his attempt to characterize ethnicity, Weber concluded that it is not feasible to go beyond vague generalizations (Weber 1997, 22, 24; see also Hughes 1994, 91). Indeed, contrary to what many think, it is not even necessary that the members of the group name themselves in any particular way or have a conscious sense of belonging to the group. Some of them may in fact consider themselves so and even have an awareness, or sense, of themselves as a group, but it is not necessary that all of them do.

Members of an ethnos are tied by the same kind of thing that ties the members of a family, as Wittgenstein would say (Wittgenstein 1981, §67,

32). They belong to the same group because they are historically related, as a father is to a daughter, an aunt to a nephew, and grandparents to grand-children. Wittgenstein's metaphor of family resemblance is particularly appropriate in this case, but the metaphor of the family must be interpreted correctly to avoid any misunderstanding of it as requiring genetic ties. One does not need to be tied genetically to other members of a family to be a member of the family. Indeed, perhaps the most important foundation of a family, namely marriage, takes place between people who are added to a family through contract, not genesis. And in-laws become members of families indirectly, again not through genesis. This means that the very notion of resemblance used by Wittgenstein is misleading if it is taken as requiring a genetic connection. It also means that any requirements of coherence and homogeneity do not apply. Families are not coherent wholes composed of homogeneous elements; they include members that differ substantially from each other and may clash in various ways. Physical features vary widely within the same family, and views of the world, politics, and religion, for example, can be quite opposed. Contrary to Corlett, descent does not appear to be a necessary condition of membership in *all* ethnic groups, even if it may be so in some. Families are related clusters of persons with different, and sometimes incompatible, properties, and homogeneity is not one of their necessary conditions.

This does not entail that other factors do not play roles in particular contexts in the constitution of ethnic groups, contributing both to their creation and preservation. To deny that they do would be to be blind to reality. According to the Familial-Historical View, history generates relations that in turn generate properties among members of groups and serve to unite them among themselves and to distinguish them from others in particular contexts. But what would these features have to do with but political organization, territorial boundaries, language, religion, culture, race, genetic lineage, experience, self-awareness, and other-group identification? Indeed, this is the reason why ethnicity is frequently confused both with nationality and race, and why it is often also understood in purely cultural terms. It is easy to think of an ethnic group in terms of national origin (e.g., Cuban), race (e.g., "Black"), language (e.g., Catalan), religion (e.g., Jewish), or culture (e.g., Arab) precisely because these are factors in ethnic unity.

Consider, for example, that the use of the Spanish language is one of the properties that unites many Hispanics and can serve to distinguish them from other ethnic groups in certain contexts. Some Hispanics in the Southwest are united by their knowledge of Spanish, and this serves also to distinguish them from Anglos who live in that part of the country. These people speak Spanish as a result of certain historical events, such as the invasion and colonization of the Southwest by Spaniards in the sixteenth century. Had these events not occurred, these people would not know any Spanish or have any claim to be Hispanics. Certain historical events, then, established particular relations that in turn generated a linguistic property. And it is only in this context that language makes sense as an ethnic marker for the group.

Although historical events and relations tend to generate common properties, such properties might not go beyond certain periods, regions, or subgroups of people: *a* may follow *b*, and *b* may follow *c*, and *c* may follow *d*, implying a connection between *a* and *d* even when *a* has no property in common with *d*. Let me explain this further. Consider the case of *a*, *b*, *c*, and *d* in which *a* has a relation (aR_1b) with *b*, *b* has a relation (bR_2c) with *c*, and *c* has a relation (cR_3d) with *d*, but the relation between any two of these is not the same. This does not entail that there is an immediate relation between *a* and *c* or *d*, or between *b* and *d*. (In order to simplify matters, I assume that the relation between *a* and *b* is the same as the relation between *b* and *a*, and so on with the others.) Now the mentioned relations allow us to group *a*, *b*, *c*, and *d* even though there is no property common to all of them, not even a relation that unites them directly. There is, however, a relation between *a* and *b*, another between *b* and *c*, and another between *c* and *d*. At the same time, these relations allow us to separate the group *abcd* from other groups, say *mnop*, because none of the members of *abcd* has relations with the members of *mnop*, or because, although they may have relations with *mnop*, the relations between *a*, *b*, *c*, and *d* are different from the relations between *m*, *n*, *o*, and *p*. Group identity entails both unity and distinction in a world of multiplicity such as ours, and unity and distinction are easily understandable when there are properties common to all the members of a group, but such properties are not necessary. The unity and distinction of a group can be explained as long as there are relations or properties that tie each member of the group with at least one other member without assuming that there are properties common to all members.

This is the kind of unity in terms of which the Familial-Historical View proposes to explain ethnic groups. The unity of these groups does not involve commonality; it is a familial-historical unity founded on relations and the properties to which they give rise in context. Sarmiento has nothing in common with me, except for very general properties such as being human, but both of us are tied by a series of events that relate us and separate us from Shakespeare and Ghandi. This is what makes us Hispanics. There is no need to find features common to all Hispanics in order to classify them as Hispanics. This is one reason why these groups are neither permanent nor closed communities. Ethne are fluid, open, and changing; members come and go, enter and leave, as they forge new relations among themselves and with members of other groups, depending on particular and contingent circumstances. The fluidity of ethnic groups has been recognized by many authors, including Vincent, Thompson, Jenkins, and Corlett (Vincent 1974, 376; Thompson 1963, 9; Jenkins 1999, 90; Corlett 2003). Du Bois, then, had the right idea when he talked about history and family, except that he applied it to race rather than ethnicity, and he did not flesh out what it entailed: an ethnos is like a family, tied by a history. Keep in mind, however, that I am no historicist. Ethnic groups are not trapped in their history, albeit history cannot be denied. Nor am I proposing a kind of neo-essentialism. There is no essence here; there is only a complex historical reality. Only a misguided sense of group unity, based on notions of coherence and purity, leads to essentialistic conceptions of ethnicity.

Now that we have a general categorization of an ethnos as a family, we can ask the same question of ethnicity, and the answer should not be difficult: ethnicity appears to be the feature that characterizes members of an ethnos qua ethnos. Hispanicity appears to be the feature that characterizes members of the Hispanic ethnos qua Hispanic. However, ethnicity is not a feature like "having a heart" that characterizes certain entities independently of other entities. It is rather like "sibling" or "mother," which depend on something other than the entity to which they apply. For X to be a sibling, there must also be a Y who stands in a certain relation to X. And the same applies to mother. These are relations or relational features, and ethnicity is one of these insofar as it depends on those who have it being related to others. In order for X to have ethnicity, it must be related to others who, with it, constitute an ethnos. Relational features are predicated of the relata, but they are contingent on the relation. This is clear in the case of nations, for example. "American" is predicated of individual persons, but only insofar as these persons hold the relation of citizenship to the group of other Americans and the country. This means that relational features, and consequently ethnicity, are not really anything other than the relations holding among certain things. The ethnicity of a Jew is nothing but his or her relation to other Jews, namely that he or she belongs to the group of people we call Jews.

This relation, unlike the relation "being-in-love," appears to be symmetrical, for although I can "be in love" with you and you do not have to "be in love" with me, I cannot be related qua Hispanic to others without these others being also related to me qua Hispanics. A relation is symmetrical only when the relata are such that, if one stands in some relation to another, the other stands in the same relation to one. The relation "shorter than" is not symmetrical because if I am shorter than you, you cannot be shorter than I, but the relation "next to" is symmetrical because if X is next to Y, Y is also next to X.

The view that ethnic relations are symmetrical, however, is inaccurate to this extent: ethnic relations, when subjected to analysis, break down into relations that are not symmetrical. This is similar to what happens in other families. I am a member of the Gracia family because I am related to my father as a son, say, but my father is not related to me as a son, but as a father. To speak with greater precision, then, we need to distinguish between two levels of relations: higher-order relations, such as membership in a family or in an ethnos, and lower-order relations, which are those into which these higher-order relations are analyzed. The first are symmetrical, but the second are not.

The question of transitivity can be dealt with in a similar fashion to that of symmetry. A relation is transitive if it is passed on, as it were. If Peter is stronger than Paul and Paul is stronger than Juan, necessarily Peter is stronger than Juan. Motherhood by contrast is not transitive, for if María is the mother of June and June is the mother of Ellen, María cannot be the mother of Ellen. Now the ethnic relation "being-Hispanic," say, would appear to be transitive in this sense: if María is related as Hispanic to Juan and Juan is related as Hispanic to Jorge, then María appears to have to be related as Hispanic to Jorge. However, to say this is actually deceptive insofar as the higher-order relation "being Hispanic" is cashed out, in the view I have proposed, in terms of lower-order, changing historical relations, and the latter need not be transitive. The actual relations that tie María to Juan need not be the same relations that tie Juan to Jorge. So, strictly speaking, one cannot say that the relations between María and Juan, in virtue of which they are both Hispanic, are the same that tie María and Jorge. They could be the same, but they need not be. This means that the relations in virtue of which members of an ethnic group belong to it need not be transitive, even if the relation of belonging to the ethnic group is. This is very much, again, as what happens with a family. I am a member of the Gracia family because I am related to my father as a son, but my wife is a member of the Gracia family because she is married to me; she is not my father's son, or even his daughter. The relation of belonging to the Gracia family is transitive, but the relations in virtue of which this relation obtains are not. This is another way of saying that belonging to an ethnic group does not entail the same thing always, or to say, in our example, that to be Hispanic (or Jewish, or Han) does not always mean the same thing.

One last point needs to be clarified before I summarize the view I have proposed. I have claimed that an ethnos is a kind of family, but perhaps I have not made sufficiently clear how it differs from other kinds of families. Earlier, I mentioned two other kinds of families: nuclear and extended. The nuclear family is composed of just parents and children, and perhaps grandparents. The extended family includes persons from many generations who carry the family name as well as persons who do not carry the family name, such as concubines, distant relatives (a very significant term), in-laws, and so on. It is quite clear that ethnic groups are not like a nuclear family, but how are they to be distinguished from extended families? Where can we find the distinguishing factor?

Consider time first: although extended families can last for long periods of time, they need not do so, whereas ethnic groups necessarily must extend over many generations. This is important to them because their genesis is slow. Another factor is their composition. Extended families are composed of individuals many of whom also belong to other extended families, but there are no extended families within extended families. By contrast, this is not only possible, but also seems necessary in ethnic groups; it is characteristic of them to contain many extended families, and not only this, but it is also possible for ethnic groups to include other ethnic groups. The Hispanic ethnos includes not only the extended families of Gracias and Silvas, but also Puerto Ricans and Catalans. Extended families, of course, do not include ethnic groups within them, even if they can, and often do, include members from different ethnic groups.

Let me now summarize the view I have proposed in two formulas:

An ethnos is a subgroup of individual humans who satisfy the following conditions: (1) they belong to many generations; (2) they are organized as a family and break down into extended families; and (3) they are united through historical relations that produce features that, in context, serve (i) to identify the members of the group and (ii) to distinguish them from members of other groups.

Ethnicity is the relational property of belonging that characterizes the members of an ethnos.

Both of these formulas integrate parts of the definitions and metaphysical categorizations of ethnos and ethnicity, in order to present metaphysical analyses of these notions that serve our present purposes. Ideally, the analyses would be complete, but this has not been my aim. I seek merely analyses that are sufficient to distinguish ethnicity from race and nationality, and this will become clear after I discuss the latter two.

Now we can see how this position is different from the one recently defended by Corlett. For him, as we saw above, there are two concepts of ethnicity: one for purposes of public policy, based on descent, and one metaphysical, based on a set of cultural features such as language, combined with a certain ethical attitude, namely respect, toward them. The view I have defended is familial and historical, but not necessarily involving descent. The important elements in it are kinship and history. My position, then, is more open, for practically any feature can count toward uniting an ethnos, including racial and national ones. Ethnicity is not just a matter of descent, culture, or an ethical attitude, although it could be so for particular ethne. In this sense, my view makes room for Corlett's position, but not vice versa.

HISTORICAL ORIGIN AND LOCATION

Families are historical entities originating in historical events, such as marriages, that occur at particular times and having particular locations where their members reside. So if ethnic groups are families of a sort, we are entitled to ask if there are points in history where ethnic groups come to be, and if there are places associated with them. These are historical questions concerned with the contingent conditions that apply to individuals, and are therefore contextual. In the case of historical entities, such as ethnic groups, the questions involve factors that lead to the formation of the groups, the moment or moments of group origin, the relative unity and diversity of the groups throughout history, and the location of these groups.

To answer that the Gracia family began in the twelfth century in a little town of Aragon, when the name Gracia was given for the first time to some long-forgotten ancestor of mine, is not to contradict that to be a Gracia does not entail a feature common to all those people who are called Gracia and belong to the Gracia family. It is merely to confirm the fact that, metaphysically, the Gracia family is a historical entity united by a set of changing relations throughout history. Likewise, to say that the use of the term "Hispanic" for an ethnic group begins to make sense only after 1492 is to confirm that Hispanics are an ethnic group, that they do not necessarily share a feature common to all Hispanics, and that members of the group are tied by a series of relations that are historically contingent. So, yes, to be

Hispanic it is necessary to be tied in some way to a point (or points) of origin in time, whatever that may be, but this tie is historical and contingent, and serves its purpose only contextually.[7]

Insofar as ethnic groups originate in historical locations, there is always a place (or places), and sometimes a time (or times), that is associated with them. Moreover, such times and places often live in the collective memories, actual or mythical, of the groups (Smith 1991, 21). For the Jews, the place is Israel; for Latinos, it is Latin America; for Poles, it is an area in central Europe; and so on. And, as with the place, there is a time (or times) somewhere in the past that is often deemed crucial for the origin of an ethnos. This is important because it contextually sets apart the first members of the group, even if it cannot be used to distinguish subsequent members of the group who live at later dates and never live in the original location. It is for this reason that the places and times in question cannot constitute conditions for membership in ethne. The membership in the group has to be explained in contextual terms, and the unity of the group has to be explained in terms of familial relations throughout history.

Note, for example, the case of ethnic Cubans in Miami. Many of these people were born in the United States and have never been in Cuba. Yet the sense of Cuba they have is part of their ethnicity. In some cases, it is not present-day Cuba, for most of them despise the Cuba of Fidel Castro; it is rather the Cuba of the '50s, a place and time that is past and of which they have no immediate experience. Indeed, it is quite likely that this Cuba of the '50s, as it lives in the consciousness of ethnic Cubans in Miami, is no more than a myth developed by the nostalgia of exile. This furnishes another reason for rejecting particular times and places as essential to the unity of ethne in that it is more often than not the case that the particular times and places ethnic groups identify as the coordinates of their origin are in fact mythical.

All this naturally leads to questions about origin: How does an ethnos come to be? What factors bring it about? Do these factors involve human decisions, or are they independent of what humans might do? These are important and interesting questions that need to be addressed, but they must be answered in context and in reference to particular ethne.

Let me illustrate the point with reference to a related issue, concerned in particular with history. As we have seen, history is very important for the view of ethnicity I have proposed. But one may want to ask: What kind of history is pertinent for the development of ethne? What sort of history creates ethnicity? Can any kind of historical event do so, or is it only a certain kind that is effective? Furthermore, is there a dif-

ference in the kind of history that produces ethne and that which produces other groups, such as nuclear families, faculty committees, religious
groups, races, and nations?

Clearly, these questions raise an important issue concerning the Familial-
Historical View of ethnicity, and its resolution is based on the very point that
the view stresses. This point is that there is no feature or kind of feature,
whether single or composite, that is essential to ethne. Yes, ethnic groups are
conglomerates of extended families, and they are the result of historical relations that generate distinguishing features in context. But there is nothing
other than this that is characteristic of all ethne. Indeed, this very lack is peculiar to them, distinguishing them from other groups. We shall see later in this
book how it serves to distinguish them from races and nations, but it is also
quite obvious in the case of appointed committees and religious groups, for
example. There is something common to all appointed committees, namely,
that they have been appointed; and there is something common to all religious
groups, namely, they all have a set of beliefs and practices. But nothing of the
kind can be said of ethne across the board, even if it may be said of certain
ethne. For some ethne, for example, it is descent that is essential; for others it
is language; and for still others it is a certain religion. But it cannot be said of
all ethne that any of these, or anything at all for that matter, beyond the conditions specified in the formulas given earlier, is essential to them.

If this is so, then it makes no sense to think that one can determine any
kind of historical event as necessary for the production of ethne if such
events are intended to explain how a certain type of necessary characteristic
or feature arises. Of course, it should be clear that, as ethne are groups of
people of a familial sort, anything that tends to contribute to bring people
together in a very extended way can be regarded as influential in the formation of ethne, and anything that does not works the other way. But the pos-
sibilities of what does are too great, and depend too much on particular circumstances, for us to be able to identify them. The general openness and
contextual determination of ethne makes it impossible to pinpoint any kinds
of historical events that would go beyond those that apply to particular
ethne. We can certainly understand how the English, for example, came to
be the ethnos they are due in part to the Norman invasion. But it would be
a rather obvious mistake to argue that invasion is the kind of historical event
that is essential for the formation of ethne. Again, we can easily see that the
sexual union between two people is essential to the formation of a nuclear
family, but nothing as clear as this can be found in the case of an ethnos. And
we can also establish that the act of appointing is necessary for the constitution of a committee, but the case with ethne is quite different.

OBSTACLES TO THE PROPER
UNDERSTANDING OF ETHNICITY

If the familial-historical understanding of an ethnos makes as much sense as I have claimed, we should ask ourselves why it is that so far it has not been widely adopted by those who have talked about this topic, particularly when quite early Du Bois had already suggested a similar notion in the context of race. There are at least five assumptions that have stood on the way. The first assumption is that the effective use of a common name requires the identification of an essence, that is, a feature or set of features that necessarily and sufficiently characterize the things called by the name; if no essence can be identified, the name is meaningless, merely a sound without substance, and therefore must be abandoned lest it cause confusion.[8] The second assumption frequently made by those who discuss ethnicity is that ethnic categories must have clear and strict boundaries, so that their membership is never in doubt—everything that can be considered is, or is not, a member of the category in question (Zaibert and Millán-Zaibert 2000; Corlett 2003). A third assumption is that ethnicity involves both homogeneity and internal compatibility; members of an ethnic group must be alike and constitute a coherent whole in which the members and their features are compatible (see, e.g., the case of the Chinese, Dikötter 2002, 495). The fourth is that ethnic groups are, or were, pure in some sense (Alcoff 1995, 261, discusses this approach). The fifth is that ethnicity is restricted to groups that are not mainstream (or dominant) within a particular body polity; accordingly, Poles are ethnic in Germany, but not in Poland.[9]

The view that the effective use of names requires a feature, or a set of features, that can be identified has been effectively challenged in contemporary philosophy. This does not mean that there are no names whose use is justified by an essence. Surely the effective use of the term "triangle" assumes that a triangle is a geometrical figure with three angles, and that this is both a necessary and sufficient condition of triangularity; it constitutes the essence of triangularity. Rather it means only that not all names are of the same sort, and therefore their use need not be justified in this way. Some names can be effectively used even when there is no single feature, or set of features, they connote every time they are used. Wittgenstein gave the example of "game" (Wittgenstein 1981, §75, 35). This term is effectively used in English, and yet when we try to identify even one common feature to all games that also distinguishes them from other things, we can never find it. Some games use balls, some do not; some games give pleasure, some do not; some games take a long time, some do not; some games require high concentration, some do not; some games involve physical effort, some do not; and so on.

The conception of an ethnos as a family of a kind implies that there are no features that need to be common to all those persons whom we wish to include in an ethnic group, but this does not mean that the use of a common term is unjustified or meaningless. In general, my point is that there is a way to understand an ethnos that allows us to speak meaningfully of, and refer effectively to, the group, even when the people named by the ethnic term do not share any feature in common at all times and places. More particularly, my thesis is that the notion of ethnos should be understood historically, that is, as a concept that involves changing relations over time.

The second assumption, namely, that ethnic categories must have clear and strict boundaries so that their membership is never in doubt, is quite out of step with the conditions under which we accept many of our most valued categories and concepts, so there is no reason why we should impose on ethnicity conditions without which we are willing to do in other cases. Consider, for example, as common a concept "most of the X's," as we use it when I say "Most of the students who are taking my course in ethnicity this semester will pass it." Everyone understands what this means, but when one looks at the situation more closely, it is clear that the membership of the category is clear in some instances but not in others. Say that the course has twenty students enrolled. In this case, it is clear that "most of the students" does not refer to one, two, three, four, five, six, seven, eight, nine, or ten students. Nor is it twenty, for that would be all of the students. It is also clear that most of the students would cover nineteen, eighteen, and seventeen. But once we get below seventeen, questions arise. Can one consider eleven, twelve, thirteen, fourteen, fifteen, and sixteen to constitute most of the students? Interestingly enough, the total number of students affects also the numbers in doubt. If the course has an overall enrollment of ten, then clearly one through six and ten are not most of the students; nine and eight do constitute most of the students; but what do we make of seven? Here it is only one number that seems to be in doubt, rather than the six numbers in the case of twenty. Now if we increase the number of students to fifty, then we will find that the number in doubt is even larger than in the case of twenty.

Two things are clear from this. First, the category "most of the X's" has members that are in doubt and members that are not. Second, the exact number of members that are in doubt depends very much on the particular number that constitutes the totality, which means that it results from contextual factors particular to the situation. None of this, however, stands in the way of our using the concept "most of the X's," and certainly we do not think any less of the category to which this concept refers because of it. There is no reason, then, to assume that, because a particular category has an undetermined membership, it is useless or must be abandoned. And this applies to many other categories.

Consider such categories as healthy, human being, and dead. Healthy is particularly ambiguous and relative to context. But even categories such as human being and dead have cases in which determination is not clear in spite of recent scientific developments. Do we count as a human being an embryo three days old, an implanted fourteen-day-old embryo, and a twelve-week-old fetus? Is a human body with life support and no brain waves alive or dead? The category of ethnos is not different from these—some of its members are clearly identifiable, but others are not.

With respect to the third assumption, namely, that of the homogeneity and internal compatibility of ethnic groups, I have said enough. These groups are composed of members that are never quite alike, and neither they nor their features are always compatible. Ethnic groups are not like cream of broccoli soup; they are more like minestrone. Each part is different in some ways, but they share relations with other members of the group, just as happens with families. Members of families do not always get along with each other, and some of their characteristics might be incompatible with those of other members of the family. For different members of a family may have different colors of skin, different values, different political views, different religions, and so on, and some of these may be incompatible with each other. There are members of Cuban families who favor Castro and others who are opposed to him. Further examples could be easily given, but there is no need to elaborate the obvious. Suffice it to say that the assumption of homogeneity and compatibility leads to all sorts of misunderstandings concerning ethnic groups, just as it does with families. If several members of a family are crooks, that does not mean all members are, although it is often the case that some people may treat them as such. With ethnic groups, this leads to stereotypes that can be harmful to individual members of the groups.

The fourth assumption, concerning purity, is often tied to a racial conception of ethnicity. Thus the notorious myth of the Aryan involves both a race and an ethnos.[10] I do not believe the purity of ethnic groups can be taken seriously insofar as even the most isolated of these have relations with other groups and many of the elements of their ethnic makeup can be traced to these other groups. Their purity, then, must be racial. Because I discuss race later, however, I leave the issue of purity for that context. Suffice it to say for now that the notion of racial purity makes no sense either.

Finally, the fifth assumption, namely, that ethnic groups are found only within certain political boundaries, is common among some sociologists in the United States: ethnicity refers to certain traits associated with social groups of alien origin within a country (see, for example, Dinnerstein and Reimers 1975, 140). Thus, for example, we can speak of ethnic Poles in Germany, ethnic Russians in Estonia, and ethnic Latinos in the United States because they form identifiable social groups that have common features derived from societies foreign to the countries where they currently reside. The conditions of ethnicity, then, appear to include at least the following:

1. the existence of a group of persons (individual persons by themselves are not ethnic unless they belong to an ethnic group);
2. the group has distinct and identifiable cultural or social traits;
3. the cultural and social traits that distinguish the group come from outside the country where the group resides; and
4. those traits are considered alien to those generally accepted as mainstream (or dominant) in the country of residence.[11]

Poles living in Germany are ethnic because they constitute a group with identifiable cultural and social traits distinct from those of German society, traceable to Poland, and thought by Germans to be alien. Likewise, Latinos are ethnic in the United States because they form a group with identifiable cultural and social features that are foreign to Anglo-American society—and considered to be such by Americans who are not Latinos—and that originate in their ancestral homelands in Latin America.

Of course, at least three of the four conditions of ethnicity mentioned, namely (2), (3), and (4), can easily be challenged in the case of many ethnic groups. For example, (2) fails in the case of Hispanics in that it is questionable, as we saw earlier, that all members of this group share distinct and identifiable cultural or social traits. Condition (3) fails in the case of Mexican Americans in that, for many of them, the ancestral homeland is the very territory where they actually reside, namely the American Southwest. It also fails for Poles, because political boundaries have changed so often in central Europe that some Poles have found themselves in different countries at different times, sometimes in a country in which they were distinct from the mainstream (or dominant) group, and sometimes in a country in which they were not. Indeed, the connection to a foreign ancestral homeland poses serious problems and does so not just for the reasons given, but also because in a country such as the United States, largely composed of immigrants, mainstream cultural traits also come from outside the country. Anglo-Saxon cultural traits are not native to the territory that constitutes the United States today.

These difficulties indicate that ethnicity must be understood differently. There is no reason one could not speak of an ethnos that transcends political lines. Murguia, for example, has proposed the notion of panethnicity, and Padilla speaks of different levels of ethnic organization (Murguia 1991,12; Padilla 1985, 62). Why should Poles in Germany constitute an ethnic unity and Poles in Poland not? Why can't Poles in Germany and Poles in Poland be part of the same ethnic group? There is no reason to think of ethnicity solely within the context of a particular polity. Indeed, there are problems of demarcation that arise and make such a restricted view of ethnicity unacceptable. What happens, for example, when an ethnic group becomes larger than the dominant group? Could not a situation like this turn the tables in such a way that the dominant group becomes ethnic and the large group nonethnic? Or does ethnicity have to do with dominance and political and social power? But the reins of power also are subject to change. There is also the question of the sources of the ethnicity of an ethnos. If it is culture, which is the view of most of those who accept the conception of ethnicity under discussion, then how can one distinguish an ethnic group within a country from an ethnic group outside the country when both have the same culture?

There are other difficulties that can be raised, but let me dispense with them and propose instead to distinguish between ethnic groups in three different contexts: national, regional, and global. Nationally we could speak of Poles in Germany as ethnic, but regionally (say in Europe) and globally (in the world) we may speak of Poles as forming also an ethnic unity. Likewise, we may speak of Hispanics as forming an ethnic unity in the United States and also as forming an ethnic unity in the world or in the Americas. There is no particular reason why one must restrict the notion of ethnicity to the context of a nation, a region, or the world considered as a whole. Of course, sometimes it is convenient to distinguish Poles in Germany from Poles in Poland. And one way of doing it is to speak of ethnic Poles (in Germany) and just Poles (in Poland). But this is confusing because it unduly restricts the notion of ethnicity. It is much better to speak of Poles in Germany and Poles in Poland. In all cases, it is important to be clear about the context. For present purposes, I shall use the more globally encompassing context.

OBJECTIONS AGAINST THE FAMILIAL-HISTORICAL VIEW

There are several specific objections to the view I have proposed that I must take up. The first attacks it by arguing that it does not do justice to the fact that ethnic groups are, indeed, different from other groups, and that this difference cannot be explained merely in terms of historical relations. Hispanics, for example, are different from Han Chinese, French Basques, and certainly Anglo-Saxon Americans. We can tell who is and who is not Hispanic, and we are quite aware of the differences that separate Hispanics from other ethnic groups. A good explanation of these differences must refer to deep ways of thinking and acting. It will not do to argue, as I have done, that there are actually no features that ethnic groups have in common, for if this were the case, then it would not be possible, as it in fact is, to tell members of particular ethnic groups apart from members of other groups. Of course, uncovering such common features might be difficult, or even factually impossible at times, but this does not entail that such features do not exist. That those that may have been suggested thus far do not work does not imply that the task is logically impossible.

The answer to this objection is that I do not claim that there are no common features to ethnic groups and, therefore, that we can never in fact tell members of an ethnos apart from members of other ethne. Rather, I have argued that it is not necessary for ethnic groups to have discernible features common to all members at all times and in all places. This view does not prevent one from holding that there are features common to some members at all times and in all places, at all times and in some places, or at some times and in all places, or features common to all members at all times and in some places, or at some times and places. Nor can my position be construed as implying even that there are no common features to members of ethnic groups at all times and places. My point is only that there are no features that can be shown to be necessarily common to all members of ethnic groups at all times and in all places. Indeed, I believe there are features common to members of some ethnic groups at some times and in some places, and it is precisely such features that serve to identify them at those times and places. At every time and in every period, some members of ethnic groups have features in common that distinguish them from other groups, but these features do not necessarily extend beyond those times and places, and indeed they do not need to extend beyond them to account for their membership in the groups and their distinction from other groups.

At any particular time and place, there are familial relations that members of ethnic groups have and that both distinguish them from members of other groups and are the source of features that also can be used to distinguish them from others. Particular physical characteristics, cultural traits, language, and so on can serve to distinguish Hispanics in certain contexts, although they cannot function as criteria of distinction and identification everywhere and at all times. For example, in a place where all and only Hispanics speak Spanish, the language can function as a sufficient criterion of Hispanic identification even if, in other places, it does not. Likewise, in a society or region where all and only Hispanics have a certain skin color, or a certain religion, and so on, these features can be used to pick out Hispanics, even if elsewhere there are Hispanics who do not share these features. Even though ethnic groups are not homogeneous, particular features can be used to determine who counts as a member of the group in particular contexts. Ethnic membership does not entail a set of common features that constitutes an essence, but this does not stand in the way of identification. We can determine who counts as a member of an ethnic group in context. Just as we generally and easily can tell a game from something that is not a game, we can tell, say, a Hispanic from a non-Hispanic in most instances. But there will be, as with games, borderline cases and cases that overlap.

In some situations, such as that of Hispanics in the United States, there are added reasons that facilitate an answer to the question, Who counts as Hispanic? Two of these may be considered. First, Hispanics are treated as a homogeneous group by European Americans and African Americans; second, even though Hispanics do not constitute a homogeneous group, they are easily contrasted qua groups with Anglo and African Americans because they do not share many of the features commonly associated with these other groups. The source of identification of ethnic groups, then, need not always be positive or exclusively positive; a *via negativa* is also helpful and used. Indeed, in context it may be quite sufficient. My sons-in-law can be distinguished from George W. Bush not only because they are married to my daughters, but also because George W. Bush is president of the United States and they are not. Likewise, members of some ethnic groups can be distinguished from members of other ethnic groups not because they have certain features other groups do not have, but because they lack features other groups have. And, in this, the consciousness of difference between groups also plays a role. Even though ethnic groups are not homogeneous, the thought that they are contributes, albeit paradoxically, to their identification and separation. The identification of members of ethnic groups, then, is not just possible, but also relatively unproblematic in most cases. The contrast between groups in particular circumstances, together with what other groups think of a particular ethnic group, whether justified or not, often serves to distinguish them.

The answer to this objection is important because the motivation for Corlett's view based on descent is precisely that it provides a clear demarcating sign that can be used for public policy purposes. But as we saw, descent does not work as intended. Indeed, we must understand that there is no fixed, clear, and certain mark of membership for all ethnic groups in all places and times. This means that there are always going to be difficult and even undecidable cases. What can we do in such situations? What we do with similar categories, such as "healthy," "human being," and "dead." Society devises ways of dealing with these matters in particular circumstances and with those circumstances and the knowledge available at those times in mind. The solutions are not always neat and clear. They do not work like criteria in mathematics or geometry. But the world is not a mathematical or geometrical entity. Most of the time we have to muddle through in murky waters.

This clarification of my position serves also to answer a second objection. This objection is that the criterion for membership in ethnic groups I have proposed is too weak because it could describe a situation in which only a single feature is shared by any two individuals belonging to the group, and that would not be enough to set the group apart from other groups. Consider two groups of, say, six individuals each that we wish to distinguish from each other: group 1 is composed of members a, b, c, d, e, and f; group 2 is composed of members g, h, i, j, k, and l. According to the view I have proposed, there would be nothing wrong with a situation in which each of the members of each group had only two features. For the first group, the features would be as follows (in parentheses): $a(A, B)$, $b(B, C)$, $c(C, D)$, $d(D, E)$, $e(E, F)$, and $f(F, G)$. For the second group, the features would be as follows: $g(G, H)$, $h(H, I)$, $i(I, J)$, $j(J, K)$, $k(K, L)$, and $l(L, M)$. Now the point to note is that the last member of the first group has one feature in common with the first member of the second group. The significance of this fact is that it appears to make the break between the two groups arbitrary. That is, there seems to be no more reason to end the first group with f and to begin the second group with g than to end the first group with b and begin the second group with c. True, the set of features of the first group (A, B, C, D, E, F, and G) is different from the set of features of the second (G, H, I, J, K, and L). But the fact that there is at least one common feature (G) between the first and the second group makes the break into the two groups appear arbitrary, for we could say that the first group, rather than being composed of a, b, c, d, e, and f, is composed of a, b, c, d, and e, and the second group, rather than being composed of *g, h, i, j, k*, and *l*, is composed of *f, g, h, i, j, k*, and *l*. And, of course, other combinations and breakdowns would also be possible.

The situation appears to be even more serious when one considers that in reality the members of any ethnic group, and certainly the members of a group such as Hispanics, share not one, but more than one feature with members of other groups that presumably we want to distinguish, as ethnic groups, from the group of Hispanics. In short, the view I have presented, so the objection goes, is too weak.

One way to answer this second objection is to modify the view as follows: instead of speaking of members of a group, each of which shares at least one feature with at least one other member of the group, one may propose a set of features several of which are shared by each member of the group. We could call this position the Common-Bundle View of ethnicity.[12] Say that we identify a group with six members: *a, b, c, d, e*, and *f*. And let us propose a set of six features also: *A, B, C, D, E*, and *F*. According to this view, each member of the group would have several of these features as, for instance: $a(A, B)$, $b(A, B, C, F)$, $c(C, D, F)$, $d(B, C, D, E, F)$, $e(A, E)$, and $f(B, E, F)$.

The advantages of this answer should be obvious. Here we have a position that appears to solve the weaknesses pointed out earlier. Clearly, now we have a tighter bond between the members of the group we want to distinguish, and we can also easily set the group apart from other groups by simply showing how individuals who are not members of the group do not have any, or a sufficient number, of the set of features used to define the group.

Now let us, by way of illustration, apply the Common-Bundle View of ethnicity to Hispanics, say, and point out that there is a set of twelve features several of which all Hispanics have (the selection presented here is purely arbitrary and should be given no significance): speaker of Iberian language, Iberian descent, born in Iberia, born in Latin America, Amerindian descent, African descent, citizen of Iberian country, citizen of Latin American country, resident in Iberian country, resident in Latin American country, Iberian surname, lover of Latin American music. Using this criterion, Juan de los Palostes qualifies as Hispanic because he is of Iberian descent, was born in Latin America, and speaks Spanish. His daughters also qualify because they speak Spanish, are of Iberian descent, have Spanish surnames, and love Latin music, although they were not born, nor do they reside, in an Iberian or a Latin American country. And some children from Anglo-American fathers and Latin American mothers who do not speak Spanish and were born in the United States can also be considered Hispanic because of their partial

Latin American descent and their love of Latin American music. At the same time, we can distinguish this group from those who might have one of these features—say, they speak an Iberian language or were born in Latin America—but do not have any other. Moreover, it would exclude, for example, children of Anglo-Saxon missionaries in Latin America and African Americans who have learned Portuguese in school.

Clearly, adopting the Common-Bundle View is a promising way of answering the objection against my original position, the Familial-Historical View. And there is in fact no reason why it cannot be integrated into my view, except that, upon further reflection, there are problems with it. I see three difficulties in particular that make me hesitate. First, there is the problem of determining the particular set of features we should identify as pertinent. How and on what bases do we decide on the set of features that members of an ethnic group share? Indeed, even in the rather innocuous list I provided as an illustration, there are some features that are bound to create difficulties. For example, why should the child of Anglo-Saxon American missionaries who was born in Colombia, holds Colombian citizenship, and speaks some Spanish, not be considered Hispanic? And we might keep in mind the problems raised earlier concerning political, territorial, cultural, racial, and other such features.

A second problem with this way of answering the objection that should also be obvious from the example is that, even if we were able to settle on a satisfactory list of features some of which all members of an ethnic group share, we have no easy way of determining the number of these features required for someone to qualify as a member of the ethnic group. Two? Three? Four? Twenty? And does it make a difference which features are involved? In the earlier example, does it make a difference whether we include love of Latin American music and Amerindian descent or not? Indeed, are two of some kinds of features sufficient (e.g., lover of Latin American music and Amerindian descent), whereas of other kinds three or four are needed? Obviously, this complicates matters tremendously, and it is not clear on what basis a decision can be reached.

The third problem is still more vexing. It has to do with the fact that, even if we were able to settle on a set of features and on the number that needs to be shared, this could turn out to be of use only for the past and the present and not the future. We do not know what features will be pertinent for membership in a particular ethnos in the future. The set of features that a group shares could change, and so could the proportion of features necessary for qualification. After all, we are speaking of a historical reality, and historical realities are in a constant process of change. Group membership is

flexible and subject to evolution and transformation, as Schutte has effectively argued in the case of Latin American identity (Schutte 1993, 240). We
can easily illustrate this point with a reference to language. Suffice it to say
that the English spoken in the Middle Ages would be unintelligible to an
American today, and yet we still consider it to be English. So whatever we
think pertinent for membership in an ethnic group in the past and present
could in time change. If tigers can be bred to lose their stripes, there is no
reason why Hispanics could not become quite different than they are today
or were in the past.

In short, the view we have been discussing as an answer to the second
objection raised is simply too unhistorical and inflexible. There cannot be a
fixed list of features in which members of a particular ethnic group share.
There can be, of course, a list at any time, but the list must always remain
open-ended. This is why it is still better to think in terms of history and family ties than in terms of a set list of features. Ethnic groups are part of a historical reality, and therefore the criteria to identify them must take cognizance
of that fact. Note that I began by allowing the possibility that in principle
there could be such a list of features even if we cannot identify it. Now, however, it should be clear that I do not think this is possible even in principle.
This does not mean, however, that members of ethnic groups cannot be identified as such in particular contexts. Even though there are no essential features, there can be criteria in context. Consider, for example, that knowing
how to swim is not an indication of being human. But in a place where only
humans know how to swim and all humans know how to swim, knowing
how to swim can function effectively as a criterion of being human.

Finally, we come to the circularity objection, raised by Appiah in the
context of the individuation of races, but certainly applicable to my view of
ethnicity. It argues that the Familial-Historical View relies in the individuation of races by history, but this does not work, because the individuation
of a race by its history presupposes the individuation of the history by the
race. He puts it thus:

> [W]hen we *recognize* two events as belonging to the history of one race,
> we have to have a criterion for membership in the race at those two
> times, independent of the participation of the members in the two
> events. To put it more simply: sharing a common group history cannot
> be a criterion for being members of the same group, for we would have
> to be able *to identify* the group in order to identify *its* history. . . . Du Bois'
> reference to a common history cannot be doing any work in his *individ-
> uation* of races. (Appiah 1985, 27; my emphasis, except on "its")

Applying this objection to the Historical–Familial View of ethnicity, we can say that the individuation of an ethnos presupposes the individuation of its history, but the individuation of its history presupposes the ethnos.

In spite of *prima facie* appearances, Appiah's objection is not impregnable. A fatal weakness in it is that Appiah equivocates on the meaning of "the history of a race." This expression can have at least three senses. In one, it refers to the history of an ethnos once the ethnos is constituted, that is, the history that follows the constitution of an ethnos. In another sense, it refers to the history within which the ethnos becomes constituted. And in a third sense, it refers to the history that precedes the constitution of the ethnos.[13] Ethne, just like other social groups, are established in time and under particular circumstances, and there is a history that precedes them, a history in which they develop, and a history that follows them. The history that precedes them consists of the set of events that happens before the ethnos is constituted. The history in which they develop consists of the events that directly or indirectly affect the ethnos throughout the process of its constitution and after. And the history that follows the ethnos consists of the events that follow after the ethnos has been constituted. And keep in mind that what I mean by history here refers to actual events that happen, rather than to what we think of what happens or to a narrative we produce about it.

It might be helpful to present the three cases I have suggested schematically, where "e" stands for an ethnos and "$E_1 E_2 E_3 E_4$" stands for (the events that constitute) a history, as follows:

1. The history of a constituted ethnos:
   e E1 E2 E3 E4
2. The history within which an ethnos is constituted:
   $E_1 E_2$ e $E_3 E_4$
3. The history preceding the constitution of an ethnos:
   $E_1 E_2 E_3 E_4$ e

Now, let us consider the group of Latinos as an example. Sense 1 of history refers to the series of events ($E_1 E_2 E_3 E_4$, all coming after the Latino ethnos L) that occurred after the ethnic group of Latinos, say, became distinct from other groups. Sense 2 of history refers to the series of events ($E_1 E_2 E_3 E_4$, where L is between $E_1 E_2$ and $E_3 E_4$) within which the group of Latinos became distinct from other groups. And sense 3 refers to the series of events ($E_1 E_2 E_3 E_4$, coming before L) that preceded the distinction of Latinos as a group.

Now it certainly makes sense to argue that an ethnos could not be individuated by the history that follows the constitution of the ethnos, for that history presupposes the ethnos. However, the history that is regarded as individuating in the Familial-Historical View need not be this history, but rather it can be the history that precedes the constitution of the ethnos or even the history within which the ethnos develops. The history that precedes an ethnos is not contingent on the ethnos and can be described without reference to it, so the problem of circularity does not arise concerning it. We can individuate that history by referring to things other than the ethnos, such as other events, other entities, and so on. The history that precedes Latinos can be distinguished by reference to the events that constitute it, for example, and not the group of Latinos. So, it is possible to claim that history individuates the ethnos without falling into circularity in that it is in the context of certain events in that history that the ethnos emerges. Something similar could be said about the understanding of the history of an ethnos as the history in which the ethnos develops. A developing ethnos may not yet be considered to be an ethnos, and so the factors involved in its individuation do not appear to require the ethnos as fully constituted. But this case is not as clear as the previous one.

Perhaps a more detailed example will clarify the point. Let us turn again for a moment to the ethnic group we call Latinos or Latin Americans. There was surely a time at which this group did not exist. Indeed, before 1492 there was no such group of people. What was there? In the Iberian peninsula there were Catalans, Spaniards, Galicians, Portuguese, Basques, and Andalusians. Some of these groups had political independence—the Portuguese, for example—but most of them did not. In pre-Columbian America also there were many groups of indigenous people: the Maya, Aztec, Inca, and so on. But surely before 1492 there was a history. Events were happening in both Iberia and pre-Columbian America. There were wars, invasions, and the formation of political units among many other happenings. And these events were individual and can also be identified and distinguished from other events. For example, the marriage of Ferdinand and Isabella brought the kingdoms of Castile and Aragon together. Montezuma became the king of the Aztecs. These events were historically unique and could be identified as such by any observer who had access to them. But neither the individuality nor the identification of these events as individual requires a reference to the future that is Latin America or the group we know as Latinos or Latin Americans. Yet these very events, as well as others, set the stage for the encounter between Iberia and pre-Columbian America. And this encounter, or encounters, as I have argued elsewhere, generated events that slowly created the conditions for the development of the group of people we now refer to as Latin Americans or Latinos (Gracia 2000b, ch. 5). Latin Americans are certainly not Iberians, but they are not pre-Columbians, either. So much for the history that preceded Latinos.

Now let us consider the history within which Latinos emerged. This is the history that begins in 1492 and continues to the present. At first, there were no Latinos, but slowly, as a result of many events there came to be. And this happened in different places, contexts, and circumstances. In this history, there are events that can be identified without reference to Latinos, for the formation of this group is not uniform in every place in Latin America. So there may be places where historical events may be individuated and we can identify them as such without reference to Latinos. In other places, however, there are events tied to the group because the group had already emerged. So the history within which Latinos emerge is sometimes dependent on the group, but at other times it is not. This makes possible reference to some of this history, or part of it, without involving the group, and thus again precludes circularity.

Finally, there is the history that follows the group's formation, and this one clearly is tied to the group. Yet even here one could speak of this history as molding and changing the group and thus as influencing the group. Consider a natural disaster in Mexico that elicits a sense of solidarity throughout Latin America. The national disaster can be indicated without reference to Latinos, or even Mexicans. But it can be a force in the formation of a feeling of solidarity between the people directly affected by the disaster in Mexico and the people not affected by it in Chile, thus strengthening Latino ties.

NEED FOR, AND ADVANTAGES OF, ETHNIC CATEGORIES

In spite of all that has been said, one may still want to question the need for, or advantage of, using general ethnic categories if one adopts the Familial-Historical View. If there are no common features to all members of an ethnic group, what can we get out of an account of the group that is not already present in accounts of other groups and individual persons who are gathered under the category? In short, does using an ethnic term such as "Hispanic" and its corresponding category help us know anything that we do not already know through the study of, say, other groups such as the Spanish, Catalan, Mexican, Argentinian, and Hispanic-American peoples or of the individual persons Juan, Pedro, and Lupita? The answer is that in this way we understand better a historical reality that otherwise would escape us.

The study of peoples involves the study of their relations and how they influence each other. In particular, a historical account must pay careful attention to the events and figures that play important roles in history, avoiding artificial divisions in the account. Keeping this in mind, I submit that ethnic concepts allow us to understand certain historical realities that would otherwise elude us.

Ethnic concepts allow us to grasp aspects of reality that would otherwise be missed because the conceptual frameworks used would be either too broad or too narrow. Concepts are windows to reality, and an ethnic concept is indeed a window to the history of a chapter in universal human history. In the vast panorama of humankind, it introduces a frame that directs the attention of the observer toward something that, under different conditions, would be given little attention, or be overlooked altogether, because of the vastness of the view. Thanks to it, we see more of less. "Hispanic," for example, opens for us a window that yields knowledge we would otherwise not have. At the same time, it allows us to notice things that we would miss if we used only national, racial, or religious concepts, such as Belgian, "Black," or Roman Catholic. These are also windows, but like any window, they reveal something by excluding something else. By using these narrower concepts, we lose a larger view. The use of ethnic terms, concepts, and categories, then, reveals something unique by simultaneously narrowing and widening our view.

This does not mean that such use should be exclusionary. To speak and think about Jews, for example, should not prevent us from speaking and thinking in other ways as well, that is, from using other principles of organization, and therefore from including the consideration of other unities. For these other organizations and unities will surely explain, emphasize, and reveal other facts that, under different arrangements, would go unnoticed. We need not look out only through one window. The perspective based on the notion I have proposed explains, emphasizes, and reveals aspects of a reality that would otherwise be neglected. I do not mean to exclude other arrangements. Indeed, there are many other enlightening ways of thinking about the world. We could think in regional terms, such as Latin American, Iberian, Asian, and North African; in linguistic terms, such as Quechuan, Castilian, and French; in political terms, such as Brazilian or Nepalese; and so on. And all these would, if the notions are historically warranted, reveal to us aspects of reality that, under different conceptions, would be overlooked.

Ethnic categories themselves are not necessarily mutually exclusive. One can be Han Chinese and Cuban (just visit New York City's Chinese/Cuban restaurants and you will meet some examples) or Mayan and Mexican, or Argentinian, Latino, Hispanic, and Italian. As could be expected, in cases of multiple ethnicities, there is usually one that dominates over the others, and one with which individual persons tend to identify, but this does not mean that the others are not present and could not, in certain circumstances, come to the forefront, as Schutte (2000) has effectively argued in the case of Hispanic and Cuban. Ethnicity is fluid and changing, not solid and immutable.

Note, moreover, that the use of ethnic terms is not intended to reflect just that some persons choose to refer to themselves under these terms. Applying a contemporary name theory to ethnic names, it is sometimes argued, as we saw earlier, that self-naming (or self-identification, as it is often put) is both a necessary and sufficient condition of the appropriate use of an ethnic name.[14] If I choose to call myself Hispanic, others should call me so. But, in fact, self-naming is neither necessary nor sufficient in this way. It is not sufficient, because the use of a name calls for a rationale for its use. There must be a reason why I choose to call myself Hispanic, and the reason must be a good one, otherwise the name will be rejected. And it is not necessary because, even if I do not choose to call myself Hispanic, it may be appropriate to call me so. Indeed, there are names we reject even though we deserve them. Not many criminals, for example, would be willing to call themselves so, even though the epithet may be appropriate. The Familial-Historical View does not face these objections for, although it does not accept that there are common features to all members of an ethnic group at all times and in all places, it allows for common features at certain times and places arising from particular historical relations. My view, then, does not suffer from emptiness or circularity.

CONCLUSION

The category ethnos is useful when thinking about certain groups of people. It also serves to refer to much of what they produce and do, for this product and these actions are precisely the results of who they are, and they are in turn the result of their history. Particular ethnic categories and the terms we use to refer to them serve certain purposes at certain times and often continue to serve such purposes in the study of the past. At other times, however, they may cease to be useful for the description of a reality current at that time. Ethnic terms and categories are justified because of certain dimensions of historical reality, that is, the relations among human beings; if those relations diminish considerably or are superseded by others altogether, then the terms and categories become obsolete. The extension of an ethnic term should not be understood to be strict and closed, for human relations are anything but that. There is constant regrouping, and our understanding of these relations requires the constant realignment of our conceptual framework.

The strength of the Familial-Historical View lies precisely in that it allows us to speak of ethnic groups without imposing a homogeneous conception on who, or what, they are. It is an open-ended, historically based conception of ethnicity that permits multiplicity and development. It recognizes diversity within an ethnic group, and it respects differences among its members; it acknowledges the past; and it prevents totalizing attitudes that could be used to oppress and dominate some, or all, members of particular ethnic groups. It is meant to provide understanding in the recognition of both the strength and weakness of ethnic ties. Moreover, this view makes it possible to distinguish ethnicity from race and nationality, as we shall see later.

Part of my task has been to do a bit of conceptual analysis to clear the way for a more precise understanding of ethnicity. My argument has been that the use of ethnic terms and categories, as I have understood them here, does not strip ethnic groups of their historical identity, reduce them to imputed common traits, or imply their false homogenization. Indeed, I have argued just the reverse, for use of ethnic terms and categories, rightly understood, helps us respect diversity, is faithful to historical reality, and leaves the doors open to development in many directions. Moreover, the lack of a homogeneous conception should be sufficient to preclude the oppressive and discriminatory application of ethnic terms and categories. My most powerful answer to the objections against their use is that they work by helping us understand the bases of ethnic families.

Finally, let me point out two further advantages of the Familial-Historical View of ethnicity. One is that it allows fully for the participation in the cultural diversity of ethnic groups without losing their more particular identities. The diversity, variety, and mixture that characterize ethnic groups are enormous. Conceiving ethnicity in the terms I have outlined helps us understand this phenomenon and allows us to share in each other's cultural riches.

The other advantage of the conception of ethnicity I have proposed is that it is not hegemonic; one ethnos does not rule out others, for my position does not conceive an ethnic group as sharing a set of features that actually conflict, or necessarily conflict, with other features shared by members of other groups or subgroups. My conception of ethnicity is open and pluralistic, allowing the coexistence of many and variegated ethnic groupings. Its social implications are substantial, then, for this way of conceiving ethnicity undermines intolerance and any attempt at imposing on others narrow conceptions of who we are. Now let us turn to race, a considerably more controversial and difficult notion than ethnicity.

NOTES

1. For the emphasis on language as a unifying factor of Hispanics in the United States, for example, see Padilla (1985, 151–54). This view is widespread in the press, for example, "A Minority Worth Cultivating," *Economist* (April 25, 1998): 21. For a similar linguistic emphasis outside the United States, see Heredia (1987, 43–59). For the importance of language for ethnicity in general, see Sartre (2001, 121).

2. The cultural criterion is sometimes coupled with descent or, alternatively, perception. For discussions of this criterion, see Appiah (1990a, 498); Geertz (1973); Peterson (1982); Glazer and Moynihan (1975, 4); Smedley (1993, 30); Barth (1969); Eriksen (1993, 10–12); Jenkins (1999, 88); and van den Berghe (1967, 9–10) and (2001, 104). Culturalist attempts to define ethnicity have been made by many authors in Spain and throughout Latin America. In Spain, see Heredia (1994, 135). In Mexico, Samuel Ramos (1963) and Octavio Paz (1961) stand out. For other examples, see chapter 5 of Gracia (2000b). For the U.S. context, see Padilla (1985, 57).

3. I do not assume that extra-mental existence of the object of reference is a necessary condition of reference. This is a matter I leave open here.

4. The issue of whether features and relations are individual, or even whether there are any things at all that are individual, is hotly disputed in the literature. See Gracia (1988, 57–115).

5. Rex classifies ethnic groups together with races, classes, and nations as "quasi-groups," in part because they are brought together in situations of conflict (Rex 1986, 80–81).

6. There is considerable controversy concerning the proper name for this group. Many favor speaking of Latinos/as instead of Hispanics. In fact, however, the denotations of the two terms are different. "Hispanics" is more inclusive in that it denotes the people of Iberia also. I chose "Hispanics" here precisely because it is more inclusive and has a cultural connotation that is also often associated with ethnicity. For discussions of these terms, see Gracia (2000b, chs. 1 and 3); (2005); Alcoff (2005).

7. Contrary to Gooding-Williams's contention, identifying a point of origin for an ethnic group does not imply a different theory of ethnic-group identity than the one I have proposed, nor does it contradict my theory (Gooding-Williams 2001a, 3–10).

8. For a discussion of this view and pertinent texts, see Gracia (2000b, 56–57, 66–67).

9. This is standard in the media. Italians are ethnic in the United States, but not in Italy; Russians are ethnic in Latvia, but not in Russia; Spaniards are ethnic in

Germany, but not in Spain. Examples are commonplace, but see also Glazer and Moynihan (1975, 1ff.).

10. For the development of the Aryan myth, see Poliakov (1974). The myth of purity with respect to Germans goes back to comments by Tacitus (Poliakov 1974, 81).

11. For some sociologists, the ethnic group must also be a minority in terms of numbers, that is, constitute less than 50 percent of the total population. See Jordan and Rowntree (1997, 316) and McKee (2000, xv). But others correctly see this as an unwarranted assumption and are willing to speak of both minority and majority ethne (Guibernau 1997, 9; Smith 1997, 29; Chapman et al. 1989, 17). For a view of minorities as "dominated groups," see Wagley and Harris (1958, 10). Spoonley notes that the notion of minority has nothing to do with numbers, for a minority can actually be a majority in numbers. Minorities, in his view, have to do rather with being treated unequally and as inferior in some way (Spoonley 1993, 4).

12. I first discussed this view in Gracia (2000a), and it has been picked up by García (2001a).

13. One can also speak of the history that follows the disappearance of a race, but it would be hard to construe this as in any sense being "the history of the race."

14. The philosophical foundation of this view goes back to some Wittgensteinians, for example, Bambrough (1960–61). Among sociologists, Brown includes self-naming as a condition of ethnicity, as noted earlier (Brown 1997, 81).

4

RACE

What is race? Is there an answer to the objections to it that were formulated in the first chapter of this book? Perhaps the best-known
response to these questions is given by Anthony Appiah in his influential
essay, "Race, Culture, and Identity: Misunderstood Connections," published in *Color Conscious*, a book that has made history in race studies. Appiah's view is not only that a biological conception of race makes no
sense factually or conceptually, but also that an ethnic one, centered
around culture, does not either. Rather than speaking about races, then,
we should turn to the concept of racial identity. As he puts it: "First, . . .
American social distinctions cannot be understood in terms of the concept of race. . . . Second, replacing the notion of race with the notion of
culture is not helpful. . . . And third, . . . we should use instead the notion
of racial identity . . ." (Appiah 1996, 32).

Appiah's attack against the notion of race is framed in terms of two
contemporary theories of meaning, the ideational and the referential, because in order to make credible claims about race one must establish a
meaning for the term. The ideational account, taken strictly, requires that
there be something that satisfies a set of criterial beliefs or, if taken loosely,
requires that there be something that satisfies a good number of those beliefs (Appiah 1996, 35, 36). The referential account requires that we find
something in the world that provides an effective causal explanation of the
use of the word "race." Appiah argues, however, that when the history of
the concept of race in the United States is investigated, we find no identifiable objective phenomenon to which people respond when they talk
about race that can effectively function causally (Appiah 1996, 40, 72). Nor
do we find a uniform set of coherent beliefs about race (Appiah 1996, 72).

There is, then, neither a proper referent of the word "race" nor a proper idea of it. As Appiah concludes:

> [Y]ou can't get much out of a race concept, ideationally speaking, from any of these [American] traditions; you can get various possible candidates from the referential notion of meaning, but none of them will be much good for explaining social or psychological life, and none of them corresponds to the social groups we call "races" in America. (Appiah 1996, 74)

In place of races and the concept of race, Appiah proposes the concept of racial identity. This, according to him, adheres much better to what we do when we speak about races, racial phenomena, and racial groups. He defines racial identity as:

> a label R, associated with [1] *ascriptions* by most people (where ascription involves descriptive criteria for applying the label); and [2] *identifications* by those who fall under it (where identification implies a shaping role for the label in the intentional acts of the possessor, so that they sometimes act *as an R*), where there is a history of associating possessors of the label with an inherited racial essence (even if some who use the label no longer believe in racial essences). (Appiah 1996, 81–82)

The conditions of racial identity are clear: ascription by others, self-identification by the labeled, and a set of descriptions, used both for ascriptions and as norms for action, that has a historical association to a label involving a racial essence. It does not matter for racial identity, then, that there be no reality of race, or even a consistent concept of race. What matters is that people label some other people and themselves and that the labels include a notion of inherited racial essence. A racial essence is a set of conditions regarded as necessary and sufficient for a particular race, whether in fact such a set exists or not. In this context, then, it is important to realize that the labeling, for Appiah, who follows Ian Hacking in this, is crucial. Indeed, the label comes first, and it is only afterward that other features, such as cultural traits, are associated with it and used for action (Appiah 1996, 89). As he puts it: "Collective identities . . . provide what we might call scripts: narratives that people can use in shaping their life plans and in telling their life stories" (Appiah 1996, 97).

This is Appiah's proposal, but is he right? Can he answer the objections raised in chapter 1? He embraces some of these objections insofar as he agrees that we must abandon the belief both that race is a reality and that there is a cogent concept of race. He wants us to use instead the concept of a racial identity, which in his view reflects accurately the way we function with respect to racial phenomena. There is neither race nor a consistent concept of race; there are only certain procedures of labeling, varying descriptions, and attempts by those described to tailor action to those descriptions. This is racial identity. But does this proposal make sense?

Appiah seems to be on the right track in many ways. Indeed, in a discussion of race the best way to proceed seems to be by asking for the set of necessary and sufficient conditions of racial groups. To ask this question is to a great extent like asking if the notion of race makes any sense, that is, if it has conceptual limits and is coherent. An affirmative answer requires identifiable differences between races, and this in turn can be broken into two requirements: first, ontologically there must be differences; second, epistemically, the differences must be discernible. These requirements should not be confused: one thing is to talk about what there is, the other to talk about our knowledge of what there is. There are all sorts of things that exist but that we do not know, and there are all sorts of things we think we know but that do not exist. Still, if there were differences that we cannot discern, then it would be impossible for us to talk about them. So, in effect, we need to consider only differences that are discernible, even if there may be some that are not, but this does not mean that the differences are to be regarded as merely epistemic. In short, the correct question is whether there are differences such that they can function as necessary and sufficient conditions for a race, not just epistemically, but also ontologically.

Appiah's response faces at least two main challenges: first, in spite of his claim to the contrary, there seem to be some constants to the notion of a race, such as hereditary features; and second, some scientists cite evidence that suggests that human groups can be divided along what some would argue are racial lines. References to supporting sources were given in chapters 1 and 2.

Many authors, however, going all the way back to the nineteenth century, follow Appiah in claiming that there are no necessary and sufficient conditions for races. We need only mention Du Bois, Martí, and Alain Locke (Du Bois 1897; Martí 1946; Locke 1992, 10–12; see also Zack 1993; Harris 1999a; Outlaw 1996; and notes to the section "The Factual Argument," in chapter 1 of this book). In their view, the concept of race cannot be cogently articulated, for a variety of reasons. One frequently cited, and to which I referred earlier, is that human beings have so much in common that the so-called racial differences between them are negligible. Studies of DNA suggest, for example, that all human beings descend from the same mother and that the number of common characteristics to humans is extraordinary. As Nei and Roychoudhury have shown, we are fundamentally the same biologically (Nei and Roychoudhury 1982; 1972; see also Hoffman 1994, 4). But this should not be surprising. Indeed, it would be difficult to argue otherwise insofar as members from what are considered to be different human races can mate and produce offspring and the offspring are fertile themselves. Human races are not like dogs and cats, or even like horses and donkeys. As King points out, it is undeniable that we all belong to the same biological group (King 1981, 135–38). So the question is whether, having accepted this, it still makes sense to speak of different races within this group. After all, we do not consider black, white, and yellow cats different races of cats, although we do consider Siamese and Pekinese cats to belong to different "breeds." So why should we consider "Black," "White," and "Yellow" humans different races of humans?

One answer frequently given these days, and shared by Appiah and a score of scientists, is that we should not. There is nothing biological that justifies the notion of different human races, or even different human "breeds," and therefore we should just drop the concept (Appiah 1985; Lewontin 1972; Livingstone 1993; Cavalli-Sforza et al. 1994). As Montagu argued a while back, the notion of race, like the old notion of phlogiston, is baseless (Montagu 1964, xli). Indeed, many of those who make this claim argue that race is a social construct, and as such can, and because of its pernicious effects should, be eliminated (Appiah 1985; Lewontin 1972; see also Cavalli-Sforza et al. 1994, 19–20).

At the outset, this response makes considerable sense, but upon closer inspection several problems come up. First, there is a problem with respect to the issue of social construction, for this is a complicated matter. Indeed, further reflection reveals that the issue is not a matter of just construction versus nonconstruction, for the line that separates these alternatives is not very sharp. For the moment, it should suffice to say that, even if one were to accept that human races are social constructions, this would not necessarily mean that the notion of race is incoherent, that it is indistinguishable from such other notions as ethnicity or nationality, or that its use is necessarily pernicious. Certainly, chess is a social construction insofar as chess is a game resulting from human ingenuity—the rules that make up chess are the result of human design and have been adopted by humans who have decided to do so. Yet this does not imply that the notion of chess is incoherent, that chess cannot be distinguished from other games and things, or that it is necessarily a bad thing to have such a notion. The same could be true of the notion of race.

The argument that the strong commonality among humans does not justify dividing them into races can also be challenged. If we accept this argument, why not accept that the commonality among humans is such that the distinction among individual human beings is unjustifiable? Yet no one would want to go that far. Indeed, an emphasis on individuality seems to be prevalent among those who reject the notion of race, including Appiah. Besides, we divide humans in all sorts of ways that are generally thought to be both justified and useful. We separate them according to age, intelligence, moral character, beliefs, cultural heritage, ethnicity, religion, language, political affiliation, physical abilities, nationality, profession, gender, talents, skills, and so on. So, why not according to what has come to be called race?

In principle, it makes sense to say that, even though humans are mostly the same biologically, there are differences among them: some of these are found between individuals, say Mary and Peter, and some are found between groups, say Jews and fundamentalist Christians. So why not say that humans can also be grouped racially? Only if we were to find that we cannot identify conditions of distinction concerning race, either because there are in fact no such conditions, or the ones that appear to be there are incompatible, would we be able to argue soundly that the notion of human races is empirically unjustified or logically incoherent, and therefore that it must be rejected, just as we reject the notions of an existing square circle and an existing Aphrodite. But in fact empirical evidence, according to some scientists, does point to differences, even if not of the magnitude that some used to think. Nei and Roychoudhury, for example, point out that, although "interracial genic variation is small, it is important to realize that the genetic differentiation [between races] is real and generally statistically highly significant" (Nei and Roychoudhury 1982, 41). And geneticists have reached remarkable agreement on genetic groupings of humans, even if many are opposed to calling such groupings "races" or associating these groupings with any kind of nineteenth-century biological notion of race, or the various notions of race used in ordinary discourse (see the discussion of this issue in Cavalli-Sforza et al. 1994, 79).

Finally, one could also argue that the gap between humans and non-human animals is not so great either, and yet not many rush to question the distinction between them. Recent genetic studies have shown that humans and primates have most of their genes in common. Indeed, even the genetic distinctions between humans and lower animals is surprisingly minor. So if this low percentage is sufficient to distinguish between certain animals and humans, even smaller genetic differences could justify other distinctions as well, including racial ones (cf. Levin 1997, 21).

In short, we cannot altogether dispose of the notion of race on the basis of these arguments, although this by itself cannot be considered an argument in favor of race. Appiah's argument cannot be easily dismissed. So we are back where we started: What is race, and is there an answer to the objections against it mentioned in chapter 1?

I propose to answer this question through a metaphysical analysis. I am primarily interested in the categorization of race rather than in the way we come to know or speak about it. The concern is not with the word "race," or even with the concepts knowers may have of it. Rather, I am interested in what we think about when we think of race. So what are the general categories into which race falls? That "race" is a term that can mean either the feature shared by those persons that belong to a race or the group of persons themselves that are characterized creates a complication.[1] I begin with race understood as a group of persons and return to the feature later.

THE GENETIC COMMON-BUNDLE VIEW

In asking about a race, I mean to ask about such things as "Blacks," "Whites," and "Yellows." I am not concerned with particular races, but rather with race as such.[2] And I begin by borrowing some ideas from the discussion of ethne in the previous chapter, for after all, races and ethne are frequently thought to be indistinguishable or inseparable. So they must have much in common.

A race, like an ethnos, is a group of human beings, and again, as in the case of an ethnos, the members of the group are individual (cf. Hirschfeld 1996, 20). But this is not enough for our purposes, insofar as ethnic groups and a faculty committee are also groups of individual humans and yet are not races. We need more specificity. First, we need to ask whether, like an ethnos, a race falls into the category of family; and second, if so, we need to ask what it is that sets this kind of family apart from other kinds.

To say that a race is a kind of family seems *prima facie* quite promising, a fact that Du Bois noticed a century ago (Du Bois 1897, 7).[3] After all, races are groups of individual humans that appear to be tied in the ways families are, and like families, races seem to involve genetically transmittable physical features. As he put it:

> the history of the world is the history, not of individuals, but of groups, not of nations, but of races. . . . What then is a race? *It is a vast family of human beings*, generally common blood and language, *always common his-*

tory, traditions and impulses, who are both voluntarily and involuntarily striving together for the accomplishment of certain more or less vividly conceived ideals of life. (Du Bois 1970, 74; my emphasis)

A race is a family that always has a common history, traditions, and impulses, although other things, such as language and blood, also enter into the mix. Elsewhere Du Bois returns to the kinship provided by history:

> But one thing is sure and that is the fact that since the fifteenth century *these ancestors of mine and their descendants have had a common history*; have suffered a common disaster and have one long memory. The actual ties of heritage between the individuals of this group vary with the ancestors that they have in common with many others. . . . But the physical bond is least and the badge of color relatively unimportant save as a badge; *the real essence of this kinship is its social heritage* of slavery; the discrimination and insult; and this heritage binds together not simply the children of Africa, but extends through yellow Asia and into the South Seas. (Du Bois 1940, 117; my emphasis)

Still, this is not enough. Du Bois does not dwell much on what exactly he means by a racial family, nor is he sufficiently specific about what he means by history and the pertinent aspects of it for his view. This has led to a number of criticisms and interpretations of his position. Is he an essentialist or a nonessentialist? He seems to waver (see the discussion in Appiah 1992, ch. 2). Even if it turns out that races are families, we still need to specify what sort of families they are in order to distinguish them from other kinds of families, such as ethnic groups, nuclear families, and extended families.

Conceiving races as families would seem to explain that there is no feature that all members of a race share, although Du Bois himself did not draw this inference. The features that members of races have would always be the result of historically contingent events and, therefore, would be temporal and historical, with the further consequence that not all members of the races in question would share them. It is for this reason that these features cannot constitute necessary and sufficient conditions of a race for all times and places. A "White" can be as dark in skin color as a "Black"; a "Yellow" can be as dumb as a "White"; a "Yellow" can be as physically gifted as a "Black"; a "White" can be as intelligent as a "Yellow"; and so on. There are no common features to all members of a race; there are only features shared in certain circumstances, as happens with families.

Still, this explanation of the unity of a race is not quite satisfactory. We saw earlier that families come in at least three varieties: nuclear, extended, and ethnic. And it makes sense to say that races are like these families in that their members share features with at least some other members, even if not with all of them. However, races are unlike these families in at least one feature, that every member of a race is taken to be related by descent to some other member of the race. In nuclear, extended, or ethnic families, this is seldom, if ever, so. In the case of nuclear families, a husband and a wife are not related by descent (although there are exceptions), and if they have no issue, at least one of them would not be related by descent to any member of the spouse's family. And adopted children are not related by descent to their adoptive parents, and yet they are very much members of nuclear families. The case of extended families, of course, is more obvious. And when it comes to ethne, the point is still more clear, for persons completely unrelated genetically can join ethnic families, but this is not possible in a race; no one can join a race. Membership in a race can result only from birth.

Some may want to argue that this last point is disputable insofar as, in fact, people from one race are said often to leave their race and join another. In South Africa, for example, it is known that individual persons have officially changed their racial characterization in the past. In the United States, again, we are told many light "Blacks" go "White" every year. So perhaps one can leave a race and join another at will. But this is not quite right, for in fact one cannot do this simply as a matter of choice. As Smedley, Banton, and Boxill have pointed out, one cannot shed, as it were, one's racial skin, as one can shed one's ethnic skin (Smedley 1993, 33; Banton 1983, 1–15; Boxill 2001a, 40). To change my ethnicity in the case of many ethne, I may need only to sever my relations with members of my ethnos and establish relations with members of another ethnos, for this can result in turn in the eventual elimination of the features I have that are the result of ethnic relations. But this is not the case with race, in that I cannot change all of the features that make me a member of a race or my ancestry. So there is, after all, an important difference between races and the kinds of families we have considered thus far. I shall come back to this later and give an account of what actually happens when people are said to change races.

Another important difference between races and families of the sort we have discussed so far is that, although cultural features are frequently associated with races, physical differences seem to be of the essence. In order to be a member of a race, it is not sufficient to share certain cultural elements, even if sharing them is part of what is taken to characterize the race in certain places and circumstances. Physical features always appear to be necessary conditions of racial membership, although the features in question may vary. This means that, if races are to be considered families, they are families of a special sort.

Now the same analysis that was made in the case of ethnos and eth-nicity applies to race, except that "race" is used to speak of both a group of humans (just as "ethnos" is) and of the feature that characterizes the mem-bers of the group (just as "ethnicity" is). In the first sense, we also have a group composed of individual persons as noted before, and in the second sense we also have a relational feature ("White" or "Yellow") that is cashed out in terms of a relation to the group.

Let me propose two formulas to describe a race. The first posits a no-tion of race as a group of individuals. This is the counterpart of an ethnos.

> A race is a subgroup of individual human beings who satisfy the follow-ing two conditions: (1) each member of the group is linked by descent to another member of the group, who is in turn also linked by descent to at least some third member of the group; and (2) each member of the group has one or more physical features that are (i) genetically transmit-table, (ii) generally associated with the group, and (iii) perspicuous.

The second formula presents a conception of race as what characterizes members of a group. This is the counterpart of ethnicity.

> Race consists in the relation of belonging that characterizes members of a race.

The two key conditions presented in these two formulas are metaphysical in that they describe what race is through a general categorization of it. In order for something to be a race, in either of the two senses stated, the members of the group have to be linked by descent and have one or more physical features that are genetically transmittable, generally associated with the group, and perspicuous. Indeed, Boxill argues that inborn, inherited traits are essential to the notion of race, even when race is taken as con-structed (Boxill 2001a, 32). But these conditions can also function epis-temically. For knowing that a particular person satisfies them with respect to a particular race entails that one has identified that person as a member of that race.

Neither one of these conditions, taken by itself, is sufficient for racial membership, unless one adopts the infamous One-Drop Rule (see Mal-comson 2000), but this view is inconsistent and therefore unacceptable. The One-Drop Rule is inconsistent as a racial marker because it can function ef-fectively only if applied to some races and not others. This means that be-ing related by descent to a member of some race, who is in turn related by descent to at least some third member of that race, is not sufficient for some-one to be a member of the pertinent race, for the person in question may not share in any of the features generally associated with members of it. This is the reason why we say that people can change races. I would argue that, strictly speaking, there is no such racial change. There is only the recognition that the persons in question do not satisfy the conditions sufficient for belonging to a particular race, while they meet the conditions of belonging to another race. The change is, then, one of labeling, that is, of what we call the persons, rather than of being, that is, of what the persons are.

Likewise, having features associated with a certain race does not automatically make a person a member of the race or serve effectively to identify the person as such. Indians, from India, are frequently as dark as "Blacks," but they are not generally regarded as being "Black" and they do not consider themselves to be "Black." Italians from southern Italy are frequently as dark as "Blacks" and have some features that satisfy the nondescent conditions of membership in the "Black" race. Yet, because they do not satisfy the descent condition, no one thinks of them as "Black."

To be a member of a race, one has to be linked by descent to someone who is a member of the race and who in turn is linked by descent to still another member of the race. For A to be "Black," she has to be linked by birth to B, who is both "Black" and linked by descent to C, who is also "Black." In addition, A must share in a pool of physical features that are genetically transmittable, generally considered to be racial indicators, and perspicuous, such as skin color, hair texture, and nose shape. For A to be "Black," she must be dark skinned, or have curly hair, and so on. It is not required that A have all the features generally associated with the race imputed to her, but she must have some. If she has some of them and is related by descent to other members of the race, then A is considered to be a member of the race.

The view that members of a group share in some, but not all, features contained in a set, I called the Common-Bundle View in the previous chapter. I rejected this view in the case of ethnicity, but I believe it applies well to race. Because I explained this view earlier in some detail, I need only offer the brief reminder that it can be explained thus: Say that we have a group with six members—a, b, c, d, e, and f—and a set of six features—A, B, C, D, E, and F. According to this view, each member of the group would have several, but not necessarily all, of these features as, for instance: $a(A, B)$, $b(A, B, E, F)$, $c(C, D, F)$, $d(B, C, D, E, F)$, $e(A, E)$, and $f(B, C, E, F)$.

The general advantages of this view were mentioned earlier. So let us see how it works in the case of race. Let us apply the Common-Bundle View to "White," say, and stipulate that there is a set of ten features several of which are generally associated with being "White" (the list presented

here is purely arbitrary and should be given no significance—an appropriate list would have to be established on the basis of sociological data): pinkish skin color, light olive skin color, inability to get a tan, pointed nose
shape, straight nose shape, hooked-shaped nose, thin lips, straight hair, wavy
hair, and much body hair. Using this criterion, John Irish qualifies as
"White," because he has pinkish skin color, thin lips, a straight nose, wavy
hair, and lots of body hair. His daughter also qualifies because, although she
does not have much body hair and her nose has a different shape, she shares
in several of the features of the group: pinkish skin color, thin lips, and wavy
hair. At the same time, we can distinguish John and his daughter from Mary
and her son, who are "Black," because they share in a different set of features associated with "Blacks," even though Mary has a hooked-shaped nose
and wavy hair, and her son has much body hair and, as an albino, is unable
to tan.

The kind of unity I have been describing is the key to race. As with an
ethnos, we are speaking here of a group of people who do not share common nonrelational features. But, unlike an ethnos, their unity is founded
both on a kind of relation—a descent link—and participation in a pool of
features of a particular kind. Alain Locke has nothing in common with Martin Luther King Jr., but both are tied by birth to other "Blacks" and share
in a pool of physically perspicuous features that are considered indicators of
the "Black" race, even though they may not share in the same features from
the pool. This ties them together and also separates them from members of
other races, such as Mao Tse-tung and Margaret Thatcher. This makes them
"Black," rather than "Yellow" or "White." There is no need to find features
common to all "Blacks" in order to classify them as such.

Lest there should be any misunderstanding, let me make clear two
points. One is that the descent requirement cannot be taken as a feature in
which all members of a race share. The reason is threefold: First, the descent
link is no more than a birth relation between each individual member of a
race and one other individual member, who is in turn tied by birth to some
other member and therefore not a feature properly speaking. Second, although the relation in the abstract is of the same general kind, in the concrete it is actually an individual link between three individual persons: it is
the genetic relation between a, b, and c and, therefore, numerically different
from the genetic relation between a and d, b and e, or f and g. And third, the
kind of the relation in general breaks down into many different specific relations—fatherhood, motherhood, sisterhood, and so on.

The second point I need to make clear is that, if one thinks of the set
of features associated with a race as a single disjunctive feature, then the

members of the groups should share a common feature. But surely this would not go contrary to my position, for the feature in question would not be anything like hair color or bodily shape.

Keep in mind that I have not claimed that racial phenotypes are, or must be, transmitted genetically. Clearly if, as noted earlier, genotypic factors are affected by the environment in the production of phenotypes, it makes no sense to claim that all phenotypes are always transmitted genetically. The point is rather that the concept of race includes the notion of physically perspicuous features that in principle either are able to be transmitted genetically or have that potential, so that, under appropriate circumstances, they result in the same phenotype.

In sum, part of what ties members of a race is the same kind of thing that ties some members of a family. There may be no common features to all of them, but nonetheless they belong to the same group of persons because they are genetically related, as a father is to a natural daughter or grandparents to natural grandchildren. Moreover, they share in a pool of features that need not be common to all the members of the group. It also means, as with ethnicity, that any requirements of coherence and homogeneity do not apply. Racial groups are not coherent wholes composed of homogeneous elements. Like families, races are related groups of human persons with different, and sometimes incompatible, features. Homogeneity is not one of their necessary conditions.

Du Bois was on the right track with his familial view of race, although he missed some key points.[4] Among these are the following: first, he completely ignored the matter of language and names; second, he did not develop the notion that there are no common features to races; and third, he failed to make clear the difference between a race and an ethnos.

Our list of family groups, then, has to be expanded to include races. Now we have four kinds of family groups: nuclear, extended, ethnic, and racial. They all share that the members of these groups are individual human beings tied through historical, contingent relations in the ways I have made clear, but they differ in the specific conditions that apply to them.

But what does this conception of race tell us about the question of whether particular racial categories are mutually exclusive and thus the use of racial terms used to refer to them exclusionary? In concrete terms, is being "Black" incompatible with being "White," and does the use of the name "Black" exclude the possibility of using "White" for the same persons? Recall that ethnic incompatibility and exclusion were not necessary or even the rule. Can we say the same of races?

The way most people think about this is quite confused and inconsistent, and depends very much on the races in question and on cultural location. In the United States, it is clear that being "Black" and being "White" are considered incompatible, and the use of the terms "Black" and "White" is inconsistent when applied to the same person. As Zack has pointed out, one is either "Black" or "White," but not both (Zack 1993, 5). This is a result of the notorious One-Drop Rule, according to which anyone with a drop of "Black" blood is "Black" and not "White." And the same incompatibility seems to apply when it comes to "Yellow" and "White," although the matter is not as clear-cut as it is with the previous case.[5] At the same time, the attitude with respect to relations between races other than "White" is different. One can be both "Black" and "Yellow," for example.[6]

This general attitude toward the relations between races is sometimes carried over to certain ethnic groups that are regarded as "races" or are racially understood, such as Hispanics. If one is Hispanic, then some people think one cannot be "White," whereas they have no difficulty thinking of Hispanics as "Black." It also reflects the view that the "White" race is regarded as superior to any other race and as somehow pure. "White" purity is defiled by even a minimal mixing with other races, whereas the situation does not apply to races other than "White," because as Alcoff notes, they are all considered to be impure to some extent (Alcoff 1995).[7]

The attitude toward races in places other than the United States is not quite the same as what has been described.[8] In Latin America, for example, there has always been great sensitivity to the notion that a racial mixture is not equivalent to any one of the elements that went into the mix. A mixture of "Black" and "White" is neither "Black" nor "White." During the colonial period, attempts were made to catalog the various possible mixes between the races present at the time in Latin America, such as *español* (Spanish), *negro* (Black), and *indio* (Indian). Note that two of these categories are not primarily racial, although they have racial connotations. "Spanish" is certainly not a racial category, even though it was taken to imply "White" at the time, and "Indian" has never been a completely racial category in Latin America.[9] "Indian" frequently has more to do with the way people live, that is, with culture, than with race.

The various mixes between the categories were called *castas* (castes) and included extraordinarily detailed possible combinations and mixture proportions.[10] For example, the mixture of *español* (Spanish male) with *india* (Amerindian female) results in *mestizo* (mixed male), *mestizo* with *española* (Spanish female) results in *castizo* (Castilian male), *castizo* with *española* results in *español*, *español* with *negra* ("Black" female)[11] results in *mulato* (mulatto male), *mulato* with *española* results in *chino* (Chinese male), *chino* with *india* results in *salta atrás* (skip backward male), *salta atrás* with *mulata* (mulatto female) results in *lobo* (male wolf), *lobo* with *china* (Chinese female) results in *jíbaro* (wild male; sometimes spelled *gíbaro*), *jíbaro* with *mulata* results in *albarazado* (whitish male), *albarazado* with *negra* results in *cambujo* (also spelled *canbujo*; reddish black male), *cambujo* with *india* results in *sambaigo* (also spelled *zambaigo*; precisely, this mix), *sambaigo* with *loba* (female wolf) results in *calpamulato* (precisely, this mix; *calpamulo* also recorded), *calpamulato* with *cambuja* (reddish–black female) results in *tente-en-el-aire* (stay on the air), *tente-en-el-aire* with *mulata* results in *no-te-entiendo* (I do not understand you), and *no-te-entiendo* with *india* results in *torna atrás* (turn back; sometimes *torna atraz*).[12] The development of the generally widespread notions of *mestizo* and *mulato* in particular are attempts at dealing with racial mixture.[13]

Several things are revealed by these attempts at the classification of racial mixtures in colonial Latin America. First, clearly there is nothing such as the American One-Drop Rule. People of mixed race occupied a unique place that was not identified with any one of the elements that went into the mix, unlike in the United States, where having a drop of "Black" blood automatically is supposed to make one "Black." Second, there is no sense of incompatibility between the components of a racial mixture.[14] On the contrary, racially mixed people are kinds different from the originals, but quite consistent and operational in themselves. Third, the notion of "White" racial purity is undermined insofar as a consistent standard of purity applies to every race and not just to some. It is not just "Whites" who can be pure, but also "Blacks" and "Indians." Fourth, the category at the top is not "White," but "Spanish male." This is important because this is not exclusively or even primarily a racial category, and it includes a gender element. The Spanish part points to ethnicity or nationality, and the male part indicates a notion of masculine superiority. The implications of this could be rather startling and merit further reflection, but I do not have the space to do justice to it presently.[15] Fifth, the category of *negro* ("Black" male) does not appear at all—giving the impression that mixing with a "Black male" was not to be considered at all. Sixth, although there is a sense of hierarchy, in which "Spanish male" stands at the top, the lowest caste seems to be the one that, instead of staying with what it has "gained," goes back to a former stage. Moreover, the position of "Spanish male" is not taken as absolutely different from those of other races; to be a "Spanish male" is obviously the best thing one can possibly be, but the rules that apply to race apply to it as well. This is different from the situation in Anglo-Saxon societies, where

"White" is treated in an entirely different way from the ways other races are treated.[16]

Clearly, exclusionary attitudes toward races are idiosyncratic and also inconsistent, insofar as they are based on confused or incoherent notions of race. There is no reason why general and basic criteria of racial membership should vary from race to race, but as Zack has repeatedly noted, there is asymmetry in the views about "Black" and "White" (Zack 1993, 5). Now if we adopt the Genetic Common-Bundle View of race, these confusions can be pinpointed and eliminated. The understanding of race I have presented is not exclusionary and, in my view, actually corresponds to the underlying social reality of race, even if it does not fit the "standard view" of race widespread in American society. According to my conception, anything like the One-Drop Rule is absurd. You may have all the drops of so-called "Black" blood you may want, but that does not make you "Black," or exclusively "Black." To be "Black," one has to satisfy the conditions stipulated earlier: one must be related by descent to someone who is also "Black" and who is in turn related by descent to some other "Black," and one must share in some of the perspicuous and genetically transmittable physical features associated with being "Black." If one is related by descent to other "Blacks," but has none of the features generally associated with "Blacks," one is not "Black," or as some others like to say, one "passes" for "White." Of course, in such a case one needs also to be linked by descent to "Whites" or some other race.

The notion of "passing" is curious, because it may be that one generation does "pass" insofar as it knows it has "Black" blood and believes itself to be "Black," but the next generation may not know it at all. The next generation may simply be members of a race different from that of some ancestors. "Passing" involves an epistemic dimension: in order "to pass" one has to know one is not what one presumes to be.[17] Moreover, it carries the connotation of dishonesty on the part of the one who "passes," for obvious reasons. In fact, the notion of "passing" is quite absurd, and has been generated precisely to enforce such discriminatory and inconsistent notions as the One-Drop Rule; it makes no sense. If we adopt the Genetic Common-Bundle View, then one can understand why one "passes" as a member of a race, for the reason is that in fact one *is* a member of that race, insofar as one is linked by descent to some members of that race and one shares in some of the perspicuous features that are generally considered to characterize the race. However, if certain persons have features that appear to put them in the category "Black"—and by golly there are many Italians and Spaniards who qualify—but they do not satisfy the descent requirement, then they are not "Black." The persons become "dark Italians," "dark Spaniards," or something along those lines.

This also means, according to the Genetic Common-Bundle View, that one can be a member of two or more races at once, which is in fact the case of mulattoes who have, say, facial features associated with "Whites," a skin color associated with "Blacks," and descent links to both "Whites" and "Blacks." To think about a person as "White," then, should not prevent us from speaking and thinking in other racial ways as well about that person, that is, from using other principles of classification. These other classifications reveal other facts that, under different arrangements, would be ignored. We need not frame reality always in the same way, because reality is complex and subject to multiple understandings. The perspective opened by the notion of race I have proposed uncovers aspects of both reality and our experience of reality that would otherwise go unnoticed.

As with ethnic categories, the use of racial categories does not exclude other nonracial arrangements. Indeed, there are many helpful ways, other than racially, of thinking about the reality denoted by racial terms. We could think in regional terms, such as West African, Asian, or European; in linguistic terms, such as Chinese, Arabic, or Castilian; in political terms, such as Cambodian, Italian, or South African; in ethnic terms, such as Hispanic, ethnic Polish, or Jewish; and so on. And all these would, if the notions are historically warranted, make clear to us aspects of the world that otherwise might be overlooked.

Another significant consequence of the Genetic Common-Bundle View is that the use of racial terms is not intended to reflect just that some persons choose to refer to themselves by these terms. It is popular today to say that self-naming (or self-identification) is both a necessary and sufficient condition of racial membership. If I choose to call myself "Black," others should call me so because this means that I am "Black." But, in fact, self-naming is neither necessary nor sufficient in this way. The view I have put forth is immune to these difficulties. Although it does not accept that there are common features to all members of a race at all times and in all places, it allows for common features at certain times and places arising from particular historical relations. In short, the conception of race I have put forth is, like the view of ethnicity presented in the previous chapter, neither vacuous nor circular, and it is also consistent.

The two formulas proposed, then, provide us with the basis for a categorization of race. Race, in one sense, falls into the category of a group of individual persons who are distinguished from other groups in that they are tied by descent and in that they have some features that are generally associated with a race. In this, they also constitute a subcategory of family. In another sense, race consists in the relation of belonging that unites members of racial groups. Obviously, race is metaphysically very similar to ethnicity, so we may ask, as we did with ethnicity, whether race, considered as a relation, is symmetrical and transitive.

The answer is that, again like ethnicity, one must distinguish between the higher-order relation of belonging to the group and the lower-order relation and features on which the former is based. The higher-order relation appears to be both symmetrical and transitive, but the lower-order relation and features on which the higher-order relation is based are neither. Indeed, the relation of descent that is fundamental for racial membership is neither symmetrical nor transitive insofar as it breaks down into different relations that are not themselves symmetrical or transitive. If X is related by birth to Y, Y is not related by birth to X. A daughter is related by birth to a father, but the father is not related by birth to the daughter. And the same applies to transitivity. Birth relations cannot be passed on, even though they are at the core of descent. The situation is similar to the other condition, namely, participation in a list of genetically transferable and perspicuous physical features, for although the condition is both symmetrical and transitive, the features in question vary and so cannot sustain symmetry or transitivity. I return to the similarities and differences between race and ethnicity later in the book.

To sum up, it should now be clear how my position differs from that of Appiah, and how it constitutes an alternative to it. Like Appiah, I reject biological and cultural conceptions of race as incoherent and inaccurate. But unlike Appiah, I do not believe that the concept of race need be incoherent. Properly understood, the concept of a race is coherent and can be distinguished from the concepts of ethnos and nation. We do not need to reject all concepts of race in favor of the notion of identity, as Appiah proposes doing. Indeed, to speak of racial identity without a proper concept of race appears untenable. Appiah's view avoids most of the objections against race formulated in chapter 1, but it fails to do justice to the need for a concept of race that would help us distinguish race from ethnicity and nationality and could be used to account for human history and oppose the abuses perpetrated on the basis of race. The Genetic Common-Bundle View I have proposed, as I shall show in chapter 6, effectively answers the objections of chapter 1 without having to give up the concept of race.

HISTORICAL ORIGIN AND LOCATION

Families are historical entities established by historical events of various sorts and must reside in particular places. So, in order to complete our analysis, we need to ask whether there is a point in history where a race comes to be and whether there are particular places that must be associated with particular races. Let me go back to what I said in the previous chapter concerning ethnic groups and summarize it, with appropriate modifications, in the context of race, for most of it is applicable here as well.

The issue concerns contingent conditions surrounding groups of individual persons found in particular contexts and has to do with historical location. In the case of races, this involves factors that lead to the establishment of the groups, their origin, continuity throughout history, and spatiotemporal location.

To say that the use of the term "Black" for a racial group begins to make sense only at a certain time in history (1) confirms that "Blacks" constitute a racial group, (2) does not imply a shared feature common to all of them, and (3) supports the view that they are tied by a series of historically contingent relations that include descent links and also share in a pool of genetically transmittable perspicuous physical features generally associated with the race. Races have beginnings, but these beginnings are historical and contingent and serve their purpose only contextually (Harris 1999b, 443). Insofar as races develop in historical locations, there are always places, and sometimes times, that are associated with them. Moreover, the times and places sometimes survive in the collective memories, actual or mythical, of the groups. For "Blacks," the place is Africa; for "Yellows" it is East Asia; and for "Whites" it is the Caucasus (Senghor 1961, 1211).

This is important because the place and time contextually separate the first members of the racial group, even if they cannot be used to distinguish subsequent members of the group who lived elsewhere at later times and never lived in the original location. For this reason, an original place and time cannot constitute a condition, whether necessary or sufficient, for membership in a racial group, just as they do not constitute conditions of ethnic groups. Rather the unity and membership in a race has to be explained differently. Most "Blacks" in the United States, for example, were born here and have never been to Africa. Yet Africa is part of the racial consciousness of many of them to such a degree that some leaders of the community decided to change the terms commonly used to refer to themselves and begin to use "African-American" as a way to emphasize the relation of the group to the place of their origin (Alcoff 2000a). This place of origin often is not even the present Africa, but some mythical place lost in time. It may not even be the historical Africa from which the slaves were brought to America, but rather an Africa that probably never existed.

The issue of historical origin and location naturally leads to questions concerned with the way in which races come to be, but this is a complicated issue that will have to be left for another time. More space than I can devote to it here is required to deal with it adequately. Moreover, as with ethnicity, this matter concerns particular contexts and groups, rather than race as such.

OBSTACLES TO THE PROPER UNDERSTANDING OF RACE

There are at least four obstacles in particular that stand in the way of a proper understanding of race. Three of these are similar to three of the five we saw that stand in the way of a proper understanding of ethnicity. The first is the assumption, noted by both Smedley and Appiah, that the effective use of a common name requires the identification of an essence, that is, a feature or set of features that necessarily and sufficiently characterizes the things called by the name (Smedley 1993, 32; Appiah 1996, 55). For example, for Senghor there is an essence to "negritude," which is cashed out in value terms—cultural, economic, and political (Senghor 1961, 1211; see also Sartre 2001, 119). The lack of an essence is thought to indicate that the name is vacuous and therefore useless and even misleading. The second assumption that constitutes an obstacle to the proper understanding of race is that categories require clearly defined limits so that their membership is never in question—there are members and nonmembers of a category, but there is never a case in which membership is in doubt. The third assumption is that race entails both homogeneity and a compatibility in its members (Darwin 1874, 219). Members of a race are all the same and compatible with each other. And the fourth is that races, at least in their origins, are pure.[18]

In the previous chapter, I examined and rejected the view that the effective use of names requires a feature, or a set of features, that can be identified as common to the entities of which the names are truly predicated, so I refer the reader to that discussion. The inference from it is that there is no set of necessary and sufficient conditions that must be satisfied at all times and places for racial names to be used effectively (Boxill 2001a, 39). The conception of a race I have proposed implies that there are no features necessarily common to all those persons included in a racial group, and yet this does not mean that the use of all racial terms is unjustified or meaningless. There is a way to understand the concept of race that allows us to speak meaningfully of, and refer effectively to, racial groups, even when the peoples named do not share any feature at all times and places. More concretely, I claim that a race, like an ethnos, should be understood historically and contextually, thus allowing for diversity within unity.

But is this consistent with the requirements identified earlier? Don't all members of a race share at least two common features, namely, (1) they need to be tied by descent to at least some other member of the race who is in turn tied by descent to at least some third member of the race and (2) they have to have more than one feature from a set of physically perspicuous and genetically transmittable features generally associated with the race? Aren't these two requirements in fact features shared by all members of a race?

The answer is no. To be tied by descent does not count as a feature insofar as it is a relation that can be analyzed in more than one way. This means, first, that it does not characterize the members of the race themselves. Relations do not characterize relata themselves but merely situate them with respect to other things. That X is to the left of Y or even the mother of Y is not something in X or Y, but rather something in between X and Y.[19] Moreover, this relation can differ insofar as it can be that of father to child, mother to child, grandparents to grandchildren, or vice versa, and so on. So not everyone is related in exactly the same way, even if the number of relations in question is finite, or even small. Likewise, sharing in one or more of the features that constitute the set associated with a race does not entail that all members of the race have the same features, even if some members do share some features. A "White" person can have light skin and thin lips, but she may not have bodily hair or a thin nose.

With respect to the issue of strict boundaries and questionable members, we noted in the case of ethnicity that there are many categories to which we refer and that we find unproblematic that have no strict boundaries and whose membership is not completely clear. The case with race is one of these, but this does not interfere with its use. Indeed, Boxill has argued that, although the boundaries of races are not strict, they have not fluctuated much (Boxill 2001a, 38). Because the features associated with a race constitute a set, and not all members of the race have all these features, it is clear that there will be cases in which membership will be in doubt, although there are other cases in which it will not. What I said about this matter regarding ethnicity also applies to race.

This helps us respond in turn to the misconceptions of homogeneity and compatibility. If both the descent links and features that characterize members of a race are not necessarily the same for all of them, then certainly races cannot be claimed to be homogeneous: the members of a race can differ in important ways. This, in turn, opens the doors to incompatibility as well, for difference may involve incompatible features.

With respect to purity, a response similar to that given to the assumptions of homogeneity and compatibility can be given. But there are other answers as well. For example, genetically, the same alleles are found in different racial groups, even if their frequency might differ. So how could the notion of purity be sustained? Purity requires complete isolation from contaminants, that is, no overlapping of elements, and this, genetically speaking, is a myth, as has been proven in a number of cases concerning American "Blacks" and "Whites" (King 1981, 112–16).[20]

NEED FOR, AND ADVANTAGES OF, RACIAL CATEGORIES

One may question the need for, or advantage of, using racial categories, as we did with ethnic categories. If, as I have argued, there are no common features to all members of a race, what can we understand about them by positing racial categories that we do not already understand in terms of other group categories or of individual persons? For instance, is there any epistemic advantage in using a category such as "Black"? Can this category help us get to know anything that we do not already know through other categories such as African, American, Mandinga, and dark-skinned, or individuals such as Mobutu, Thomas, and Jorge? The answer is the same we gave in the case of ethnic categories: through it, we are able to understand better a historical and social reality that otherwise would be difficult or impossible to grasp.

Senghor and Fanon are right when they point out that racial categories allow us to understand certain historical phenomena that would otherwise escape us (Senghor 2001; Fanon 2001). Racial concepts make it possible for us to grasp aspects of human experience that would otherwise be missed, in part because the conceptual frameworks we use are either too broad or too narrow. A racial concept is a unique window through which we can look at a section of human history and social reality. In the extensive field of human experience, it introduces a means to frame the observer's gaze and leads it toward something that, under other conditions, might not be noticed, or might be noticed insufficiently. We can see more detail, even if we miss a greater perspective. "Black" directs our attention toward something that, without this concept, we might miss altogether, and that we could not fathom were we only to consider national, ethnic, linguistic, religious, or similar concepts. These are also frames, but like any frame, they reveal something by excluding something else. The use of racial concepts and terms, then, reveals something unique by simultaneously narrowing and widening our perspective.

But this is not all. As we saw earlier, the paradox of race is that it appears to be socially constructed and perhaps even invented, and yet it is real insofar as it has had and continues to have enormous historical and social effects (Omi and Winant 1994, 55; see also Kant 2001, 40). Much in the history of African slavery cannot be explained without reference to race; the American Civil War cannot be adequately grasped without it; and the present condition of many members of American society, or other societies for that matter, cannot be understood without recourse to it. We need, then, the notion of race to grasp human reality both in the past and present. And it is doubtful that we will be able to dispense with it in the near future. Our immediate future is tied to our past and, if our past is unintelligible without the use of the concept of race, the immediate future also will be unintelligible without it.

Finally, race has been the source of much oppression and abuse. To correct this requires not only that we refer to race, but also that we have an appropriate understanding of it. Without a concept of race, we cannot fight the ghosts that populate our social consciousness or overturn the oppressive, racist structures that are embedded in our social institutions. Bernasconi, Alcoff, and Outlaw have argued that without an understanding of race, we cannot set right much that is wrong in our society, and Sartre made consciousness of race a condition of liberation from oppression (Bernasconi 2001a; Alcoff 2001; Outlaw 1996, 157; Sartre 2001, 118). Of course, no wrong can be set right with another wrong. So we need an appropriate and adequate understanding of race to understand the root of much evil and conflict in human society; we cannot rely on a faulty one.

One can envision a time when the notion of race will have no use except for the historical purpose of understanding the past. If racism ceases and human society becomes racially blind, if no one finds satisfaction and fulfillment in identifying with a race, if inequities on the basis of race become absent in the human community, if racial segregation and discrimination are eliminated, then the concept of race will cease to have value. And if I am correct in saying that race involves only a descent link and some perspicuous and genetically transmittable features selected from a socially constructed list, then what would be the use of referring to racial categories? What would saying that someone is "Black" tell us about that person that we would not learn from the use of nonracial categories, including those of descent link and perspicuous and transmittable physical properties? Nothing, or nothing much, I believe. Race, as a category, has no great metaphysical or epistemic significance when separated from its ethical and political dimensions. So if the latter two are absent, the former two are of no consequence. In such a world, the category of race would become no more than a historical curiosity (Sartre 2001, 137).

OBJECTIONS AGAINST THE GENETIC COMMON-BUNDLE VIEW

Several of the important objections that may be raised against the theory of ethnicity I proposed in chapter 3 can also be raised, *mutatis mutandis*, about the view of race I have proposed in this chapter. Let me begin with one that argues that the Genetic Common-Bundle View does not adequately account for the differences between racial groups; something stronger and more specific must be supplied than the conditions I have stipulated. Consider, for example, "Blacks" and "Whites." We can tell who is and who is not "Black" or "White," and we can tell—so the argument goes—because we have clear criteria for these based on features that all members of the groups in question share. The reference to a descent link and to a set of features, only some of which are shared by some members of the groups, is not enough. A good explanation of the differences between races must refer to consistent and constituent features of all members of these, otherwise the unity of each group is jeopardized. It will not do to argue, as I have done, that there is actually no feature that members of a racial group have in common, for if this were the case, then it would not be possible, as it in fact is, to tell members of different racial groups apart from members of other groups. Mind you, establishing such common features might be difficult, or even impossible at times, but that does not entail that the features do not exist. Logic and reality are two different things.

Again, as I said in my answer to a similar objection in the context of ethnicity, this objection is misdirected, for nowhere have I claimed that there are no common features to members of racial groups and that as a consequence we can never in fact tell them apart from members of other groups. Instead, I have claimed that members of racial groups need not have features in common at all times and in all places that are necessary, sufficient, and discernible. My view does not prevent one from maintaining that there are features common to some members at all times and in all places, at all times and in some places, at some times and in all places, or even at all times and places, or features common to all members at all times and in some places, or at some times and in all places. Nor is it fair to construe my position as entailing that there cannot be common features to members of racial groups at all times and places. I argue only that no features are necessary and sufficient and can be shown to be common to all members of racial groups at all times and in all places for the groups to exist. In fact, I have also argued that there are features common to members of racial groups at some times and in some places, and that it is in terms of such features that we can identify them at those times and in those places. At every time and in every place, some members of racial groups have features in common that distinguish them from other groups, whether racial or not, but these features do not necessarily extend beyond those times and places or need to do so in order to account for their membership in the groups and their distinction from other groups.

The various relations that members of races have among themselves provide the foundation for features that also can be used to distinguish them. Particular physical characteristics can be used to distinguish "Blacks" in certain contexts, although they may not function as criteria of distinction and identification everywhere and at all times. In a society or region where all and only "Whites" have a certain skin color, this can be used to pick out "Whites," even if elsewhere there are "Whites" who do not share in this particular skin color. Races are not homogeneous, but particular features can be used to determine who counts as a member of the group in particular contexts. Apart from the descent-link requirement, racial membership does not entail one or more common features that constitute an essence, but this is not an obstacle to identification. Generally, we can determine who counts as a member of a race in context. Just as we generally and easily can tell a game from something that is not a game, we can tell, say, a "White" from a "Black" in most instances. But there will be, as with games, doubtful cases and cases that overlap. This is very much like what happens with the cases of healthy, human being, and dead mentioned before, and it is exacerbated in the case of race because one can belong to more than one race.

What I have said may be illustrated with reference to "Blacks" in the United States. Where is the uniformity of the people that go by that name in the country? Consider skin color, which is the factor most often pointed to, and used, for determining "Black" racial membership. There seems to be an endless range of different shades of skin color that American "Blacks" have, from the very light to the very dark. And other features are as, or more, varied and confusing. "Blacks" have as many shapes of noses as "Whites," and something similar applies to other features usually associated with "Blacks." Yet, in most cases, "Blacks" can be identified, and when they are identified, this is done in terms of descent taken together with participation in some set of genetically transmittable perspicuous physical features generally associated with them.

A second objection argues that the criterion for membership in racial groups I have proposed is too weak because it could describe a situation in which only a single feature is shared by any two individual persons, and that would not be enough to set the racial group apart from other groups. I presented a detailed discussion of this objection in the last chapter in the context of ethnicity. What was said there seems to be quite sufficient, *mutatis mutandis*, to answer it in the race context as well, so I shall not dwell further on it here. But I should point out that in the case of race, there is also the descent-link requirement; this makes the case of race even stronger than that of ethnicity.

A third way of attacking the Genetic Common-Bundle View of race is to refer back to the three difficulties I raised in the previous chapter against the part of the Familial-Historical View of ethnicity I also called the Common-Bundle View and apply them, *mutatis mutandis*, to my view of race. The first difficulty is that it is not clear we can come up with a particular set of perspicuous physical features pertinent for races. How and on what bases do we decide on the set of features that are to be associated with a race? Indeed, even in the rather innocuous list I provided as an illustration, there are some features that are bound to create difficulties. For example, why should the shapes of the nose I listed be associated with "Whites" when they can be had also by members of other races? Are these features merely a matter of what people think? And if so, don't these thoughts change from time to time? There is plenty of evidence that public opinion changes with respect to what are considered features associated with any one race. And if the features in question are not a matter of public opinion, where do they come from? Science? As we have seen, science has failed to provide strict demarcating racial criteria.

The second difficulty directed specifically against the Common-Bundle View is that, even if we were to settle on a satisfactory list of features, some of which all members of a race share, we would have no easy way of determining the number of these features required for someone to qualify as a member of the race. And does it make a difference which features are involved? In the earlier example given, does it make a difference whether we include skin color and thin lips when we are speaking of "Whites"? Indeed, are two of some kinds of features sufficient (e.g., skin color and hair type), whereas of other kinds three or four are needed? This seems to complicate matters, and the basis on which a decision can be reached is not clear.

A third difficulty originally raised against the Common-Bundle View is the lack of assurance that the set and number of features needed to be shared at a particular time by members of a race would be helpful at another time. If my theory is taken seriously, then we do not know what features will be pertinent for membership in a particular racial group in the future, for example. The set of features in which members of a particular race share could change, and so could the number of features necessary for qualification. Keep in mind that we are dealing with historical phenomena, and historical phenomena are in flux. Group membership is open. So why can't we say that a certain shape of the nose pertinent at some point in history for membership in a race is no longer so at some other point in history? Whatever we think is required for membership in a particular race at a certain period could change. If ethnic groups can become different through time and space, why can't races do likewise? Would it be possible even that skin color, that most historically important racial marker, can change? Is it possible for "white" skin to become a marker for "Blacks" and for "black" skin to become a marker for "Whites"?

The answer to the first difficulty is that, in contrast with ethnicity, which is wide open in terms of the features that can count for membership, the list of features that can count in the case of race is rather limited. Indeed, the problem with ethnicity was that practically anything can count, in context, for it. So the list of features is very large, if not endless. In the case of race this is not so, for the features in question are always physical. Moreover, these features are fairly well established in the minds of both members of the racial groups and those who are not members of them, so that the epistemic problem does not arise with the same severity. Of course, there will be cases in which membership is disputed, and indeed with reason, but in the majority of cases membership will not be disputed or seriously disputable.

Of course, there is a human element involved, but to what extent it remains to be determined. For present purposes, I need only point out that, if a list of features associated with a race exists at any one time, even if the list is different from that used at another time, it is epistemically possible to identify members of the race at that time. This entails the possibility that one may be considered a member of a particular race at one time and not a member of the same race at another time. My view allows for this possibility; indeed, it makes it essential to the conception of race I adopt. Otherwise the view would not adequately account for our experience of race, which vouches for this variability.

The issue of number, again, can be answered fairly easily because it does appear that some features have more weight than others, and the combination of some again count more than the combination of others. Also, the intensity or perspicuity of certain features, such as skin color, make a difference. In some cases, it appears that even one feature is enough in context as long as it is accompanied by the descent link that is a necessary condition of racial membership. The descent link, missing in ethnic groups, is often enough for membership in a racial group, even if accompanied by only one physical feature associated with the race. Keep in mind that we are speaking of two things here: one is the metaphysical issue concerned with the conditions of membership in a racial group; the other is the epistemic issue involved in the determination of membership in a racial group. For the first, the descent link is sufficient if accompanied by some features, but in certain circumstances more than one feature may be required for discernment. In some cases, two features may be sufficient for classification, but in other cases more are needed. It is clear, however, that one feature by itself is never sufficient for racial classification unless it is accompanied by knowledge of descent link. Even skin color, the feature that seems to be given more weight in racial classification, can be overridden by other factors if it stands by itself.

The answer to the third difficulty is that this is no difficulty at all. There are plenty of recorded cases of "Blacks" who have "White" skin, red hair, and blue eyes.[21] There is no reason, then, why the lists of features associated with particular races need to be constant, or why features associated with one race at a particular historical juncture might not be associated with another race at a different point in history. This may sound strange, but it is actually very much a part of the social experience of race and, therefore, cannot be ignored.

Finally, I need to say something about the relation of the Genetic Common-Bundle View to the scientific notion of race. The reason is that, whereas the scientific notion is cashed out in terms of measurable genotypes—never mind the disagreement within the scientific community about this, for my concern is with the strongest formulation of this view—these do not always correlate with the morphological differences visible to the naked eye that are central to the social view of race for which I try to account. Does this mean, then, that we have two different notions of race? Yes and no. The scientific notion is narrower but is related to the social conception and therefore related to the view I am proposing, for my position incorporates available scientific information while taking into account social factors ignored in genetic studies. The strict separation between biology and social practice, advocated by Gooding-Williams and others, is artificial (Gooding-Williams 2001b, 240–41). Science is a social enterprise, and its conclusions affect, and are affected by, social perceptions and realities.

CONCLUSION

Let me bring this chapter to a close by noting that a race is best understood as a group of individual persons organized as a family. The bases of its unity, however, are different from those of other kinds of families. They consist in a descent link and a set of perspicuous and genetically transmittable physical features generally associated with the race. An ethnos is also a kind of family, but its unity differs from that of a race in that it is entirely based on a particular history and the contingent features that develop as a result of that history. Races also differ from professional associations and clubs in that the latter two are not based on descent at all, but rather in agreements of some sort, and they differ from nations in ways that will become apparent in the next chapter.

But have I said anything that would preclude our speaking of humanity as a race? Yes and no. The fact that the understanding of race is cashed out in terms of a subgroup of human beings precludes the identification of the group of all humans with a race. However, one could still argue that, were it not for this stipulation, the Genetic Common-Bundle View could apply to the whole of humanity. And this is true, but it is not a serious objection for at least two reasons. First, the Genetic Common-Bundle formula is not intended as a strict definition of race, but only as one sufficient to distinguish races from ethne and nations. Second, the definition of the human "race" would necessarily include the kinds of biological conditions that are not possible for the socially constructed notion I have provided. The human species is a biological reality, human races are not.

The conception of race I have presented is to be contrasted with the purely biological notion of it prevalent in most of the nineteenth and twentieth centuries, for it maintains that race is a social category. At the same time, unlike many of the notions of race that have been proposed in opposition to the biological model, it includes a descent element and also genetically transmittable physical features, even if the particular features in question are socially conditioned.

Finally, as proposed here, races are distinguishable and identifiable. All races involve descent, but the sets of genetically transmittable perspicuous features associated with particular races do not coincide and, therefore, make possible the distinction between particular races.

The notion of race I have presented has the advantage that it can be integrated, as often happens in fact, into the notion of an ethnos. That is, a particular ethnos, owing to its concrete history, can incorporate race as one of its distinguishing features at certain times and places. Moreover, this notion explains how race can be an important factor in the development and preservation of an ethnos. All kinds of social phenomena, then, become intelligible, such as the racial and ethnic understandings of "Blacks," the notion of a "Black" becoming "White," the confusion of ethnic groups, such as Hispanics, with races, the changes in the notions of particular races over time, and so on. Finally, the view for which I have argued takes into account and makes sense of many of the intuitions and views that have been presented concerning race in the past.

NOTES

1. Smedley (1993) gives a third alternative: race is neither a feature that people have or are thought to have nor a group of people. Rather, it is a "knowledge system" (15) or "world view" (25–29) through which people look at humanity (21). This is an understanding of race as a concept.

2. To date, the only systematic attempt to discuss various metaphysical understandings of race is Mills's (1998).

3. The element of kinship in race and ethnicity has been explored by van den Berghe (1981, 18ff.).

4. Boxill argues, however, that Du Bois had two different views of race rather than just one (Boxill 2001a, 30–35), the first presented in "The Conservation of Races" and the second presented in "The White World."

5. There are instances in which "Yellows" are lumped together with "Whites" and contrasted with "Blacks," although the terminology might differ. See Nei and Roychoudhury (1974) and Cavalli-Sforza et al. (1994, 79). And there are also cases in the United States in which "Black" is excluded from "Indian" (i.e., Native American), whereas "White" is not (Patterson 2000, 16).

6. Zack refers to the case of the 2000 Census, in which, now that it is possible, people are portraying themselves as belonging to more than one racial group (Zack 2002, 85–86).

7. For the myth of racial purity, see Poliakov (1974) and King (1981, 112–16). Contrary to those who think that the idea of racial purity applies only to "Whites," this idea and the search for purity are present in many racial groups. See Patterson (2000, 16) and Malcomson (2000).

8. Although lip service is frequently paid to this notion, in fact when most American race theorists talk about race, they merely consider American attitudes toward it. This is frequently misleading. See for example, Boxill's argument based on "ordinary language" (Boxill 2001a, 41), by which he means American English

usage. Similarly, Zack (2001) argues that the concept of race is inconsistent, whereas in fact she only succeeds in showing that the American concept of race (the One-Drop Rule) is so. See also Appiah (1996).

9. In fact, Spaniards and Southern Europeans in general posed problems for early attempts at racial classifications. See Bernier (2000) and Blumembach (2000). For a racial view of "Indians" in the United States, see Malcomson (2000).

10. The term "caste" should not be understood in the Spanish colonial context as it is in India. The Spanish *castas* are not racially distinct kinds, presumed pure and separate, that are supposed to be kept segregated from each other, and whose contact (even occasional) results in the contamination of the higher by the lower. The classification into *castas* is rather an attempt at developing a taxonomy of the extraordinary degree of racial mixing in Latin America. The Latin American castes, then, reveal a social reality completely different from the reality of India and lack the social consequences that India's castes have, so that some of the nefarious effects of India's caste system are missing in Latin America. For the issues surrounding the notion of castes in India, see Dumont (2001).

11. Some lists, such as that displayed at the museum of the ex-Convento de Santo Domingo, in San Cristóbal de Las Casas (Mexico), read *morisca* (Moorish female) instead of *negra*, and *morisco* (Moorish male) instead of *mulato*.

12. Apart from the list of the ex-Convento de Santo Domingo mentioned in the previous note, Mörner and Mendieta reproduce lists (Mörner 1967, 58–59; Mendieta 2000, 53). Banton has a chart for Mexico (Banton 1983, 26). The terms *chino* and *china* do not actually entail Chinese or Asian ancestry, but a mixture of *mestizo* and Spanish female. Kendall lists *china* as a Quechua term for female (Kendall 1973, 45). These terms continue to be used today, but they have a variety of meanings, although in many parts of Latin America the connotation is of mixed blood and of lower status in society. Note also that many of the terms used for the *castas* were taken from different breeds of horses. Indeed, the term *mulato/a* appears to derive from *mulo/a* (mule) so that at one point mixed breeds of this sort were thought to be infertile (Poliakov 1974, 135).

13. I discuss these in Gracia (2000b, ch. 5).

14. Smedley brings attention to the lack of rigid boundaries (Smedley 1993, 40).

15. In passing, I might note that, in contrast with the horror with which Anglo-Saxons generally looked at liaisons between "White" females and any males of "mixed blood" of whatever kind, the given classification openly acknowledges pairings of Spanish females (presumably European "Whites") and both *mestizos* (males resulting from pairings of Spanish males and Indian females) and *mulatos* (males resulting from pairings of Spanish males and "Black" females). There are, of course, many gaps in the list, some of which might be significant. For example, there is no account of pairings between a *negro* ("Black" male) or *indio* (Indian male) with "White female"; "White" females are paired only with mixes, even though the mixes are always in equal proportion. In case anyone doubts the veracity of the opening claim in this note, consider that at one time various states in the United

States had laws against the marriage between a "White" and a "Black," and still in the year 2000, there was a law in Alabama that barred such marriages: "The Legislature shall never pass any law to authorize or legalize any marriage between any white person and a Negro, or descendant of a Negro" (Constitution of Alabama, Article IV, Section 102, cited by Sengupta 2000). Note, by the way, that (1) only "Whites" are referred to as persons in the text of the law; (2) it is assumed that the laws that apply to a "Black" also apply to his or her descendants, no matter how far removed; and (3) "Negro" is capitalized but "white person" is not.

16. Not everyone agrees with this conclusion. Although some anthropologists believe that views toward race change with context—for example, between the United States and Brazil—others think that this is not so. For the pertinent literature and a challenge to the view that Brazilians in particular think differently than Americans about race, see Gil-White (2001a).

17. See Gooding-Williams's discussion of Walter Benn Michaels (Gooding-Williams 2001b, 238–41). See also Williams (2001). The problems raised by the notion of passing are many. Consider the case of someone who fits the criteria for being "Black" but does not know he is "Black." Does he pass when he presents himself as "White"? Now consider someone who meets the criteria for being "White" but thinks himself to be "Black"—not knowing his real ancestors—and presents himself as "White." Does he pass? Now consider someone who knows himself to fit the criteria of being "White," but presents himself as "Black" for the sake of solidarity with "Blacks." Does he pass?

18. For the myth of purity, see Poliakov (1974) and King (1981, 112–16). The idea of racial purity has been under fire for a long time. Du Bois questioned it early on (Du Bois 1968, 13ff.).

19. For this understanding of relations, developed by Frege, Russell, and others, see Weinberg (1965). Even scholastics, such as Suárez, treated relations differently than qualities, for example. Indeed, Suárez identified four elements in a relation: (1) the subject of a relation, (2) the term of the relation, (3) the foundation of the relation, and (4) the relation itself. In the relation of similarity in whiteness between X and Y, the elements are, respectively, (1) X, (2) Y, (3) the white in X and the white in Y, and (4) the similarity in whiteness between X and Y. For more on this, see Gracia (1992b).

20. There is substantial evidence that American "Blacks" have a significant number of "White" genes and vice versa. See Reed (1969); Lewontin (1998); Banton (1983, 16–17).

21. Further support could be found for this point if it were true that some ethnic groups, such as the Irish, at some point in their history in the United States have been considered "Black." However, Boxill has argued that this is not true (Boxill 2001a, 36–38). For the argument about the "Blackness" of the Irish, see Ignatiev (1935) and Patterson (2000).

5

NATIONALITY

The conceptions of ethnicity and race proposed in the previous two chapters make it possible to see better their similarities and differences, and the reasons why they are so frequently confused. They also illustrate where some of the leading views about them have gone astray. Still, so far I have said nothing substantive about nationality and, without this, the analysis is incomplete insofar as nationality is also frequently and inadvertently confused or purposefully identified with race or ethnicity. I turn to nationality in this chapter and ask the same questions I asked about ethnicity and race: What is it, and can the objections raised in chapter 1 be answered effectively? David Miller's well-known book *On Nationality* presents an answer to these questions that goes a long way toward a satisfactory view, but falls short of it. So I begin with this book.

Miller is aware both of the case against nationality we saw articulated in chapter 1, as well as of the various ways in which people think about this concept. His view is presented as prescriptive: "I am concerned to establish how to think about nationality" (Miller 1995, 4). And his concern is grounded on the same concern that has motivated this book, namely, to provide a cogent and effective view that can serve to prepare the way for the discussion of some of the ethical and political dimensions of it (Miller 1995, 10–12).

Two aspects of Miller's view are particularly pertinent for us. First, nationality is part of what constitutes one's personal identity; our nationality is part of who we are. Nationality is a kind of identity that, together with other identities, constitutes our personal identity. I am who I am because I am Canadian, Cuban, and American, just as I am who I am because I am the son of Ignacio and Leonila, the father of Leticia and Clarisa, and the husband of Norma, among other things.

Second, nationality is based on a notion of nation as "a community (1) constituted by shared belief and mutual commitment, (2) extended in history, (3) active in character, (4) connected to a particular territory, and (5) marked off from other communities by its distinct public culture" (Miller 1995, 27). These features, according to Miller, distinguish nations from other "collective sources of personal identity." Nations are in some ways like football teams, cities, and religious groups, but this set of conditions separates nations from them. Of course, the conditions identified by Miller imply and result in others. An important requirement for them is communication. If a nation requires common beliefs, then it is necessary that there be means of communication to make possible the sharing of those beliefs. A result of these conditions is that nations develop views about themselves that are often mythical. National identities contain considerable elements of this sort, although this does not in any way undermine them or make them illegitimate (Miller 1995, 34–35).

There is much that is commendable in this conception of nations and nationality. It seems indisputable that nations are communities, are connected to a territory, have a history, share some beliefs, and have some common public culture. I do not believe it possible to name a nation that does not display these elements. Moreover, Miller is quite right in saying that nationality is closely related to who we are as individual persons. Great acts of heroism, for example, would be unexplainable without reference to a feeling of personal belonging to a nation. There cannot be patriotism without nationality, and patriotism is a powerful force in personal motivation and action. He is also right in claiming that nations are fluid entities, changing with times, and that they have views of themselves that contain mythical elements. Still, Miller leaves us with questions that he does not answer. His view is not specific enough to demarcate effectively the notion of nation. Here are some of the problems with his position.

Consider the second condition: shared beliefs. Beliefs about what? Clearly nations have common sets of beliefs, but we need to know the nature of these beliefs before we can say whether we are talking about nations, religious groups, ethnic groups, or football teams. Are the beliefs about religious matters? Are they about ways of dressing? Do they include rules about hygiene? Are they aesthetic? Do they involve ethical norms about personal behavior? Without guidance in this we are lost. And matters are further complicated because we know, as Miller is aware, that there are certain nations that hold religious and cultural beliefs to be essential to their nationality. Are they right? Insofar as Miller is telling us that he wants to prescribe how we would think about nations, don't we need to know whether these groups of people, who call themselves nations and believe that religion is part of their nationality, are right?

Next comes the requirement of extended history. Again we have a problem of unspecificity. How extended is the history required to be? Extension by itself means simply that we have more than just an instant in question. Is this what Miller means? No, it is clear that he has in mind a long period of time. But if this is so, then we have nations only if they have lasted a long time. But how long is long? Fifty years? One hundred years? Two hundred years? Extension is a problem, but it becomes more of a problem if we interpret it to involve a long period of time. For what are we going to make of the American nation, for example? When did it begin to be a nation? How many years did the group of people we have come to know as Americans have to hold on together before they became a nation? Were they a nation before the Declaration of Independence? Were they a nation after they won the War of Independence? I think the difficulty is clear.

Miller also cites that nations have to be active in character. But does this tell us anything substantive? Active in what sense? In religious worship? In communal eating? In ceremonial events? In sports? He needs to come up with more than he has given us. Moreover, the players in the activity have to be identified. Who is to be active? Every member of the community? Some members of the community? And if only some members, who in particular?

Territory poses problems as well. It is true that nations seem to be connected to a territory. But Miller needs to tell us something about the nature of the territory in question and also about the connection between the community and the territory. Does the community have to reside in the territory, or is it enough that the community has a sentimental attachment to it? Think about Palestinians and Jews at various times in their history. And can the territory change with time? How fixed must its boundaries be? If we are going to talk about a territory, we need to know something about its identity. What is essential to it? And are nomadic peoples not nations? Miller answers none of these questions. Again, this condition is too unspecific to be of help.

Last, we have what Miller calls a distinct public culture, but what does this mean exactly? Public culture in what sense? Religious culture? Etiquette? Sports? Languages? Foods? Sexual behavior? Ethical behavior? What exactly is relevant here? Is every part of public culture relevant? As is clear, we have the same problem here that we had with shared beliefs. Nor am I convinced that a distinct public culture, even if we were to accept Miller's claim, is really required. Why does it have to be distinct? Could we not have two nations that have the same public culture and yet, because of other factors such as territory, history, and beliefs, are not the same nation? I think the case could be made that this is so in certain countries in South America. Consider, for example, Uruguay and Argentina. Uruguay was part of Argentina at some points in its history, and its public culture is very similar to that part of Argentina immediate to it. Indeed, in many ways, there are greater differences between the public cultures of different populations in Argentina than between those of the population of Uruguay and Argentinians from Buenos Aires. And yet Uruguayans constitute a different nation than Argentinians.

The imprecisions in Miller's formula have a particularly undesirable consequence: they undermine the formula's effectiveness in distinguishing between ethnic groups and nations. Miller attempts a distinction in terms of descent: ethnic groups involve descent, whereas nations do not (Miller 1995, 19). But clearly not everyone in an ethnic group is tied by descent to everybody else, and some ethnic groups do not require descent for membership. This should be clear from the discussion in chapter 3 above. Moreover, Miller complicates matters by adding that ethnic groups are a source of national identities (Miller 1995, 20). Doesn't this suggest that nations are fundamentally ethnic groups, after all?

In short, Miller has provided us with a good formula to begin a discussion of the concepts of nation and nationality, but he has fallen short of the specific details needed for an effective view. We need to go back to our original question and see if we can supply a more effective answer: What is a nation, and how can we answer the objections raised in chapter 1 against it? Following earlier procedure, my answer will be given through a metaphysical, rather than an epistemic or a linguistic, analysis. The view I propose is fundamentally political and thus supplies the specific element missing in Miller's position.

THE POLITICAL VIEW

At the outset, let us recall that some nations and ethnic groups share the same name, as for example, happens with Mexicans and the Irish. When we use the expression "a Mexican," sometimes we have in mind a Mexican national, but at other times we mean someone who is ethnically Mexican. And the same is true of the Irish. Our topic here, however, is not ethnic groups, but nations.

A nation, like an ethnos and a race, is a group of individual human beings, but this is not enough to distinguish it from these and other groups, including religious communities, professional associations, cities, and clubs (Smith 1991, 9). So what is distinctive of nations? We can begin by pointing to two factors that appear essential: a system of laws and a certain territory.

A system of laws is one of the things most commonly associated with nationality. Indeed, this is the way most eighteenth-century political theorists viewed a nation. As Abbé Sieyès pointed out in 1789, a nation is "a union of individuals governed by one law, and represented by the same law-giving assembly" (Benn 1967, 5:443). The idea here is that the laws under which a group of persons live unite them into a nation. All other features a nation may have—primarily common interests, goals, and the consequent duties and rights—are taken to follow upon this, although sometimes the laws are taken to be also a reflection of a moral consciousness (Renan 1996, 50).

One can arrive at the view that laws are essential to nationality in several ways, but perhaps the most common is by pointing to the way one can join a nation, that is, how we can become, say, a Greek or a Spanish national. We saw earlier that the only way to become a member of a race is by being born into it. By contrast, one can become a member of an ethnic group by establishing close relations with the group, which can be of various kinds and, unlike in races, do not necessarily include a descent link. The situation with nations is quite different, however. So let us ask how the conditions of membership in a nation differ from those of races or ethnic groups and, in short, how one becomes a member of a nation.

This happens in various ways, but generally the most common way is by birth. One can generally be born into a nation, but this can take two different forms: (1) if one's parents are part of a nation (*jus sanguinis*) or (2) if one is born within the territorial boundaries of a nation, even if one's parents are not members of the nation (*jus solis*). Of course, there are exceptions to both rules. In some countries, being born in the national territory is not a sufficient condition for nationality, and in other countries, having parents who are members of the nation does not automatically grant one membership. And there are also other ways of becoming a member of a nation. For example, one can ask to become part of a nation, and one can be granted membership, on the basis of particular rules that are operative for that nation but do not include birth. One thing is common to all these ways, however, namely, that the procedure through which one becomes a member of a nation—whether by birthplace, descent, residency, a combination of these, or something else—depends on laws explicitly formulated and adopted by the nation. This is not necessary or even frequently the case when it comes to racial or ethnic groups. For race, the conditions of membership have to do with descent and genetically transmittable and physically perspicuous features; and for ethnicity, they concern certain relations that tie the members of the group in context and separate them from other groups, which frequently are not matters of law. So here we have an important distinguishing mark of nations. Note that the issue of how groups of people become nations is not what concerns us here, for the causes in question could vary considerably. The issue for us rather is about the conditions of nationality. The laws to which we are referring regulate the relations among the members of the group, and for that reason are political; they involve the organization and governance of the group—the city-state or *polis* in ancient Greece.

This distinguishes both ethnic and racial groups from national groups, for in neither of the former two is it required that there be laws that determine how one becomes or is a member of the group, even if in some cases laws have been used to determine racial or ethnic inclusion. In particular, race and nationality appear to be very different kinds of groups—recall that we have classified them as families of sorts.

Still, the case with ethnicity does not appear to be so clear for two reasons. First, one may argue that most, even if not all, ethnic groups, have rules that determine how one becomes a member of the group, even if these rules are sometimes explicitly formulated and sometimes not. One way in which I can become ethnically Mexican, for example, is to marry into a Mexican family and become integrated into the group in various ways. So how can national groups be distinguished from ethnic ones?

The answer is that nations are tied by laws, not just rules, and although all laws are rules, not all rules are laws. In order for a rule to become a law, it is required, among other things, that it be formulated and promulgated by an appropriately recognized governing authority. If a rule is not formulated, it is a mere custom. If it is not promulgated, then it cannot be justly enforced insofar as those who are supposed to obey it have no way of knowing it. And if it does not have behind it an appropriately recognized governing authority, it lacks legitimacy. Besides, rules may apply to a single individual— I may establish a certain rule for my behavior in certain circumstances, for example—but laws apply only to members of groups.

The second argument that seeks to undermine the distinction between ethnic groups and nations based on a system of laws points out that part of what unites an ethnic group could be precisely the laws it explicitly formulates and adopts, including some about membership qualification in the group. But this is to miss two points: first, the rules adopted by an ethnic group are not laws in that an ethnos is not a political entity, and therefore its rules are not formulated and promulgated by a governing authority; second, an ethnic group may develop rules that become part of what unites the group and distinguishes it from others, but the adoption of such rules is a matter contingent to the particular ethnos—it is not necessary for all ethnic groups to develop such rules, whereas to have laws is essential for nations. A nation is principally a political organization, and part of the glue that holds it consists precisely in the laws that the group accepts or practices.

Moreover, unlike the rules that may be used by a particular ethnos, the laws that unite a nation into a polity must be intended to constitute a system. A single law, or even an aggregate of disparate laws, does not suffice. The laws that unify a nation must form a body intended to be coherent, integrated, orderly, interrelated, interdependent, and comprehensive.

The conception of a nation as a group of people linked by a system of laws is not sufficient to set nations apart from all other groups of persons. It appears to be enough *prima facie* to distinguish nations from ethnic and racial groups, but it is not enough to distinguish nationality from all sorts of organizations that satisfy this condition and yet are not nations, such as professional associations, private clubs, cities, and provinces. One could argue that these groups are governed by systems of laws (often called "bylaws") they have explicitly formulated and adopted, and membership in the groups is determined by some of those laws. So how can nations be distinguished from these?

A factor that has been identified as a possible source of this distinction is territory: nations seem to require a territory; a nation has to have a piece of land that it calls its own, the so-called homeland.[1] Territory seems to be an easy way of distinguishing a nation from other groups also tied by laws, such as professional associations and clubs. Moreover, territories have boundaries, and these can easily serve to distinguish among nations as well.

Four problems arise with this condition, however: one concerns boundaries; a second concerns the case of nomadic nations; a third has to do with particular groups, such as cities and provinces; and a fourth involves the fact that different nations frequently claim the same territory.[2] Clearly, national boundaries shift from time to time. Part of the current territory of the United States belonged to Mexico or Russia less than two hundred years ago. So, one may wonder, if boundaries shift, is not the identity of the nation, or even its very existence, in peril?

One answer is that they are not, because the territory of a nation does not require fixed boundaries throughout history as long as it has some boundaries at any particular time. The territorial condition of a nation is not that it have a particular territory at one time or the same territory throughout its existence. The condition is that it have some territory at any time in which it exists.[3] This is similar to the requirement of having air to breathe for a person to be alive. Air is a necessary condition of being alive, but the air in question does not have to be particular, or the same, throughout the person's existence.

This response also takes care of the counterexample of nomadic nations, for these do have, at every particular time in their existence, a range of territory over which they exercise some control and which they consider their own, even if it is not rigidly defined and the territory changes with the passage of time. And something similar can be said about territories that are claimed by different nations. Because fixed boundaries are not a requirement of nations, territorial disputes can arise, and yet this does not affect the viability of the view that nations must have territory.

The territory requirement, then, also serves further to differentiate nations from ethnic groups and races. Consider ethnic groups first. Although the members of ethnic groups are located in a territory, the territory does extend beyond the boundaries occupied by the members of the ethnos at any particular time, unlike that of a nation, which does. The U.S. territory covers the space that its citizens occupy plus all sorts of other spaces and places, including rivers, lakes, the oceans, air space, and even underground. The land between my wife and me, when we are sitting at our dining-room table having lunch, is part of the U.S. territory, and so is the Alaskan wilderness, where no Americans are present now, or have been present perhaps ever.

Territory is directly tied to the notion of nation, whereas territory is not directly tied to the notion of ethnos. An ethnos occupies a territory in that the members of the group are spatial entities and thus have particular locations. But this is not because it is of the essence of an ethnos, qua ethnos, to do so. By contrast, it is of the essence of nations to have a particular territory, and this has nothing to do with the locations of the members of the group.

Territory often plays an important role in the formation and development of ethnic groups. Latin America is not a condition of Latinos, or the land of Israel of Jews, but these lands contribute to strengthening the ethnic bonds of these groups. A territory can be instrumental in the development of relations among people, for proximity unifies and distance separates, although all this is incidental and accidental. In the case of nations, however, territoriality is essential: A nation without a territory, in which the people in question reside, is not a proper or true nation, although it may be an ethnic group or a race.

What has been said about nations and territoriality in relation to ethnic groups applies, *mutatis mutandis*, to races. Even the notion of an ancestral homeland, so common in the memory of races, is not a condition for them. Africa is not a condition of "Blackness," just as the Caucasus is not a condition of "Whiteness," even if these places were causally instrumental in their development. These places are merely accidental to these races, and the same applies to other races and the places from where they are supposed to have come. This point was discussed in the preceding chapter, so there is no need to engage it again here.

Laws and territoriality appear to effectively distinguish nations from ethnic groups and races.[4] They also distinguish them from families, for a family, whether nuclear, extended, ethnic, or racial, has nothing to do with laws or territory. Different members of a family may live under different laws and in different territories. Nor is the family home, or farm, or any other kind of what might qualify as a territory essential for the existence and survival of a family qua the family it is, even if it can contribute to it.

But, we may ask, is this enough? Are the notions of law and territory as we have understood them here, even taken together, sufficient for the understanding of nationality, its distinction from other groups, and its peculiar unity? Generally, the answer one finds in the literature is negative: something else is required. And one of the reasons given for this judgment is that the notions of law and territory do not distinguish nations from entities such as cities and provinces, for these also have laws and territory and yet are not nations. But what else can account for the glue that holds nations together?

Language is one of the candidates that has often been proposed in the past to distinguish nations from other groups of people and unify nations. Indeed, Voltaire and Weber, among others, identified it as a condition of nationality (Voltaire 1965, 10; Weber 1997, 24, 26; see also Graham 1997, 3). Some go so far as to argue not just that linguistic unity is a necessary condition of nationality, but also that linguistic unity ultimately defines a nation (Poliakov 1974; Weber 1978, 1:395).[5] This idea is behind some efforts in the United States to declare English as the official language of the country, and has influenced similar moves in other countries such as Spain. Indeed, many countries have "official" languages, but can language in fact be considered a condition of nationality? Is Castilian, for example, a sufficient condition of belonging to the Spanish nation? The answer is negative, for this language is spoken by many people who are not native speakers of it.

But is linguistic unity necessary, even if it is not sufficient? Does every Spanish national need to be fluent in Castilian? The answer again is negative. Indeed, many people considered Spaniards are not fluent in Castilian as this is not their native tongue, and thus they speak it awkwardly and with a heavy accent, and sometimes not at all.

Indeed, even if the linguistic requirement is taken as referring to an original, maternal tongue, rather than one actually spoken today, say, the situation is not better, for it is difficult to find nations that fit this criterion. There is not one maternal language for all the peoples who make up nations such as France and Italy today, and many of the peoples who belong to these nations speak French or Italian poorly or not at all.

Cultural criteria in general appear *prima facie* to be more likely to account for national unity, in that they are broader and more flexible. This view was particularly favored by German philosophers of the nineteenth century who thought of culture as the expression of the Spirit of a people (Benn 1967, 443; and at the end of the eighteenth century, see Kant 1991, 97–116; Fichte 1979, § 7:13; see also Hume 1987, 197–201; Hudson 1996, 257; Anderson 1990, 19, 47).[6] And, indeed, at first it might look as if culture could function as an effective demarcating criterion between, say, Spaniards and non-Spaniards.[7] However, culture ultimately fails to define a nation. Consider the case in which we speak of Spaniards as referring to persons who share the Spanish culture. What is Spanish culture? The culture of the political unit we know as Spain? Does it include Galician and Basque cultures? Why do we separate it from Portuguese culture and not from these? After all, what we know today as Portugal was part of Spain in the sixteenth century. The cultural criterion is too vague to be of help in determining a Spaniard or the Spanish nation. And the same can be said of many other nations. It certainly applies to the American nation, for where is the so-called American culture? Does it have to do with having English as the mother tongue, eating hamburgers, and having two left feet when it comes to dancing *salsa*? Moreover, culturalist understandings of nations generally lead to various forms of essentialism, with all the negative consequences associated with that position (Jones 1999, 165).

Perhaps here I should add something about religion, for although most religions claim to be universalist, the fact is that most of them are clearly culturally relative and contain cultural elements parochial to particular societies. Some religions are openly tribal (i.e., based fundamentally on descent)—as happens with Judaism. Some religions are closely culturally bound—as is the case with Islam, for Muslims are required to learn Arabic in order to understand the word of Allah as put down by Mohamed, their religious practices are clearly idiosyncratic of a particular culture, and they are supposed to work toward the imposition of a cultural, political, and legal Islamic system in every society in which they live.[8] Even religions that try to purge themselves of cultural elements often do not succeed—as is evident in many Christian denominations.

The identification of religion with culture, and of nationality with religion, is the source of some of the most violent and pernicious conflicts between societies. Examples are common everywhere, from Afghanistan to Northern Ireland. Of course, the idea that nationality should be bound up with religion is not only the cause of much mischief, but it is also something that makes no sense, as Renan pointed out long ago (Renan 1996, 38).[9] This is particularly so for religions committed to proselytizing, for obviously their aim would be to enlist all humankind in their ranks, and this could only result in the elimination of all national divisions. Clearly, then, religious affiliation cannot be taken as either a necessary or a sufficient condition of nationality.

Sometimes it is argued that a nation requires a common experience among its members, and often this is put in terms of a sense of history or of a heritage, when this is understood in turn as the grasp and memories of a common past, although in some cases no distinction is made between history and heritage and a sense of history and heritage (Renan 1996; Miller 1998, 658). A common awareness, and particularly memories of sufferings and successes, is deemed essential for a group of persons to constitute a nation, for this creates a common bond and the desire to preserve it. And, indeed, most nations work hard to invent a past even if they do not have it. We need only recall Virgil's *Aeneid* to illustrate the process. A common experience certainly strengthens a nation and facilitates agreement on the laws under which its citizens are supposed to live. But again, it is hard to conceive a nation primarily in terms of a common experience, for it is very difficult to argue that all members of a nation in fact share a common experience. Consider the case of the Mexican nation, composed of such different peoples as the Tarahumara, the Maya, and the *mestizos* (the mix of Amerindian and Spanish). Does it make any sense to say that the Tarahumara have a common experience with all other Mexican groups, including the *mestizos* who live in Mexico City and the Maya who live in Yucatan?

Common experience, then, does not seem to be a necessary condition of nationality, and if it is not a necessary condition, it would be even harder to argue that it is a sufficient one, because examples of shared experience between members of different nations are common. Furthermore, there has to be more than experience for experience to function as a unifying factor of a nation; an awareness of the group must be included. Merely having a common experience does not entail that those who have it are aware of its common character to a group, and therefore that the experience effectively ties the members of the group as such. This leads me to the next factor.

Some have argued that the members of a nation need to be aware of themselves as a nation and to have a sense of belonging to the nation (cf. Miller 1998, 657, 658). This is thought to be a requirement because nationality depends on laws and territory and both of these require group self-awareness and perhaps even a group name. One cannot think of adopting and applying laws to a group without somehow thinking of the group as such, and this is in turn helped by a name used to refer to it. Likewise, one cannot think of the territory of a group without thinking about the group, and having a name for the group helps it.

In spite of its *prima facie* strength, however, this condition faces various difficulties, depending on how it is understood. First, there is the problem that self-awareness cannot be taken to apply to all members of the group, for children and mentally incompetent persons do not satisfy it. In order to avoid this difficulty, group self-awareness would have to apply only to some members of the group, such as perhaps those who are capable of having such awareness. But even then we would need to distinguish between two aims: one concerns conditions for the group and another concerns conditions for belonging to the group. For the first, the condition must be that there be a substantial number of members who are aware of the group and consider themselves to belong to it. For the second, the condition must be that any mentally capable person who confronts the question of whether he or she is part of the group answer it affirmatively. Of course, there may be persons who have not confronted such an issue but nonetheless qualify as members if, confronted with it, they would answer it appropriately.

A sense of national awareness on the part of some members of the group seems to be a necessary condition of nations, although it is not necessary that such awareness be general. But this requirement by itself is not a sufficient condition for a nation, for one can be mistaken about what one believes.

Other-awareness may also be regarded as necessary, if perhaps not sufficient, for a nation. But this view needs to be subdivided in terms of who "the other" is. There are at least two important cases to consider. In the first, "the other" refers to the members of a nation. In the second, "the other" refers to other nations. This gives us two cases of other-awareness. In one, some members of a nation are aware of other members; in another, some nations are aware of other nations.

There is reason to think that both of these states of awareness play a role in nationality. How other nations think of nation X certainly affects X in significant ways. Indeed, it seems a requirement of X as a nation that other nations think of it in this way, otherwise they might act as if it did not exist, take it over, destroy it, or otherwise contribute to its disappearance. In the case of an individual member of a nation, it also appears essential to have other members accept the person as a national, otherwise, and regardless of what the person thinks, she might be treated as a foreigner, expelled from the national territory, or killed. Witness the case of Jews in Germany during the period of National Socialism.

But are these requirements sufficient conditions of nationality? They do not seem to be so to the extent that there are other requirements involved as well. After all, we have been assuming that laws and territory are also conditions that need to be met for a nation to exist. Moreover, the opinion of others, whether these are foreign nations or fellow nationals, is based on the satisfaction of very specific conditions. So, again, these conditions are only part of the requirements of nationality and not sufficient for it.

Some argue that "self-awareness" is not a strong enough term to describe the attitude that the members of a nation need to have toward it. There must also be an act of identification: the explicit will to identify with the group.[10] It is not sufficient that members of a nation recognize themselves as part of the group; they need to see the group as something tied to their own identity as persons. Indeed, if this is lacking—so the argument goes—it is difficult to pass laws applicable to the group. This is why nations need symbols of national unity, such as flags, celebrations, anthems, and so on, for these contribute to unite the members of nations through loyalty and mutual recognition (Guibernau 1996, 3, 80–84).

Of course, self-identification cannot be a requirement for all members of a nation insofar as some members are incapable of it, as is clear in the case of small children and mentally handicapped persons, so the same qualifications made with respect to self-awareness apply here. And the same can be said about the issue of sufficiency. Self-identification seems to be a necessary condition of nationality with the stated qualifications, but not a sufficient one. That a person self-identifies with a nation is not sufficient for the person to be a member of a nation. And that all members of a group of people identify themselves with a nation or think of themselves as one is not sufficient for the nation to exist.

In speaking of self-identification, I used the expression "will to identify," but it is necessary to distinguish this from a common political will (Smith 1991, 10).[11] The will to identify with a group refers merely to the recognition that one is part of the group and is bound up with its identity. This is quite strong, but it is not specific enough for our purposes in that it applies to any kind of group, as we have seen that in fact it does in the cases of race and ethnicity. The will that is required in a nation must satisfy other conditions as well, and at least the following two: (1) it must be common and (2) it must be political. By "common" I mean two things: first, it must not be a matter for just one individual person or even a few individual persons, but it must be the will of all persons who are members of the group and capable of having such a will; second, it must not concern an individual matter, but a group matter—the individual will must take second place to a collective will, although every individual's will must be given a place in order to form the common will. That the will must be political means that it must be a matter of the organization and governance of the group under a particular system of laws. It is a will not just to be part of the group, but also to be subject to the laws that regulate the relations among the members of the group.

But, of course, as should be obvious, having this common political will, although appearing to be necessary for a nation, does not seem to be sufficient. This has led some to put forward still another factor, an overall aim or goal for a nation. To speak of nations as having overall aims or goals may sound quite sensible *prima facie*.[12] After all, some nations have identified in the past, and some still do in the present, certain aims or goals for themselves. Some of these are lofty, indeed, particularly when terms such as "rights," "freedom," "the common good," and "justice" are used to describe them. Others, however, are obviously dangerous and even nefarious for other nations or even for the nation in question or some of its members. These aims or goals are often described in terms of glory, victory, expansion, conquest, domination, empire, and so on.

However, these goals, whether of the first or the second sort, have little to do with nations as such, although they may have had a lot to do with particular nations in the history of the world. Nations do not require any of these kinds of goals in order for them to be nations, and it is certainly not a requirement of national membership to share in those goals. Even in cases in which certain groups among members of particular nations try to establish these goals for the nations in question, it turns out that, more often than not, other members actually disagree with these goals and even actively work against them.

This does not mean, however, that a goal is irrelevant to a nation, but the goal that is pertinent is more generic. It is the goal of living in accordance with a system of laws that regulate the relations among members of the nation. Of course, it may turn out that these laws do involve other, more specific goals, but these would be parochial to particular nations. The goal of a nation, qua nation, does not go beyond living under the laws.

This goal, which in fact reflects a political will, does not require that members of a nation actually agree with all the laws of the nation, or even that they obey such laws. The common will and the common goal require only that they will to be subject to these laws, not that they agree with or obey them. One can be a member of a nation and will to live under its laws and yet disagree with some of these laws, work actively to change them, and in fact violate them. None of this disqualifies one from national membership. However, the violation of some laws may, within particular nations, be sufficient for revocation of nationality. Treason, for example, entails such violation and such revocation in some nations. But this, again, does not go contrary to the point that has been made here.

In short, of all the factors we have considered, it seems that the only one with promise, added to laws and territory, is political will. Let me make a proposal, then, in terms of a system of laws, territory, and common political will.[13] In this conception, nations are groups of people that have a common will to be organized politically under a system of laws within a territory.[14] Accordingly, the members of nations are subject to a body of laws they are expected to accept and abide by, and that regulates the relations among them. This does not mean that they actually agree with or obey these laws. Members of nations frequently disagree with some or even many of the laws governing them, and it is obvious that they frequently violate some of them, even when they agree with them. Note also that we are speaking about a system of laws rather than individual laws or a group of unconnected laws. The systematic nature of the laws in question is important, for they are intended as a whole that is sufficient to regulate the entire body politic; this is a package, not an aggregation of disparate and unconnected rules. Moreover, as laws, these rules have to reflect the common will of the nation, and they need to be formulated and promulgated. Laws that do not satisfy these requirements are not really laws of a nation. If they fail to reflect the common will, then they cannot be national in scope, and we saw earlier that if they fail to satisfy the last two requirements, they do not qualify as laws. Finally, territory is also an important factor—there has to be a place for a nation, even if it is not always the same and its boundaries are not strictly drawn.

But is the satisfaction of these three conditions sufficient to distinguish nations from other groups of people? They are effective in doing so when it comes to race, because races have nothing to do with laws, territory, or political will; and the same applies to ethne and religions. In cases of private clubs and organizations, and of international organizations such as the

United Nations, the reason is that these do not involve territory. But are these conditions sufficient to distinguish nations from cities, provinces, and the like?

One could argue that cities and provinces are not really groups of people, but places with people in them. But perhaps this is not a sufficiently strong difference, so let me propose one further factor: sovereignty. This has been conceived in many ways, but let us understand it here as the fact that the members of a nation are subject to a system of laws that is not subordinated, except by national and voluntary agreement, to any other system of laws. Cities, provinces, and other such groups of people live under systems of laws that are subordinated to a broader system of laws, the laws of a nation. This is why they do not constitute nations themselves. But the system of laws under which a nation lives is not subordinate to any other system, unless the nation voluntarily agrees to do so under specific circumstances and preserves the right to withdraw its consent under certain conditions.[15] Nations, then, can become parts of larger groups of people, which function under more comprehensive systems of laws and may even have territorial claims, but this does not make nations of such larger groups for two reasons: first, the members of these larger groups are themselves groups of people rather than individual persons; second, the nations in question are sovereign entities, having the right (1) to enforce their own systems of laws within their territories and (2) to withdraw from the association under certain conditions.

We still, however, need to draw a distinction between a nation and a state, for today those who do not understand nations as ethnic groups tend not to draw a distinction between nations and states (Benn 1967, 443). Insofar as I have drawn a sharp line between nations and ethnic groups, I have to establish what distinguishes nations from states if I do not wish to identify them. Moreover, such distinction will allow me to point to some further conditions of a nation.

In my view, there are at least four factors that can be used to distinguish a nation from a state.[16] The first is that a state includes more than a nation and is an entity different from a nation. The latter is a group of people, but the former includes people and also institutions and organizations (particularly a government), territory, and even human-made structures, natural features such as mountains, and so on.[17] A nation is the group of people who constitute the citizens of those states when they meet certain conditions. This means that there are no nations without states, although there may be states without nations.[18]

It is common today to speak about "nation-states," and what is meant by this varies considerably, depending on what is meant by "nation" and "state," although often those who use this expression have a notion of a nation as an ethnic group. In this sense, a nation-state is a state whose citizens belong to the same ethnic group; in a mere state, the citizens do not have the same ethnicity, and a nation without a state is merely an ethnic group (Smith 1991, 15).[19] The expression "nation-state" did not originally have an ethnic connotation. It was used in the context of empires when these incorporated states preexisted the empire and were not artificially created by the empire (for various views, see Guibernau 1996, especially chs. 2, 5, and 6). In the present context, a nation-state is understood as a state—conceived as I have done—in which the people who compose it form a nation because they have the political will to live under a system of laws in a territory. If the inhabitants of a state do not constitute a nation, then we merely have a state, not a nation-state.[20] States such as North Korea do not have nations in the sense that I have proposed, even if they have ethnic groups that consider themselves to be nations. These states, therefore, are not nation-states. However, states such as France and the United States are nation-states. In no case, however, do I conceive the nation in ethnic or racial terms.

The second factor that distinguishes nations from states refers to the fact that the goal of the system of laws by which the members of a nation are willing to live is to ensure both justice for, and the good of, all the members of the nation. Why do nations have to meet this condition? Because otherwise it would make no sense to the members of the nation to will to live under the system of laws, and the nation would lack proper unity. Indeed, it is not hard to think of many states that do not meet this condition. These states enforce a system of laws on their citizens who, if given the opportunity, would leave the territory controlled by the state or overthrow the government.

But what do we make of cases in which the citizens of the state are coerced to be part of the state, even though the laws of the state are not aimed at justice for, and the good of, all its citizens?

This brings me to the third factor that distinguishes nations from states. In a nation, the members must be free to choose to be part of the nation, but in a state it is not necessary that they be free to leave the state. Many states maintain their membership through coercion. The Soviet Union under Stalin was certainly a state, but many of its citizens would have gladly left the country.

But what happens when the citizens of a state are free but indoctrinated or brainwashed, or the information they are given is selective? As long as they are not coerced, they can hardly be described as not free, although their choices are controlled and manipulated by a skillful government. Consider the case of Cuba, for example, where the citizens are mostly free, but an effective system of indoctrination and selective information distribution ensures their support for a system of laws that is oppressive to some of its citizens, namely, those who disagree with the status quo.

This points to the fourth difference between a nation and a state. The former requires that its members be informed, whereas the latter does not. But, then, surely the members of a state such as Cuba, even though they nominally can be said to will to live under the system of laws adopted in the state, cannot in reality be said to do so, for their will functions in a context in which the outcome is determined by forces outside their will.

Note that earlier I was speaking as if membership in a nation were the same as citizenship, but now we see that this is not right, for citizenship is membership in a state. Membership in a nation is rather nationality, although just as nations and states are commonly confused with each other, so are nationality and citizenship. But this is a mistake. True, all nationals are citizens of some state, but not all citizens are nationals.

The factors that I have identified, then, appear to be effective in distinguishing nations from the other mentioned groups, but what are we to say about all the other factors considered earlier that seemed to have some relation to nations, and some of which seemed to be even necessary? The answer is that some of these are conditions of one or more of the four factors I have specified and in that sense turn out to be indirect conditions of nations. This is clearly the case with self-identification (I assume that self-awareness is implied by self-identification). A nation must self-identify as such, and its members must identify with it, if the nation is to have a common political will to live under a system of laws in a particular territory. This does not entail that all members of a nation must identify themselves with the nation, for small children and persons who are mentally disabled cannot do so. Self-identification is required only of those who are capable of doing it. People who are capable of self-identification and yet do not identify consciously with the nation are not members of it. Traitors and the like cannot be considered true nationals, even if they are so in name. Such people may have actually identified with some other nation—such as a rival of the nation of which they are supposed to be members—or may not identify with any nation at all. Nationality is not necessary to the human community. Humans can live outside systems of laws and be subject instead, for example, to the will of a tyrant who rules them by whim, or they may merely gather in loose associations based on custom, such as tribes.

Other factors, such as experience, lineage, race, and culture (particularly values, language, and religion), are not presupposed by the three factors I have identified, but they do affect nations. Of these, two in particular serve both to explain and strengthen the unity of a nation. A common experience and its memory creates and strengthens bonds among members of nations. Successes and reverses, as well as their memories, can produce a strong will to be united. An external threat, a hostile attack, or even a natural disaster can do much to prop up the will of the group.

The function of culture is different from that of a common experience. In one sense, culture can explain both the laws adopted by a nation and the willingness of the members of a nation to abide by them. Clearly, values can be expressed in laws, so common cultural values may contribute to a certain nationality. Moreover, communication is of the essence among members of a nation, and so a common language can be of great help to the unity of a nation.

Still, there is another side to the cultural factor, for this can lead to a confusion between nation and ethnos, with all the ensuing disadvantages that this carries. If one of the cultural factors associated with the nation is religion in particular, then the results are even more nefarious, as is clear from the situation in such countries as Saudi Arabia, Iran, and sixteenth-century Spain. In countries where this occurs, it is almost inevitable that those members of the nation who do not agree with the dictates of the particular religion adopted become segregated to a secondary role, if not oppressed or expelled. Often, the government falls into the hands of the clergy, giving rise to systems of oppression based on the imposition of laws that are contrary to the will of the citizens.

Obviously, the political ties that unite nations tend to generate common features in them, but such features need not go beyond particular periods, places, or groups within the nations. What was said about ethne earlier applies here as well. We are speaking, then, of groups of persons who have no common elements considered as wholes, beyond their common political wills, systems of laws, and territories. The unity of a nation is not a unity of commonality; it is fundamentally a political unity within a territory accompanied by a common will to abide by a system of laws. There is no need to find features common to all Spaniards in order to classify them as members of the Spanish nation, or to all Germans to consider them part of the German nation.

At the same time, we must not underestimate that the adoption and practice of laws may require certain common elements in a population.

There has to be, for example, certain means of communication. One could not have a nation in which its members or groups of members could not effectively communicate with other members or groups within the nation. Moreover, the adoption and practice of laws entails some agreement, and this in turn requires also certain common views, understandings, and values. The adoption of particular laws concerning freedom of speech, for example, requires some common understanding about what constitutes freedom of speech and some agreement as to its limits. This means that there are factors that are not purely legal or territorial that play roles in nations, and thus could be part of an ethnicity. A certain lingua franca in the nation, for example, might both function ethnically and facilitate national communication. A certain understanding of freedom as involving the right to speak one's mind, again, could function ethnically and nationally. But it is important to understand that these factors arise as requirements or as consequences of the laws that govern the polity, and therefore do not have the same origin or function as they do when they contribute to the rise of ethne, or races for that matter. The need for a lingua franca does not require that a particular language become a "national language," as some claim. The adoption of a national language only serves to undermine the differences between nationality and ethnicity and to oppress those members of the nation who do not speak the language as natives or who wish to preserve other languages as part of their ethnicity, and the same applies to other cultural elements. Indeed, the imposition of a language and other ethnic factors only serves to undermine the very nature of true nationality, which requires self-identification with the nation, for an ethnic group that is required to abandon its own language and culture, in order to adopt what it considers to be ethnically foreign, could hardly identify with the nation.[21]

One thing is common between nations and families, then: neither derives its unity from common features among its members. Families get their unity from the particular relations that tie their individual members, which in turn produce features common to some of the members in particular contexts. These relations also serve to distinguish different families and members of different families. In contrast, nations derive their unity from a political will to live together under a system of laws within a territory.

To repeat, the unity of a nation does not involve features common to its members. Its unity should not be understood in terms of linguistic, cultural, racial, genetic, experiential, or class boundaries, even if in context these further unite the members of the nation. These are not what distinguish nations from each other.

The Political View of nations implies that nations are neither necessarily permanent nor closed communities that allow no one to leave or enter them. How open or closed they are depends on the laws they adopt. It also follows that nations are not trapped in their history, albeit their history cannot be denied. I am as opposed to every kind of national essentialism as I am to every kind of ethnic or racial one. There is no essence to nations; there is only a changing political reality, as Renan recognizes (Renan 1996, 47). As with an ethnos, only a misguided sense of national unity, based on notions of coherence, homogeneity, and purity, leads to essentialistic conceptions of nations.

Just as there is no agreement concerning the nature of nations, there is also no agreement about nationality. The various views of it available follow the relative emphases placed on various factors. But there is no need to dwell on them, although I should point out that the conceptions of nationality usually break down into three major groups: racial views, ethnic views, and political views (see Deutsch 1966; Gellner 1983; Kedourie 1961; Anderson 1990; Guibernau 1996). However, insofar as I have adopted a general categorization of a nation, I can also provide an analysis of nationality along the same lines: nationality is the feature that characterizes members of a nation as such. Americanicity is the feature that characterizes members of the American nation as such. This feature is relational insofar as it depends on group membership. Persons are American only if they are citizens of the United States. Relational features are predicated of the relata, but they are contingent on the relation. "American" is predicated of terms that refer to individual persons, but only insofar as the persons hold the relation of citizenship to the group of Americans. This is different from nonrelational features, such as having petals. That this rose has petals is independent of its relations to other roses, but a woman cannot be a mother unless she is related in motherhood to someone else (whether the person is alive or dead).

This means that nationality is not really anything other than a relation holding among certain individual human beings. The nationality of Israelis is nothing but their political relation to other Israelis, namely, that they will to be subject to the system of laws by which Israelis govern themselves qua Israelis, in Israel.

The relation of nationality is both symmetrical and transitive. If X is related to Y as a national, Y is related to X in the same way. If I am related to you as Canadian, so are you related to me. And if X is related to Y and Y is related to Z as citizens of a nation, X is related to Z in the same way. If I am related to you as a Canadian and you are related to Pedro as a Canadian,

I am likewise related to Pedro as a Canadian. And this is not a higher order relation that breaks down into lower order ones that are neither symmetrical nor transitive, as happens with race and ethnicity.

So far I have been speaking of various categories that apply to a nation and to nationality, but I have not given proper formulas for these concepts. Here they are:

> A nation is a subgroup of individual humans who satisfy the following conditions: they (1) reside in a territory, (2) are free and informed, and (3) have the common political will to live under a system of laws that (i) aims to ensure justice and the common good, regulating their organization, interrelations, and governance, and (ii) is not subordinated to any other system of laws within the territory in question.

> Nationality consists in the relational property of belonging to a nation that characterizes its members.

Both of these formulas integrate parts of the metaphysical categorizations of nation and nationality with elements from their definitions in order to present analyses that help us distinguish nationality from race and ethnicity; but the analyses presented in the formulas should not be regarded as complete. I am not aiming in these formulas to present definitions that include the complete set of necessary and sufficient conditions of nation or nationality; my aim is merely to establish some parameters on the basis of which these can be distinguished primarily from race and ethnicity. To accomplish the more ambitious task, other elements would have to be added to the formulas, but this is something I do not need to undertake here.

One thing that these formulas make clear is how the Political View differs from Miller's position. Recall that Miller's proposal had several problems: lack of specificity, the inclusion of culture in nationality, and a propensity to confusion of nationality and ethnicity. The Political View, by connecting nationality to the political will of a people within a territory who accept a system of laws, clearly distinguishes nationality from ethnicity, disengages it from culture, and specifies the fundamental element that characterizes nations.

Other considerations might pose a challenge to the view I have presented. For example, one may ask how I can accommodate the fact that we speak of nations within nations—say of the Catalan nation within the Spanish nation—with the view of nation that I have adopted. One way is to say that, when one speaks of Catalans as a nation, one is in fact speaking of an ethnic group and not a nation properly speaking. There was a time when

Catalans did constitute a nation in the political sense, but that was five hundred years ago; now, they are merely an ethnic group. This seems to make sense, particularly when the talk about the Catalan nation typically incorporates cultural features, such as a language.

But there are cases in which these so-called nations within nations are not ethnic groups, so one may wonder whether there can be nations within nations, and different nations within the same state. After all, we speak of the Seneca Nation and the American nation, and the first seems to be part of the second and both are found within the confines of the American state. In these cases, do we have true nations, that is, groups of people who have the political will to live under a sovereign system of laws in a territory? Is not the system of laws under which the Seneca live subordinated to the system of laws that govern the American nation of which the Seneca seem also to be a part?

One way to explain this phenomenon is to point out that the two groups of people in question occupy different territories and accept different systems of laws, and that their relations as groups are a matter of negotiation. The laws of the Seneca Nation are not subsumed under the laws of the American nation, or if they are subsumed, they are so by choice and the Seneca retain the right to secede, so there is an element of sovereignty in the Seneca. We could say, then, that we have two nations (the Seneca and the American), both of whom, by mutual agreement, constitute a single state, the United States of America. Of course, if the Seneca also identify themselves as Americans, this might lead one to think that they are part of the American nation. But this is not quite right insofar as the conditions of territoriality and laws have also to be satisfied. The territoriality condition could be satisfied by saying that the territory of the Seneca is part of the territory of the United States. But the issue of the system of laws remains an obstacle. As long as the laws of the Seneca and Americans are not part of a single system of laws, it is difficult to argue that they are members of one nation.

None of this interferes with the notion that individual persons in each nation may also be members of the other nation. Individual Americans may belong to the Seneca Nation and members of the Seneca Nation may belong to the American nation. This is just what happens with people who have multiple citizenship in states that contain nations. One can be Canadian and American, as long as the laws of these countries allow it and are compatible. The situation is different, however, with such groups as Catalonians and Galicians within Spain, for these groups do not have sovereign systems of laws, even if once upon a time they did and therefore constituted true nations. And the same could be said about the Scottish and the Welsh within Britain. These are ethnic groups, rather than nations properly speaking.

Of course, we need terms to speak about groups of people who have some features of nationhood before becoming truly a nation. Consider the case of Serbo-Croatians, for example. What were they before they became a nation? One term that could be used, proposed by Eriksen, is "proto-nation" (Eriksen 1997, 40). This term refers to groups—sometimes having the same ethnicity, but sometimes not (think of the Czech, who are ethnically divided into Bohemians, Moravians, and Salesians)—that under favorable conditions might form states based on a political will and thus in turn become nations. And we can also speak of groups of people who cease to be nations owing to conquest, for example, as "remnant nations." The members of these may, of course, belong to the same ethnos, as with Catalonians, or they may not, as in some cases in the Balkans. There is no reason, of course, why they cannot be described as "conquered."

From the formulas presented, it should be clear how my position differs from, and constitutes an alternative to, Miller's view. The main difference between the two is that mine includes an element of specificity missing in his: the reference to political will. Moreover, I leave out some of his constraints, such as an extended history and the cultural factors, that seem to create more problems than they solve. And this means that in the mentioned case there are two nations rather than one.

But what of indigenous groups who have become dispossessed in some ways and incorporated into certain states? Are they still nations? What do we make of the Tarahumara in Mexico, or the Eskimo in Canada and the United States? Obviously, they have become part of Mexico, Canada, or the United States. But do they maintain a nationality of their own? According to the Political View, they do only when, as groups, they have a territory, laws, and a political will of their own, distinguishable from the territory, laws, and political will of the state of which they have become part.

HISTORICAL ORIGIN AND LOCATION

Nations are historical entities established by different kinds of events and must reside in particular places. Indeed, we saw earlier that territory is a condition of nations, so we are entitled to ask: Is there a point in history where a nation comes to be, and are there particular places associated with particular nations? Let me go back to what I said in the previous two chapters concerning ethnic and racial groups and repeat it, with appropriate modifications, in the context of nations.

The question is historical and concerns contingent conditions surrounding individual persons who find themselves in particular contexts in history; it has to do with historical location. In the case of nations, the question involves factors that lead to their establishment, their origin, their continuity throughout history, and their location.

Insofar as nations develop in historical locations, there are always places and, often, times that are associated with them. These places often are preserved in the collective memories, actual or mythical, of the groups. For Cubans, the place is the island of Cuba; for Romans, it was the City of Rome; and so on, as Miller points out (Miller 1998, 658). Frequently, there is also a time somewhere in the mythical past that is deemed crucial for the origin of a nation. This is important, because it contextually separates the first members of the group from others, even if it cannot be used to distinguish subsequent members of the group who live at later dates and have never lived in the original location. The unity of and membership in a nation have to be explained in terms of the political will of the people to live under a system of laws within a territory, but not with reference to a particular territory or time, for national territories can change from time to time. This explains why one can speak of nomadic nations, even though they do not have fixed territories in which they reside or with which they identify as a place of origin.

OBSTACLES IN THE PROPER
UNDERSTANDING OF NATIONALITY

There are three obstacles in particular to a proper understanding of nationality. The first is that the effective use of a common national name requires the identification of an essence, that is, a feature or set of features that necessarily and sufficiently characterizes the members of the nation.[22] The lack of an essence indicates that the name of the nation is vacuous, and therefore useless at most and misleading at worst. The second assumption is that nationality entails both ethnic and racial homogeneity and compatibility (cf. Miller 1998, 658).[23] A nation is always composed of members similar in ethnicity or race who are, therefore, compatible with each other. The third obstacle is the view that nationality involves ethnic or racial purity (cf. Poliakov 1974; Guibernau 1996, 56–57).

These three assumptions are interrelated in that the second and third are used as ways of satisfying the first condition. The set of features, racial or ethnic, in terms of which a nation or its members is analyzed is identified as the essence of the nation. Thus the German nation has been conceived by some in terms of the so-called Aryan race and a particular history and culture (Poliakov 1974).

In the previous two chapters, I already examined and rejected the view that the effective use of names requires a feature, or a set of features, that can be identified, even if the use of some names may require it; some names are effectively used, although they connote no essence. This, I argued, is the case with ethnic and racial names; there are no features necessarily common to all the entities of which these names are properly predicated.

The conception of a nation we have put forth likewise entails that there are no features necessarily common to all the persons that constitute a national group throughout the existence of the nation, and yet that does not mean that the use of a common national term is unjustified or meaningless. There is a way to understand the concept of a nation that allows us to speak meaningfully of, and refer effectively to, a nation as a whole or to its members, even when the persons in question do not share any feature in common at all times and places. Still, national categories are different from ethnic and racial categories because they involve among the members a political will to live under a system of laws. Moreover, the acceptance and practice of these laws have important implications for the group.

One implication is that the members of the group are linked in ways that other groups may not be, and this leads to the development of historical ties and, through them, the acquisition of features that may characterize the members of the nation at various times in history. Political union can lead to ethnic and even racial homogeneity. But racial or ethnic groups are themselves not homogeneous insofar as their members may differ in important ways, so it makes no sense in turn to speak of ethnically or racially homogeneous nations. Even understanding national homogeneity in a very broad sense, however, it is only rarely found in the world, except perhaps in a few places in which nations have been isolated and the product of inbreeding, both biological and cultural. Even the most racially and ethnically unified nations today are not homogeneous, as Guibernau has pointed out (Guibernau 1996, 47). One need only travel in the Scandinavian countries to see how inadequate the homogeneous model of nationality is. Some of these nations have tried very hard at various times in their history to prevent persons belonging to racial and ethnic groups different from those with which they identify from settling in their territory and, if settled, from becoming citizens. But they have never been successful in preventing racial and ethnic heterogeneity. Even Iceland, in spite of its isolation, displays some heterogeneity. In the American context, the idea of a "common culture" frequently touted is, Appiah argues, the result of a confusion between a "common culture," which has never existed, and a "dominant culture," which has (Appiah 1996, 87). Besides, to repeat, races and ethne are not homogeneous themselves except perhaps in a passing way, so to speak about the racial and ethnic homogeneity of nations is quite misleading.

Another important implication of the conception of nationality I have proposed that needs to be taken into account in this context is that the system of laws that binds a nation together may require certain cultural commonalities, such as an effective way of communication and a set of values entailed or presupposed by the laws in question. The acceptance and implementation of laws requires either a common language or an effective mechanism to translate one language into another. Members of a nation need to communicate with each other, and this is a powerful force for the development of ethnic ties. Moreover, the very laws adopted may require the acceptance of certain values, such as respect for persons, that again can function as powerful forces of ethnicity. Indeed, the laws in question may be expressions of such values. Clearly, then, nationality may lead to ethnicity unless a nation continues to feed on ethnically diverse peoples through immigration, conquest, and other processes. There are forces within a nation that tend to promote ethnic homogeneity, but nationality does not require it. A nation may, as has happened in Canada, Spain, and China, put in place certain mechanisms to ensure both effective communication among different ethnic groups within the nation and also the survival of those groups threatened with annihilation but whose members wish to preserve their ethnicity.

With respect to purity, there is little that needs to be said. The idea that nations are, or must be, pure is based on a confusion between nation and race or ethnicity, for purity is often associated with the latter two. Apart from these, it makes no sense to talk about national purity, for what could this possibly mean? But even in terms of race and ethnicity, the notion of purity makes no sense, as we have seen in chapters 3 and 4. So there is little that this claim can muster in its favor from any quarter in which it is examined.

The issue of purity leads naturally to the questions of whether national categories are necessarily incompatible with each other and whether the use of national terms is necessarily exclusionary. In an example, is being American incompatible with being Cuban, and does the use of the term "American," in a national sense, exclude the possibility of using "Cuban," also in national sense, for the same persons?

Earlier I argued that race and ethnicity are not exclusionary. In the case of nationality, however, this general statement needs to be qualified, for it is often the case that an incompatibility of the laws that govern two nations is the basis for an incompatibility between them. In some cases, the laws are exclusionary, whereas in others they are not. For example, a few years back, the United States did not allow its citizens to have some other citizenship, and Cuba did not allow its citizens to renounce theirs. This meant that, in order for Cubans to acquire U.S. citizenship, they had to pledge a non-negotiable allegiance to the United States and, by implication, take back their allegiance to Cuba, even if formally Cuba did not recognize that they were no longer its citizens. Indeed, even today, in cases in which multiple citizenship is allowed, the United States requires primacy in allegiance. A U.S. citizen could not fight for Canada and against the United States and remain a citizen of the United States. Clearly, no general rule applies across the board with respect to this issue.

In previous chapters, I also claimed that the use of racial and ethnic terms is not intended to reflect that some persons choose to refer to themselves with these terms. In the case of nationality, however, the situation is somewhat different, for nations cannot exist without at least some members being conscious of their political identity. The political will to live under the system of laws that binds a nation requires that at least some members of the nation be aware of the group, qua group, and also identify with it. This is another important difference between nationality on the one hand and race and ethnicity on the other.

OBJECTIONS AGAINST THE POLITICAL VIEW

Several of the objections that may be raised against the theories of race and ethnicity I have proposed can also be raised, *mutatis mutandis*, about the Political View of nationality. One argues that my view does not adequately account for the differences between national groups, but that something stronger and more specific must be supplied. Consider, for example, Americans and Cubans. We can tell who is and who is not American or Cuban, and we can tell not just because of some laws under which they are willing to live, but also because of deep differences in such things as their musical tastes and abilities, their cultures in general, and their values. Americans and Cubans have different attitudes toward life, senses of humor, tastes in clothing, and so on. A good explanation of the differences between nations must refer to consistent and constituent features of all members of the nations, otherwise the unity of the groups is jeopardized. It will not do to argue, as I have done, that there is actually no feature that members of a nation have in common, and that what ties them is simply a system of laws they have adopted and by which they will to live within a territory. Much more is required, and much more is evident if we look at nations. In short, one might say that each nation has a particular ethnicity that characterizes it and distinguishes it from other nations and that ethnicity in this case involves, contrary to what I have argued, a definite set of features, including particularly cultural features (some might even wish to add racial features).

As I said in my answer to a similar objection in the context of race and ethnicity, this argument is based on a misunderstanding of my view, for nowhere have I claimed that there are no common features to nations and that, as a consequence, we can never tell members of a nation apart from members of other nations in terms of certain features. Instead, I have claimed that members of nations have no features in common at all times and in all places that are necessary or sufficient and discernible. My view does not prevent one from maintaining that there are features common to some members of a nation at all times and in all places, at all times and in some places, or at some times and in all places, or features common to all members at all times and in some places, or at some times and in all places. Nor is it correct to construe my position as entailing that there are no common features to members of nations at all times and places. I argue only that no features are necessary or sufficient and can be shown to be common to all members of nations at all times and in all places. In fact, I have also argued that there are features common to members of nations at some times and in some places and that in terms of such features we can often identify them at those times and in those places. At every time and in every period, some members of nations have features in common that distinguish them from other groups, whether national or not, but these features do not necessarily extend beyond those times and places or need to do so in order to account for membership in the groups and for the distinction of the members from other groups. Indeed, I have said quite clearly that the very laws that tie nations are powerful forces in the development of those features, and that these laws also often involve values. The point, however, is that these features have nothing to do with nations as such—they are neither necessary nor sufficient for them.

The various relations that members of nations have among themselves, and the laws under which they live, are the foundation of features that can be used to distinguish them. Particular cultural characteristics distinguish Americans, say, in certain contexts, although they cannot function as criteria of distinction and identification everywhere and at all times. In a place where all, and only, Americans speak with a certain accent, the accent can function as a sufficient criterion of American identification even if, in other places, it does not. Consider a group of Americans from Texas who are together with a group of Londoners. Would it not be easy to tell the Americans from the Londoners by listening to their drawl? But this linguistic test does not constitute proof insofar as it might turn out that some of the Londoners are Americans who have lived in London for a long time and have acquired one of the London ways of speaking English, whereas some of the presumed Americans are actually British subjects, children of British diplomats living in the United States, who have acquired the accent from Texas.

Nations are not homogeneous in any sense, but particular features can be used, more or less successfully, to determine who counts as a member of a nation in particular contexts. How successfully will depend, of course, on the case and the circumstances surrounding it.

That the unity of nations is always to be traced to the system of laws by which the group wills to live in a territory, and that it is a fact of history that these laws change, leads to the problem of accounting for the continuity of nations through time. What criteria can we use, then, for nations that go from direct to representative democracy, monarchy to republic, and so on, and nations whose territories change over time? These are important questions related to identity whose examination I must leave for another time.

NEED FOR, AND ADVANTAGES OF, NATIONAL CATEGORIES

If national categories are understood as I have proposed, we still must ask whether we need them and whether there is any benefit in using them. The answer is that the need for, and advantage in, using them are more evident even than in the cases of racial and ethnic categories insofar as national categories bring attention to the political systems under which members of nations live in the territories they inhabit and this is essential for the understanding of human society. National categories open for us a different window into the world that reveals something missing in the categories of race and ethnicity. A nation is a window through which we can look at a section of human society and its history. In the extensive field of human experience, it introduces a means to frame the observer's perspective and lead it toward something that, under other conditions, might be bypassed. "Spaniard," for example, directs our attention toward something that, without this concept we might skip and that we could not fathom were we only to consider racial or ethnic categories, such as "White" or Hispanic. National categories uncover something unique by simultaneously narrowing and widening our horizon.

Nations and nationality are here to stay, at least for a long while, although one can envision a time when the notion of nationality will have no use except for the historical purpose of understanding the past. If nationalism is extinguished, and human society becomes universally organized under a uniform system of laws, the concept of a nation, as distinct from other nations, will cease to have value. If I am correct in saying that nationality involves only a system of laws adopted by a group of people who will to be subjected to them in a certain territory, then what would be the use of national categories in a world where the laws applied to everybody and the territory would be the whole world? Under these conditions, one could not properly speak of nations, although one could perhaps speak of the human nation, something very different from what we speak about today. Nationality, as a category, has no great metaphysical or epistemic significance if it is separated from its political significance. So if the latter is substantially transformed, the former may lose consequence. In such a world, the category of nation would become no more than a historical curiosity, such as we saw would happen with the category of race in a world in which racial categories lack significance.

CONCLUSION

I have presented a Political View of nationality, based on the will of people to abide by a system of laws that is used for the regulation of the relations among members of the group within a particular territory for the aims of justice and the well-being of everyone. There are many advantages to this view of nation and nationality. It allows for a clear distinction between nationality, race, and ethnicity. It explains how nations can be instrumental in the creation of ethnic groups and even in principle of races, how races can promote the development of nations and ethnic groups, and how ethne can contribute to the development of nations and races—an important point in that so far little has been said in the pertinent literature that provides an explanation of why these notions are so frequently confused with each other. It shows how self-awareness and self-identification are fundamental for nations, but not for races or ethne. It explains the efforts that have been undertaken to make nations racially or ethnically homogenous. And, finally, it points to a course of action in which the promotion of racial, and particularly ethnic, diversity is desirable.

NOTES

1. Although Gobineau's notion (2000) of nationality is racial, he accepts the importance of territory for it. See also Stojanović (2002, 20).

2. For different versions of some of these arguments, see Renan (1996, 40–42).

3. Another answer is that the territory in question is an original homeland associated with the group—as I argued is the case with ethne earlier (Smith 1991, 9). But this does not quite solve the problem of boundaries and tends to contribute to the confusion of nations with ethne.

4. This is a traditional Enlightenment conception of nation (Smith 1991, 9).

5. But not everyone agrees. Renan argues against this view (Renan 1996, 34–38). Some have combined language with laws, as does the *Dictionary of the French Academy* (1694; see Hudson 1996, 256). This view may be behind some of the arguments proposed in the United States for the position known as English-first— that proficiency in English should be given priority in the education of children. See Pogge (2000) and my response in Gracia (2004).

6. Gellner calls this "the cultural definition" of a nation (Gellner 1997, 57; see also Gellner 1983, 7). Smith combines culture and birth into what he calls the non-Western "ethnic" conception of a nation (Smith 1991, 10). Kedourie argues that the political conception of nation cannot be separated from the cultural one (Kedourie 1961, 47–50). See also Guibernau (1996, 55–56); Jones (1999, 164).

7. Culturalist attempts to define nationality have been made by many authors everywhere in the world. In the United States, there has been a strong effort to homogenize the nation culturally (see Oboler 1995). In Latin America also, the efforts have been numerous (see Ramos 1963; Paz 1961). Often these attempts have nation-building for a goal, as happened in the 1950s and 1960s in the United States (Young 1983, 655).

8. This is most clear in the case of some fundamentalist Muslims, who speak of an Islamic nation—see, for example, the statements made by Ayman al-Zawahiri in his autobiography, in MacFarquhar (2001)—but it goes beyond fundamentalism. The idea that religion is what gives unity to nations is found in Durkheim (1987, 222–23).

9. But many hold on to the need for unity of religion in nations or in states. Treitschke is an example (see Guibernau 1996, 9).

10. Gellner calls this the "voluntaristic" definition of nation, although it is questionable whether mere self-identification requires a will (Gellner 1997, 57). See also Gellner (1983, 7) and Seton-Watson (1977, 5), where the latter adds a behavior requirement: nations are required to think of themselves, and to behave, as such.

11. This view of nations is often described as "voluntaristic" in the literature, because it involves an act of the will on the part of the members of the nation (Miller 1998, 657). Those who favor a cultural understanding of nationality sometimes oppose conceiving nations in political terms (see Durkheim 1986, 206).

12. Sometimes philosophers also speak of a spirit, soul, or self of a nation, particularly in the nineteenth century. See Fichte (1979, §7:13); Miller (1998, 659).

13. For other combinations, see for example, Smith (1991, 43); Guibernau (1999, 13–14).

14. For other proposals that combine several of the factors mentioned earlier, see for example, Gellner (1983, 55), who attempts to combine the culturalist and voluntarist views, and Smith (1991, 43) who de-emphasizes the voluntary factor.

15. This formula avoids the Paradox of Sovereignty.

16. For other ways to distinguish between nations and states, see Tamir (1993, 150) and Lichtenberg (1997, 159).

17. For Gellner, a state is "an institution or set of institutions specifically concerned with the enforcement of order" (Gellner 1997, 54; see also Gellner 1983, 4). This echoes Weber's view that it is a human community that successfully claims the monopoly of the legitimate use of physical force within a territory (Weber 1991, 78). Smith also emphasizes power (Smith 2000, 498). This sounds like government by police, but it does succeed in distinguishing a state from a nation in a way similar to the one I have proposed. Smith states that it refers exclusively to public institutions that exercise a monopoly of coercion within a given territory (Smith 1991, 14). And the Uppsala Conflict Data Project defines it as "an internationally recognized sovereign government controlling a specified territory, or a nonrecognized government whose sovereignty is not disputed by another internationally recognized sovereign government previously controlling the same territory" (Gleditsch et al. 2002, 619). Today, all states officially consider themselves "nations" (Hobsbawm 1997, 69; Miller 1998, 657), but this again is quite misleading. States are not nations and nations are not states if by nations one means groups of people and by states one means much more. See also Guibernau (1997, 131–54).

18. Durkheim holds that there are no nations without states (Durkheim 1986, 206), but Weber disagrees (Weber 1978, 1:398; 1991, 172). See also Miller (1998, 657).

19. For Walzer, however, a nation-state does not require ethnic homogeneity, but only that there be "a single dominant group [that] organizes the common life in a way that reflects its own history and culture" (Walzer 1997, 249).

20. In the literature, these are sometimes referred to as "state-nations." See Guibernau (1996, 115).

21. This point is generally ignored in the literature concerned with linguistic rights. See, for example, Pogge (2000).

22. Miller refers to this position as "the objective view of nations" (Miller 1998, 658). The term "essentialism" is also used to refer to what some believe to be the immutable character of nations (Guibernau 1996, 1).

23. For some, the task of a state is precisely to homogenize the population (Gellner 1983, 110; see also Marshall 1992). This has been called the ethnic, racial, or cultural view of a nation, and it has its origin in Germany (cf. Stojanović 2002, 14). For arguments against this and other ethnic and racial assumptions concerning nationality, see Kedourie (1961).

6

SURVIVING RACE,
ETHNICITY, AND NATIONALITY

The road we have traveled in this book has been complex, but I hope nonetheless useful to those who have stayed the course. I began, in the preface, by pointing out the need to address the roots of the racial, ethnic, and national conflicts that have plagued the history of humankind, although I am not by any means the first to draw attention to these. Many others have also been alarmed by the depth and dimensions of these conflicts and by what looks like an increase in both in the twentieth and twenty-first centuries. The ruthlessness, brutality, and extent of these conflicts in our times are perhaps unprecedented in human history, for although the attitudes on which they are rooted have not changed with time, the means whereby they are carried out have improved. Humans have learned to be more efficient when it comes to genocide, oppression, and abuse. And developments in the media, rather than helping to turn public opinion against them, seem only to serve the opposite aim, either by creating a cacophony of voices in which reason, sense, tolerance, and compassion are often lost, or by increasing the control over, and manipulation of, populations by corrupt or ideologically motivated individuals and groups.

Unfortunately, some of the ideas that have surfaced in the past two hundred years to meet the challenge to understand race, ethnicity, and nationality adequately and deal effectively with racial, ethnic, and national conflicts have proven not only ineffective but also pernicious, contributing to the increase rather than decrease of the level and extent of these conflicts. This does not imply that these ideas have always been proposed from foul motives. Surely some of them have had behind them motives of this sort, but others have been the result rather of misguided ideological commitments or of confusions of the sorts identified in chapter 2. Most of the time, their proponents have meant well, but their motives are irrelevant for our

143

purposes. A knife is not judged by the uses to which it is put or the motives behind those uses, but rather by how well it cuts. Likewise, views about race, ethnicity, and nationality should not be judged based on the motives of those who propose them or the uses to which they are put, but instead by their adequacy. And what are these views? Here are some of them.

The unqualified claim, made so frequently as a solution to oppression, domination, and abuse, that race, ethnicity, and nationality do not exist but are fictions that should be banished from discourse, is dangerous for at least three reasons. First, it leaves us defenseless. Ignoring the real dimensions of these phenomena both closes the door on their serious investigation and prevents us from fighting the abuses arising from their misunderstanding and misuse. If there is no enemy, whom are we to fight? If race, ethnicity, and nationality are mere fictions, ghosts without substance, how are we going to eliminate pernicious forms of racism, ethnicism, and nationalism? And how are we to understand ourselves and construct identities that will give meaning to our lives in a world that is increasingly characterless and homogeneous?

Second, this view of race, ethnicity, and nationality is dangerous because it seriously misrepresents the way in which these ideas originated and the motives and attitudes that influenced them. This prevents us from learning a true lesson from history and thus leaves us unprepared for similar challenges in the future.

Third, this indiscriminate claim undermines the serious and important investigations of scientists and philosophers who have studied these concepts. Caricatures of qualified and careful research lead to misunderstandings and false implications. To say, for example, that race does not exist is counterproductive unless we point out exactly what this means and in what sense. Otherwise the claim may be easily dismissed, insofar as the social reality of race is too powerful and its effects too obvious to be simply brushed aside.

As dangerous and pernicious as this idea is the notion that race, ethnicity, and nationality are realities with essences, that is, entities in the world with immutable properties. This is dangerous not only because it is false but also because it freezes groups of people in certain states and circumstances, preventing them from adapting to different situations in order to satisfy effectively the conditions imposed on them by their environment. Indeed, in many ways it necessarily leads to their demise, for an organism that cannot adapt will perish, and conflicts can be resolved only through the elimination of one of the conflicting parties.

Not less dangerous is the idea that race, ethnicity, and nationality are exclusively the products of political agendas used to advance the interests of certain groups. There is no question that there have been many attempts in this direction, but not all fit this model. This idea is dangerous in that it necessarily makes our approach to these phenomena political and ultimately a matter of power. Unfortunately, power is mostly in the hands of the few whose interest is to preserve the status quo, so we are left without recourse.

More specifically, the common view that understands races, ethne, and nations in terms of each other is particularly counterproductive and nefarious. The view that nations are the same as ethne or races turns all relations between nations into ethnic or racial ones. Thus, national conflicts become conflicts among races and ethnic groups, fueling their virulence and lending support to the position that only the complete extermination of one of the nations in conflict can solve the problem. Disputes about territory, resources, and influence, which in other contexts are subject to compromise, now become conflicts about values, racial characteristics, and cultures, which are regarded as not negotiable. Whereas losing a war between nations not understood racially or ethnically may simply mean that one nation loses some territory, when nations become identified with races or ethne, the loss of a war presents itself as an opportunity to eliminate a way of life or even to commit genocide in order to prevent future conflicts. Indeed, is not the expression "ethnic cleansing" a commonplace these days? For as long as something of the original race or ethnos remains, there is the possibility of strife.

This is the problem seen from without, as it were. But internally also the consequences of the identification of nations with races and ethne are pernicious, for no state is in fact ethnically or racially homogeneous. This means that a nation that identifies itself with one race or ethnos leaves other ethne and races out. The nation becomes an institutionalized place of privilege for some and of oppression for others.[1] Examples of this phenomenon have been so common in recent history that little has to be added; we need only look at recent events in Afghanistan and India. But, of course, we should not forget the paradigmatic case of Germany.

The alternative view, that ethne are in fact nations or races, also has disastrous consequences. Considering either to be nations leads immediately to the desire for ethnic political independence, regardless of whether the group in question has been oppressed or not. The result is the creation of conflict and the implementation of terrorism as a way to fight for ethnic independence. This is the case of Spanish Basques. But we may ask, how far can we divide the world to make national lines correspond to ethnic ones? How far do ethnic groups go? We have witnessed recently the division of Czechoslovakia into two states as a response to the desire to separate two nations ethnically conceived. But this is not sufficient, for one of the resulting divisions, the Czech Republic, contains at least three ethnic groups—Bohemians, Moravians, and Salesians. Is a further division necessary, then? And would this be enough? Since there are no countries today that correspond exactly to ethnic boundaries, should every nation on earth be broken up and new political borders be drawn? Imagine the disruption and the conflicts that might arise! Finally, how much peace have divisions of this sort brought about in the past? The track record is dismal, so optimism in this direction is unwarranted.

But this is not all. The reality is that human ethnic populations are mixed all over, so where are we to draw the lines? These divisions, as is clear from the case of India and Pakistan, lead to endemic conflicts because there are bound to be disagreements about the boundaries and resentment resulting from the resettlement of people away from places they regard as their home. And how is such an idea to be implemented in a place such as the United States, in which ethnic and racial groups are mixed over the entire national territory? Are we to ship all African Americans to Africa and all Latinos to Latin America? Are we to send all Arab Americans to the Middle East, all Cuban Americans to Cuba, and all Irish Americans to Ireland? The same would have to happen in Spain, where all Catalans would have to go back to Catalonia, all Basques to Navarre, and all Castilians to Castile. Does anyone really think this is possible, or desirable? It is as crazy an idea as humans have come up with, and one that encourages a kind of strife that cannot end in peace and harmony. Indeed, it only postpones the need to grapple with the real issue, which is to find a political solution to the survival of humankind that takes into account the variety of ethnic and racial groups of which it is composed.

Thinking about ethnic groups as races is also dangerous and pernicious, for the idea of race is tied to descent and, therefore, involves the impossibility of change. When ethnic groups become races, then they are regarded as immutable. And this is very bad, indeed, because some of the contextual characteristics of an ethnic group may be incompatible with the values and principles that a nation has adopted. If the ethnic group cannot change, then the only resolution of this situation is either genocide or expulsion. And, indeed, these procedures have repeatedly been adopted in human history, but mostly without enduring success. Of course, the temptation to racialize ethnicity is great, for doing so provides a kind of metaphysical fixity (based on descent) and epistemic perspicuity (based on gross morphology) that seem to solve all sorts of problems. But the temptation must be resisted.

There is also danger and damage in the understanding of races as ethne. When a race is conceived as an ethnos, matters that have nothing to do with heredity are regarded as such, and culture is confused with descent. Racial markers are understood in terms of ethnic ones, and this helps isolate groups and promotes discrimination. A certain performance in an IQ test that is culturally biased is taken as a measure of racial inferiority or superiority. And a particular pattern of behavior resulting from social circumstances is identified as racially constitutive. The result is that innocuous physical features, such as skin color or hair texture, become signs of what are regarded as objectionable cultural differences. We have seen enough of this, even among scientists, to be weary of this view.

Finally, the identification of a race with a nation leads to some of the same results we have been speaking about, for in this case the members of the group may want both to form a state and to have political power. And, if they succeed, they exclude members of other races from the state simply because they are racially different. The oppressors become the oppressed, as we have seen happen in Zimbabwe.

The views of race, ethnicity, and nationality I proposed in the previous chapters contrast in important ways with the views just described. In closing, then, let me turn to them in order to sharpen their similarities and differences. I begin with race and ethnicity.

RACE AND ETHNICITY

Races and ethne are subgroups of individual human beings whose members do not need to have common features in the sense of particular properties, qualities, or even particular relations throughout the existence of the groups. Both groups are kinds of families in which the members are tied through historical relations. There is much, then, that race and ethnicity share. Nonetheless, they should not be confused with each other, for fundamental differences between them can be conceptually drawn. The main differences are at least two. First, each member of a race is connected by descent to at least one other member of the race who in turn is linked by descent to some third member, but there is no such requirement for members of an ethnos. No descent link is necessary for ethnicity. Members of an ethnos may be linked by descent, and for some ethne not only is this the case, but also inclusion in the ethne appears to depend on them being so. However, this is not a requirement in every ethnos, whereas it is for members of a race.

The second important difference between race and ethnicity is that the members of a race must share in one or more of a set of genetically transmittable perspicuous physical features generally associated with the race, but this is not a requirement of ethnicity. Members of an ethnos do not have to share in some of the features making up a particular set. Nor do the features in which they may share at particular times and places need to be genetically transmittable or physically perspicuous. The features that result from the historical relations that the members of an ethnos have can be of any sort and may change. Moreover, the list of features for races are matters of social determination, whereas this need not be so with an ethnos. In an ethnos, these features are determined by historical relations that can be independent of what people may think. In the case of a race, the features are also determined by historical relations, but that they count as racial features is a matter of social selection.

In short, contrary to a widespread belief, ethnicity is less strictly determined than race but at the same time less dependent on social perception. It is much more open and historically contingent, and this is quite understandable in that race has to do with perceived physical features and perception is subject to social and environmental influences. The differences between ethnicity and race, however, do not entail that particular ethnic groups may not coincide with particular racial groups, that they may not overlap, or that they may exclude each other. It is possible, although unlikely, that the terms that refer to a particular race may be coextensive with the terms that refer to a particular ethnos. It could happen, say, that "Black American" and "African American" (when "Black American" is understood racially and "African American" is understood ethnically) have the same extensions, while at the same time having different intensions—the terms would mean something different. This is not different than what happens with expressions such as "the husband of Norma" and "the grandfather of Sofia and Eva." Both expressions refer to me, but their meanings are quite different. The first points to me considered in relation to my wife; the second points to me in relation to my two granddaughters to whom this book is dedicated. In fact, however, I do not know of any racial term whose extension is exactly the same as that of an ethnic term.

The case of overlap, however, is quite common. It is frequent that racial and ethnic terms are applied to the same persons who belong to two different groups. A person can be "Black" and Jewish, for example, just as she can be "White" and Hispanic.

Some authors, however, want to allow not just for overlap in extension, but also for overlap in intension. They argue that we need notions of ethnorace or racial ethnicity, by which they mean that the notions of race and ethnicity are hopelessly entangled and cannot be effectively separated. This claim has two parts: (1) one cannot speak sensibly about race apart from ethnicity, or vice versa, and (2) one cannot classify someone as a member of a race and not of an ethnos, or vice versa.

Both claims are misguided. Even though in the public mind the notions of race and ethnicity are often confused, it is possible to distinguish them. We can, and often do, talk about people in terms of racial categories to the exclusion of ethnic ones, and vice versa. I gave some other arguments against these views in chapter 2, which I shall not repeat here. However, after the detailed discussion of ethnicity and race in chapters 3 and 4, it makes sense to refer to some of the factors that are behind the attempt to link race and ethnicity.

At least two of these factors should be mentioned: first, the nature of ethnicity allows for the inclusion of racial features; second, race and ethnicity can affect, and be the source of, each other or be products of similar factors (cf. Sollors 2002, 98). Concerning the first, recall that indeed, according to the Familial-Historical View of ethnicity, anything whatever can, in context, and as a result of historically contingent relations, become a feature that characterizes and serves to distinguish members of an ethnos. This means that it is possible for what are considered to be racial features to become part of what can be used to distinguish an ethnos. Skin color, descent, body shapes, and so on can be used as criteria for ethnic membership. However, this does not obliterate the distinction between race and ethnicity insofar as these criteria can, and do in fact, change, but descent and participation in a set of genetically transmittable perspicuous physical features can never be dispensed with when it comes to race.

It makes sense, then, in certain circumstances, to speak of a racial or racialized ethnos. This occurs when a particular ethnic group has features that include racial ones. This is behind such conceptions as that of ethnic Germans as a race or Hispanics as a race. But these classifications are ultimately misguided if taken as more than particular, contextual, and historical. Although there may be racial, or racialized, ethnic groups, the notion of a racial ethnos does not make sense except in a particular historical context insofar as there can be ethnic groups that are not racialized.

The second source of the misguided claims noted earlier is that race and ethnicity can affect, and be the source of, each other or be products of similar factors. For example, racial identification often leads to segregation, and this in turn may result in the development of an ethnos. The segregation of "Blacks" tends to link them together in ways that separate them from other races. This strengthens their historical interrelations and tends to produce ethnic features. Thus, one may speak of a "Black" ethnos, characterized by "Black" food, customs, values, and so on (Rose 2000, 81–82). Still, this "Black" ethnos is not the same as the "Black" race, even if it is a direct result of human actions prompted in part by the "Black" race. "'Black' ethnos" and "'Black' race" are not, nor should they be considered, synonymous. This explains why "Whites" can become "Black" and "Blacks" can become "White," as the Oreo phenomenon illustrates.[2] They do so not racially, but ethnically. However, ethnic clusters can, over a long period of time, produce racial developments owing to inbreeding and isolation. Indeed, ethnic prohibitions about marriage outside a group can lead to the development or preservation of racial markers. Finally, it is quite clear that the same environmental factors, such as geographical isolation, can help the development of both ethnic and racial features.

The notion of an ethnic race in principle makes no sense, although notions of this sort are in fact frequently used and there are understandable reasons why they develop in particular contexts. Race is often taken to involve cultural and other factors frequently associated with ethnicity, but this leads to confusions. Keeping the notions of ethnos and race separate as I have suggested can help us sort out these confusions and resolve some of the controversies that plague discussions of ethnicity and race.

The distinction I have drawn between race and ethnicity should also help us understand the loose way in which the term "racism" is used. The extension of this term today clearly includes negative attitudes not only toward races, but also toward ethnic groups (Banton 1983, 2). Israeli Zionists, for example, are accused by some of racism with respect to Palestinians, and one frequently encounters talk about racism against Hispanics, when it should be clear that neither Palestinians nor Hispanics are races.[3] If the notions of race and ethnicity are confused, however, confusion about the nature of racism follows.

NATIONALITY AND RACE

Let me turn now to nationality and race. At least two main differences between these stand out based on characteristics of races that nations do not require. First, all members of a race are connected by descent to at least one other member of the race who in turn is linked by descent to some third member, but there is no such requirement for members of a nation. No form of descent is necessary for nationality. The members of a particular nation may be linked by descent, but this is not required in all nations—and it is not even the case in most—whereas it is required for members of a race.

The second difference is that the members of a race must share in one or more of a set of genetically transmittable and perspicuous physical features generally associated with the race, but this again is not a requirement of nationality. Members of a nation do not have to share in some of the features making up a set. Nor do the features in which they may share at particular times and places need to be genetically transmittable or physically perspicuous. The features that result from the historical relations that tie the members of a nation can be of any sort and may change. Moreover, the list of features associated with particular races is a matter of social perception, whereas this is not so with a nation. In a nation, if there are such features, they are determined by historical relations resulting ultimately from the laws accepted by the group, and therefore they can be independent of what people may think at particular times. In the case of race, the features are also determined by historical relations, but that they count as racial features is a matter of social selection.

Nationality also entails certain requirements that race does not. Most important among these are the following: First, a nation is the result of the will of its members to live under a system of laws in a political arrangement within a territory. Races are not matters of will, laws, political arrangement, or territory. Races have to do with descent and transmittable and perspicuous physical features. Second, the aim of the nation is to ensure justice and the good of all members of the group, but races do not have any such aims.

In spite of many opinions to the contrary, nationality is less strictly determined than race but at the same time less dependent on social perception; it is much more open and historically contingent. The differences between nationality and race, however, do not entail that particular national groups may not coincide with particular racial groups, that they may not overlap, or that they may exclude each other. It is logically possible, although to my knowledge it has never happened, that the term that refers to a particular race may be coextensive with the term that refers to a particular nation.

The case of overlap, by contrast, is quite common. It is frequent that racial and national terms are applied to persons who belong to two different groups. One can be "White" and Norwegian, for example, just as one can be "Black" and Nigerian.

Some authors, however, want to allow not just for an overlap in the extension of racial terms, but also for overlap in intension. They argue that we need notions of national race or racial nation. By this, they mean either that the notions of race and nationality are hopelessly entangled and cannot be effectively separated or that they should be—for epistemic, metaphysical, or ethical reasons—mixed (e.g., see Poliakov 1974; Omi and Winant 1994). This claim has two parts: (1) one cannot (or should not) speak sensibly about race apart from nationality, or vice versa, and (2) one cannot (or should not) classify someone as a member of race X, and not of nation Y, or vice versa.

Both claims are misguided. Even though in the public mind the notions of race and nationality are often confused, it is possible to distinguish them as in fact I have done here, and whether they should, or should not, be distinguished is another matter altogether. Moreover, one can, and we often do, talk about people in terms of racial categories to the exclusion of national ones, and vice versa.

The main reason why nationality and ethnicity should be kept separate is that to do otherwise results in the subversion of the very aims constitutive of nationality. If a nation is conceived racially, then its laws inexorably will privilege one race over others, and this will undermine the aims of justice and the good of all the members of the nation constitutive of nationality. The conception of nationality in racial terms results in the destruction of the nation.

One source of these mistaken claims is that the notion of nationality is sometimes confused with the notion of ethnicity, and ethnicity allows for the inclusion of racial features. Indeed, according to the Familial-Historical View of ethnicity, anything whatever can, in context, and as a result of historically contingent relations, become a feature that serves to distinguish members of an ethnos. Hence it is possible for what are considered to be racial features to become part of the criteria that can be used to distinguish an ethnos. Skin color, descent, body shape, and so on can be used as markers of ethnic membership. However, this does not obliterate the distinction between race and ethnicity insofar as these criteria can, and do in fact, change. But descent and participation in a set of genetically transmittable perspicuous physical features can never be dispensed with when it comes to race.

The other source of the confusion is that nations, if persistent for a long time and isolated from other groups of people, can in principle contribute to the development of races. If a group of people is separated from others for a sufficient number of years, the evolutionary process to which the group is subjected can result in the development of certain genetically transmittable and perspicuous physical features that can be socially picked to distinguish the group from other groups. But this possibility is remote both because the development of such features takes too long and because it is difficult to envision nations that endure and exist isolated for that long (cf. Garn 1993). Moreover, even if this were to happen, it does not mean that the logical distinction between race and nation would disappear, but only that the categories would overlap in this particular case.

It makes sense, then, in certain circumstances, to speak of a racial, or racialized, nation.[4] This occurs when a particular nation is composed of an ethnic group that has features that include racial ones. This is behind such conceptions as that of a German nation as a race or Israelites as a race (cf. Poliakov 1974). But these classifications are ultimately misguided if taken as more than particular and historical. Although there may be racial, or racialized, nations, the notion of a racial nation does not make sense except in a particular historical context.

The notion of a national race makes even less sense, although notions of this sort are in fact used. Race is often taken to involve cultural and other factors frequently associated with ethnicity and, through it, with nationality, but they make no sense and lead to endless confusion. Keeping the notions of nation and race separate in the way I have suggested can help us sort out these confusions and resolve some of the issues involved in nationality and race.

The identification of race and nation in particular gives rise to a confusion in the use of the notion of racism similar to the one we saw in the context of ethnicity. People will identify discrimination against certain nations or their members as racism. If we keep the notions of race and nation separate, then this confusion disappears and we can better understand the differences between racial and national prejudice and discrimination. Let me turn now to nationality and ethnicity.

NATIONALITY AND ETHNICITY

The main differences between nationality and race also distinguish nationality from ethnicity. A nation is a voluntary political organization of people based on a system of laws devised for the regulation of the relations and governance of the members of the group of people who accept it in a certain territory with the aim of ensuring justice and the good of all members. Belonging to a nation is ultimately a matter of political will, laws, territory, justice, and the well-being of its members, whereas this is not the case with ethnicity. Ethnicity has to do with historical relations of various sorts that contingently tie people into groups independently of these factors.

The identification of nationality and ethnicity, however, is widespread (Llobera 1994, 214; A. D. Smith 1986, x). Its origin goes back at least to the eighteenth century (Voegelin 1940; Smith 1994, 382). It has at least three sources. One is that nations require some foundation. We proposed that the

glue that binds nations together is the political will of a people to live under a system of laws that regulate the relations of the members of the nation, and that this in turn involves a certain degree of self-identification of
the members with the group. But this also requires that there be some common background to the members of the group. If they are going to self-
identify with the group and accept certain laws, there must be some common values and shared assumptions. Moreover, self-identification requires
symbols through which the members of the group can unite. I mentioned
flags, celebrations, anthems, and so on, but even more important than these
are traditions.[5] Naturally, these can also be part of the ethnicity of the members of the group, and can be easily considered ethnic elements because ethnicity tolerates all kinds of features, particularly cultural ones. This leads
some to think that a nation is, after all, an ethnos. The mistake here is that
the requirements for nationality are minimal if compared with the requirements for ethnicity. Agreement about living together under certain laws is
not enough to constitute an ethnos. More is required. The foundational
structure of nationality is too basic and skeletal to sustain an ethnos. This is
in fact a substantial advantage, for it makes it possible for nations to be constituted by many ethnic groups.

A second reason why ethnicity is identified with nationality is that, just
as in the case of race, nationality can give rise to ethnic features. If the key
to ethnicity is the historical relations among members of a group, then a nation constitutes a powerful factor of ethnicity generation. Nations force
their members to deal with each other, consign them to a territory helping
develop their relations further, and bring them together in all sorts of ways.
Moreover, isolation from other nations and groups helps the process. Indeed, nations often try to promote the ethnic (and even racial) homogenization of their members in order to create stronger national bonds and
make governing easier (Guibernau 1997, 5; 1996, 11).[6] Indeed, in some
cases attempts have been made to make a certain ethnicity a condition of
membership in certain nations (Guibernau 1997, 6; see also Kymlicka 1997,
240). And it is often the case that, even after the dissolution of a political
group, an ethnic feeling remains in the group (Weber 1997, 19). But, again,
this does not mean that we need to or should conflate the notions of ethnos and nation. It only means, as in the case of race, that one can contribute
to the origin of the other in particular circumstances and that the categories
may overlap or even coincide in certain contexts.

A third reason why nationality is conceived in ethnic terms has to do
with the legitimate complaints of ethnic groups in states in which they are
oppressed. The Kurds in Iraq felt for a long time that the only way to termi-

nate the oppression they had suffered in the Iraqi state because of their ethnicity was to liberate themselves and form a sovereign state. Obviously, their experience of ethnic discrimination led them to think that the only way to avoid it is by forming an ethnic state in which they are the nation.[7] Oppression, however, is not a sufficient reason for the ethnic understanding of nations insofar as there are other ways of doing away with such oppression without incurring the problems that result from the creation of ethnic states.

KEEPING RACE, ETHNICITY, AND NATIONALITY SEPARATE

If we keep the notions of race, ethnicity, and nationality separate, then we can understand and explain all sorts of social phenomena and organizations that otherwise remain inscrutable. Consider the case of Switzerland, for example. Here we have a nation, the Swiss, who are divided into at least four ethnic groups: the Italians, Germans, Rheto-Romans, and French. Moreover, all three major races are represented in the nation. And we also have a state, the Swiss state, composed of all these people, a territory, cities, institutions, and so on. Something similar can be said of Mexico. Here we have a nation that breaks down into more than fifty different ethnic groups and all major races. And the same can be said about most other countries. Certainly, this is true of the United States. Of course, attempts have been made in these and other states to exclude certain peoples from what a leading group considers to be the nation and thus to restrict nationality to the members of only one ethnic group. The Nazis in the twentieth century tried this, annihilating in the process any ethnic group that was not German: Jews, Slavs, and Gypsies, to name just three. Their idea was that a nation has to be ethnically and racially homogeneous.

No nation is completely ethnically homogeneous today, and it is difficult to find examples of nations that have been completely so except in cases in which nationality has been denied to people who do not have the same ethnicity as the dominant group that claims to be the nation. Only by artificially excluding people who are part of the state from the nation can a nation be homogeneous. The case of ancient Athens is a good example. Only some Greeks were part of the Athenian nation, even though many other Greeks and non-Greeks resided within the Athenian territory and were members of the Athenian *polis*. But even under these conditions, homogeneity is very difficult to maintain because of intermarriages, liaisons, and the like. Even states that have tried to identify their nations with particular ethnic or racial groups have ultimately failed. Nations are generally heteroge-neous, being composed of miscellaneous groups that, however, are committed to a common political order based on a system of laws (cf. Young 1990).

There is, moreover, a serious inconsistency in the ethnic conception of a nation, similar to what we saw with the racial conception of a nation. It lies in that the aim of a nation is to ensure justice and well-being for its members, but a nation conceived along ethnic lines is ultimately established on an ethnic footing, and this favors ethnic domination, discrimination, and an inequitable distribution of goods. The only way in which an ethnic na-tion can guard against oppression and discrimination is by eliminating all ethnic differences—that is, by assimilation. But, as Young has noted, this in itself may constitute a violation of the rights of many of its members and therefore can only be construed as a kind of oppression (Young 2001). Moreover, because ethnic homogeneity in states does not exist, it has never existed, and all attempts to implement it have failed, any state that thinks of itself in ethnic terms is poised for discrimination and the oppression of the ethne not identified as part of the national ethnic profile. But there is even more to it than this, for the very notion of an ethnic nation is incompatible with the aims of nationality. Ethnicity has to do with particular historical and contextual phenomena, whereas nationality involves the universal val-ues of justice and well-being.

Apart from the logical and factual reasons I have given in favor of keeping the notions of race, ethnicity, and nationality separate, there are also powerful ethical and political reasons for doing so.[8] Perhaps the most im-portant of these is that the conception of nationality I have defended makes it possible to locate ethnic and racial conflicts within nations rather than be-tween them. If nations are identified with ethne and racial groups, conflicts between these groups become international, that is, conflicts between na-tions, often turning into wars. These wars are bound to be horrendous and to end not only in the defeat of one group by the other, but also in the at-tempt at extermination of the defeated group, for there is no effective set of laws at the international level to regulate these conflicts, and the winner will want to ensure, by eliminating the ethnic or racial source of further oppo-sition, that such opposition does not arise.

International law is still in its infancy, having been born less than five hundred years ago, and to this day has no teeth.[9] War is terrible, not only because of the devastation it brings, but also because it ends only in the de-feat of one of the parties. And if the parties are separated ethnically and racially, then its end involves the defeat of one race by another and one eth-nic group by another. This is nothing less than a return to the most primitive state in which humans have lived, but at a grander and more devastating scale. Wars of this sort tend to expand and move from the local to the global level, for nations that appear to have the same or similar ethnic or racial compositions feel that they need to band together against nations that have a different composition. In fact, we have seen this happen in the case of some ethnic groups. For example, some Arabs and Muslims feel that any act that Israel commits against any Arab or Muslim nation is an act of aggression against all Arab or Muslim nations. If this attitude is encouraged and becomes widespread, then the only way to settle conflicts is by the use of force and eventually genocide. There is no alternative but for the powerful to annihilate the weak.

But there is another way. And this is by distinguishing nations from ethnic groups and races, which means that they can be ethnically and racially heterogeneous. This does not necessarily eliminate ethnic and racial conflict, but it transfers these conflicts to the bosoms of nations, where they can more easily be dealt with for at least four reasons.[10] First, the people within a nation know each other and develop ties with each other regardless of their race or ethnicity, and this makes them more reluctant to want to destroy each other. This is amply exemplified in the United States, where some "Whites" have fought very hard for "Blacks" and some non-Hispanics have fought very hard for Hispanics. Indeed, the hate crimes carried out against a few Muslims by some extremists during the conflict between the United States and Afghanistan, after the bombing of the World Trade Center, were thoroughly condemned by most non-Muslims.

Second, nations live by laws, and these laws provide for ways to deal with internal strife. There is a guide, then, a basis, for the settlement of differences and conflicts of an ethnic or racial nature within many nations that is lacking at the international level. This means that, rather than resorting to the exercise of raw power and the implementation of genocide, these conflicts can be settled through the orderly application of the law.

Third, generally, nations have the means to deal effectively with social disruption, something that again is lacking at the international level, for nations usually have forces to control social unrest and crime and to prevent abuses of some members of the population by other members. In recent years, institutions such as the United Nations have acquired some means of using the force necessary to deal with international conflicts, but these are still insufficient, largely ineffective, and subject to endless wrangling among states.

Fourth, the use of force at the international level is generally seen as an intrusion into the affairs of sovereign states and, therefore, opposed by most states—witness the recent opposition to the U.S. war with Iraq. Most states do not accept the right of other states to interfere in their internal affairs, but they accept the use of force, justified by law, within a state.

From all this, it appears that it is a good thing not only to preserve the use of the notions of race, ethnicity, and nationality, but also to promote, or at least maintain, racial and ethnic diversity within nations. It is true that racial, and particularly ethnic, homogeneity may help unify a nation. After all, a common set of beliefs and values and a common history can both help to keep nations together and help them survive the many challenges, internal and external, they face throughout their histories. But the move toward homogeneity, although conducive to the amelioration of conflict within nations, transfers them to the international arena, making them much worse, for they cease to be internal conflicts subject to the laws accepted by the nation and instead become international conflagrations. Racial and ethnic homogeneity, moreover, divert attention from truly political issues having to do with the determination of ways to live under a system of laws that ensures justice and well-being for all. Furthermore, they create confusions that are difficult to disentangle. The future should be in the direction of heterogeneity within nations, but this is perhaps the only way to respond to ethnic diversity and to ensure the survival of the human species in the twenty-first century.

Let me add that the failure to distinguish between race, ethnicity, and nationality is the source not only of the evils I have mentioned earlier, but also of much discrimination and oppression. The reason is that when these concepts are combined, they compound the reasons for discrimination and oppression. It is one thing to oppress and discriminate because of race alone, but when race is combined with ethnicity matters become much worse. Then it is not just a matter of physical appearance and descent, but also of ways of living and historical familial ties. These conflicts acquire the character of ethnic feuds. And the mixing of nationality into the pot makes matters worse still, for questions of xenophobia and political organization become part of the equation.

ANSWERS TO THE GENERAL
OBJECTIONS FROM CHAPTER 1

Apart from the specific objections against the conceptions of race, ethnicity, and nationality considered in chapters 3, 4, and 5, we saw in chapter 1 five general kinds of objections directed against them: political, moral, factual, epistemological, and pragmatic. To answer these is essential if my view is going to have any credibility and prove superior to the views of Corlett, Appiah, and Miller I criticized.

My response to the political objection is to point out that some of those who support the politics of difference, and those who oppose them, make a serious mistake concerning identity when it comes to racial, ethnic, or national groups. The mistake is arguing that these types of groups have an essence that identifies them, by which it is usually meant a set of properties that unites them. Like homogenized milk, their members are thought to be the same, to have the same consistency. Moreover, because these are essential properties without which the members of the groups would not qualify as members, these properties are regarded as unchangeable.

In order for this argument to work, these groups would need to share some essential properties—say values and beliefs—that (1) identify them as such, (2) cannot be changed if the unity of the group is to be preserved, and (3) conflict with the values and beliefs required for a polity to function. These properties would be a matter of survival for the groups or for the polity. The choice, then, is either to survive with them, by overthrowing the values and beliefs of others in the polity, or completely to abandon those values and beliefs, thereby surrendering racial, ethnic, or even national identities.

Now, if the argument I have made in this book is sound, these groups have no essence and no set of common features required of them. In the case of ethnic groups, their unity, first of all, is based on historical relations that are constantly changing and therefore do not necessarily constitute either a rallying point or a threat to other ethnic groups, cultures, or a polity (for an argument along similar lines, see Young 2001, 398–400). Because of this, second, even though these groups do develop some properties at certain times and places, the groups can continue to be what they are even when their values and beliefs change, and their survival does not depend on any particular set of values and beliefs. This in turn preempts the charge that their existence necessarily threatens democracy (or any political institution in any state, for that matter), although it does not preempt the possibility that some values and beliefs more common among these groups than in the ethnic mainstream will prevail over some commonly and presently held values and beliefs. If they do, however, it will not be necessarily because ethnic minorities impose them based on a politics of difference, but it could be because those values and beliefs have become more acceptable and are perhaps more compatible with the pertinent societies than are some of the values and beliefs commonly accepted before by the mainstream.[11] However, third, my view does not preclude the possibility of conflicts in context. It is certainly possible—and it is a reality in some situations—that certain ethnic values based, for example, on religious beliefs may clash with the principles under which a particular state is organized. Clearly, to mention one, the Islamic identification of political and religious power, considered by some essential to Arabic ethnicity, can be a source of conflict in the United States, a country in which such identification is forbidden by the Constitution. The conflict can become serious if the ethnic group in question is not willing to give up the values associated with its ethnicity for the sake of national unity.[12] But if, as I have argued, ethnicity is fluid and changeable and the members of the group recognize it, there is no reason why the points of conflict cannot be eliminated by changing aspects of the particular ethnos. The ethnos need not be eliminated or assimilated as long as it is transformed to make room for the political values upheld by the state.

In the case of race, this kind of objection makes even less sense against my view. Indeed, it would make sense only if racial groups necessarily involved cultural and value features that worked against the fabric of national unity and some social values indispensable for democracy. But I have proposed that races have nothing to do with culture or values. Races concern only descent linkage and physical features. Of course, owing to the existence of certain social attitudes toward people of certain races in particular societies, these peoples have been isolated in some ways, and this in turn has led to the development of racially caused ethnicities. In these cases, then, it would not be the races but the ethnicities accompanying the races that would conflict with the unity of the polity and its democratic organization. But even in these cases, we saw that there is a response that can be given to this objection in ethnic terms.

The second kind of objection raised in chapter 1 was moral. Consider, for example, that some objected to racial, ethnic, or national categories because they claimed these result in exploitation and oppression. Further scrutiny reveals, however, that this charge is partly based on both ignorance and prejudice. That certain groups use the categories to set themselves over, and dominate and exploit, other groups in the name of purity cannot be a good reason to reject these categories. Indeed, this objection is based on a confusion also pointed out earlier. Consider the case of Hispanics. That some groups in the Southwest appropriated the term "Hispanics" and used it to distance themselves from *mestizos* and Mexican Americans, out of racist concerns, and that other groups elsewhere also have done, and still do, so for similar reasons should not be sufficient reason for us to acquiesce and give up on the notion of Hispanic. Racial, ethnic, or national purity is a myth.

None of these groups is pure in any meaningful sense of the word. So it makes very little sense to use these terms to indicate the purity of any group.

Another moral objection mentioned is that the use of these categories helps perpetuate a sense of cultural subservience of one group toward another. This may be true in some cases, but it should not deter us from using a category that can otherwise be useful and whose justification is rooted in history. Jews have learned that it is a mistake to cease to call themselves so because some, or even many, think "Jew" means something bad; likewise, Hispanics should not surrender "Hispanic" because some, or even many, mistakenly think it means Spanish. And the same should apply to other groups.

Still, some may argue that the use of racial and ethnic categories in particular is counterproductive because it is associated with negative traits. Again, that some people put the wrong spin on certain terms should not make us avoid them if those terms reflect something historically important. Indeed, I am not sure that, under these conditions, name changes are a good thing. Is a race or an ethnos going to change its name every time someone decides to use it negatively? This is in fact giving in, accepting the judgment of others and, therefore, defeat. Moreover, is not something important lost every time a name is changed? If the use of names has important implications for identity, as many think, changing a name does affect identity. Furthermore, doesn't a name change often create unnecessary division and dissension in the community whose name is being changed (Treviño 1987, 71)? This certainly has happened in the case of "Blacks"/African Americans and Hispanics/Latinos. Finally, should not these groups concentrate rather on defending the historical bases of the terms? A term such as "Jew," which makes historical sense, should be kept even if some people choose to interpret it negatively. Rather than dropping it, Jews should wear it with a certain defiance and assertion, for this eventually does more for their image than a change of name. We need to change people's attitudes toward Jews rather than acquiesce with the rules of a game imposed on them; and a name can be an effective tool in this task. Of course, this claim has to be balanced with prudential considerations. Anyone who has seen the film *Europa, Europa* realizes that there are circumstances in which concealment is necessary for survival. Heroism is praiseworthy, but it is not a moral obligation. In all these matters, the context is as important as the goal. In short, the association of negative traits with these groups should not deter us from using the corresponding categories and terms, for we can always change these associations, although there may be circumstances in which this is not possible.

Under the moral heading, it was also objected that nations are part of an archaic system in the face of increasing globalization that stands in the path of progress, world integration, and the survival of humanity and contributes to abuses and injustice.

No doubt there is considerable power in this kind of difficulty, but two considerations should be sufficient to undermine it. First, although nations may become obstacles to progress and global integration, they need not be so. Indeed, even in a globalized world, there is still need of local governments and organizations. And nations can, if nationality is properly understood, constitute the basis for the coordination of a global system of laws for the effective governance of the world. Second, nations often serve the needs of groups and regions and function effectively as instruments of understanding those needs. The issue is not nationality as such, but the kind of nationality that can be viable and appropriate in view of the world situation. It is not necessary that nations be dismantled; it is only required that nations evolve in a way consistent with the reality of the challenges we face in the twenty-first century and the diverse aspirations of humankind.

The most important moral objection to nationality posed in chapter 1 had to do with the pernicious effects that national sovereignty has had, and continues to have, on the citizens of some nations. National sovereignty ensures all kinds of internal abuses. Consider, for example, how American nationality has been used to oppress and disenfranchise certain ethnic groups in the United States. This has been possible because American nationality has been artificially constructed as an ethnicity—implying culture, values, and even religion—and then it has been used to distinguish "true Americans" from "false Americans" (Oboler 1995; Kymlicka 1997). The latter are members of ethnic groups who do not fit the mold—at one time these were the Irish and Jews; now they are Hispanics and Asians. An even more extreme case is that of Germany, where immediately before World War II, the nation identified itself with a certain racial and ethnic profile, which was in turn used to isolate and eventually exterminate millions of people who did not fit the profile (Poliakov 1974). A consideration of these facts should lead to an attempt to do away both with nations and even with the concepts of nation and nationality—so the objection goes.

There are several effective responses to this objection. We can begin by noting that, even if one were to accept that all nations are bad, from this it does not follow that we should do away with the concepts of nation and nationality. Cancer is bad, but the concept is indispensable for understanding and fighting the disease. I can understand why, if a concept is inaccurate or incoherent, one might argue against certain uses of it, but this does not entail that we should drop the concept altogether. The concept of phlogiston is inaccurate, but it has some use in the history of science, and perhaps even in science insofar as it can illustrate bad science. The concept of a square-circle is certainly incoherent, but it does much duty in philosophy.

However, if nations are indeed pernicious, it would seem to make sense to do away with them even if we keep the concept. But are nations always pernicious, and need they be so?

Clearly there is no necessity here. That there are some bad nations does not mean that all of them have to be bad. Moreover, I submit that the notion of pernicious or bad nations, namely, nations that oppress some of their members, is in fact the result of a confusion between the notions of nation and state. If a nation is conceived as I have proposed, then it does not involve a particular ethnicity or race and presumably cannot privilege one of those over the others. The aim of a nation involves both justice and the good of all its members, and this again seems to ensure that nations do not allow the unjust oppression of some of their members by others. But, of course, if nations are confused with states, then all the pernicious consequences mentioned are not only possible, but also common insofar as states may conceive of themselves as predominantly ethnic or racial and they do not necessarily include the aims of justice and well-being for all their citizens.

To this something else needs to be added. The notion of a world ruled by a system of just and effective laws is very appealing, but is it realistic? Can we really expect that in the foreseeable future humankind will come up with a just system of laws for everyone, and that it will be implemented? First of all, there is the question of justice. Human society has yet to devise a system of laws that is unambiguously just and effectively helps to bring about a just society. Moreover, the size of the institutions required for the implementation of such a system would be enormous, and judging from past experience, the system would probably be inefficient, ineffective, and mired in bureaucratic red tape. Besides, the potential for abuse tends to increase in proportion to size. In short, the issue is not easily settled, and it is certainly beyond the boundaries of the present discussion.

I make these judgments using the Political View of nation I have defended. If, as noted earlier, the notion of nation used is an ethnic or racial one, or one that necessarily includes ethnic or racial elements, then there is no doubt that nations that fit that notion must be dissolved, for their existence can lead only to conflict, both internal and external. The common idea that colonialism is responsible for the conflicts that afflict some parts of the Third World because colonial powers carved out states without regard to ethnic and racial differences assumes that it is a good thing to have states that are ethnically and racially homogeneous and divided along ethnic and racial lines. I am not going to defend colonialism, or the way colonial powers created states in the territories that once they controlled. I do not believe these are defensible causes, and their defense appears to be morally repugnant. It is quite clear that colonial powers created artificial states without nations. But their mistake was not neglecting ethnic or racial boundaries, but rather forming states without regard for nationality. Instead of helping to develop nations out of disparate ethnic and racial groups based on a common will to live under a system of laws with the aims of justice and the good of their members, they mostly drew lines on a map based on expediency and their own national or state interests.

The assumption that ethnic and racial conflict can be eliminated by having states coincide with ethnic or racial groups is quite misguided. Indeed, the result of such a policy is that ethnic and racial conflicts become international wars, and these are surely more devastating than internal conflicts in that they have at their disposal the full power of states. Just consider the never-ending Palestinian-Israeli conflict. If this conflict had been posed in political, rather than ethnic, terms, would it not have had fewer international repercussions?

Nations also have been the source of much conflict and suffering. The correction of this situation, then, requires that we refer to them. Without this notion, we cannot fight the evils that permeate human society, and without an understanding of nationality we cannot set right much that is wrong in the world, or plan for a more just future. Of course, no wrong can be set right with another wrong, so we need an appropriate and adequate understanding of nationality in order, in turn, to understand the root of much that is wrong in human society.

Of course, there is a point to the moral argument against race, ethnicity, and nationality, but it is the wrong point. For if the issue is framed in terms of morality, giving in to morally wrong attitudes is in a sense to condone them. It is foolish to eliminate knives because they can be used to murder people, and it is morally wrong to eliminate race, ethnicity, or nationality because it can be misused and cause suffering. The moral solution to atrocities committed in the name of these is not to eliminate them but to eliminate the morally wrong judgments and actions that are the cause of the atrocities. There is nothing wrong with a racial, ethnic, or national sense of kinship; what is wrong is the attitude of those who use it to oppress and abuse others.

The third kind of objection used against race, ethnicity, and nationality was factual. And here the point was that these categories are inadequate because they identify everything that is racial, ethnic, or national with homo-geneity, exploitation, and oppression. With respect to homogeneity, it is cer-tainly the case that *de facto* the use of most of these names implies homoge-neous conceptions of the groups in question. But this need not be so. Why should we have to think in this way, if there are better ways of understand-ing the meaning of these names? If we are going to discard any term in our language that is used erroneously, or that is given bad connotations by some people, we would pretty soon have to be silent. There is nothing in the use of these names and categories that requires that we think of the groups to which they refer as homogeneous, so there is no logical reason why we should abandon the use of these names and the corresponding categories. Remember what was said in chapter 2 about unwarranted inference.

The epistemic objections raised in chapter 1 were related to the diffi-culties with the identification of racial, ethnic, and national groups and their members. These objections, I trust, have been resolved by what I have said already. These groups have contextual properties that serve to discern them and their members, although their contextual nature makes clear that infer-ences about them are not apodictic, and the force of the evidence on which they are made may vary from context to context. This is not to say they are ineffective; it is merely to recognize their nature.

Those who find this objection compelling do not grasp that knowl-edge, like reality, is not all of the same sort and, therefore, that different cri-teria apply to it. Not all knowledge is of the apodictic kind characteristic of logic and mathematics because not every thing is like logical and mathe-matical entities. Their mistake is that of the skeptics who, as Aristotle pointed out, conceive all knowledge as demonstrative, not realizing that in doing so, they destroy any possibility of it.

Finally, the pragmatic objection against race, ethnicity, and nationality argued that, considering all the trouble these notions have caused, the ef-fective way in which this trouble is ignored when these divisions disappear, and the benefits of eliminating these divisions, we should simply drop them. The answer is, first, that most of the troubles thought to be caused by them are caused by something else. Second, race, ethnicity, and nationality are not easily eradicated, and efforts to do so often can be as traumatic as the trou-bles that they are thought to cause. Third, if we adopt an appropriate un-derstanding of these social phenomena, then perhaps we can eliminate the troubles without eliminating them. And fourth, the preservation of these notions has definite advantages, as we have seen. Pragmatically, then, it makes more sense to try to understand and deal with them than to attempt their elimination.

CONCLUSION

I have been talking about the issue of keeping separate the notions of groups whose unity is based on a political will to live under a system of laws, groups whose unity derives from descent links and certain genetically transmittable physical characteristics, and groups whose unity is based on historically contingent relations that give rise to particular features in particular contexts. I have called these nations, races, and ethne, respectively. But the names are not of the essence. Whether what I call nations are called ethne by someone else, or what I call ethne are called races by someone else, is not the issue. The terminology used is not what matters, although not defining one's terms can lead to unproductive confusion. The essential thing is to keep these different types of groups separate conceptually so that we can adjudicate among the various issues that arise with respect to them. Many authors today prefer to speak of what I call ethne as nations, and this is harmless, provided that they do not go on also to attach political dimensions to these groups. And the same could be said about race. The key is to distinguish between the notions of groups united by a political will to live under a system of laws, groups united by familial-historical ties, and groups united by descent and some physically perspicuous features that are genetically transmittable and associated with the group.

The view I have proposed is a viable and comprehensive alternative to the ideas about race, ethnicity, and nationality presented at the beginning of this chapter. Moreover, it provides an explanation of the complex relations between race, ethnicity, and nationality, and of why they tend to be confused or identified with each other. This does not mean that it should be taken as the final word on these topics or that it has no shortcomings. It means only that it is a first step in the right direction, an attempt at presenting a whole and consistent picture of race, ethnicity, and nationality that avoids the counterproductive ideas mentioned, as well as their consequences, rather than dealing in an isolated and piecemeal fashion with just a few of the many issues that are raised by these phenomena.

This view of race, ethnicity, and nationality is incomplete in some important respects, owing to the limitations imposed by space, time, and the shortcomings of my own understanding. I have generally left out topics dealing with ethics and politics, for example, in order to devote more space to, and deal more effectively with, metaphysical and epistemological matters. The latter two seemed to be in more need of discussion because they constitute the foundation of the former two and they have more often been neglected in the literature. Sociologists, psychologists, ethicists, political scientists, and social philosophers are naturally impressed by the need to answer questions that immediately affect the well-being of human society, and these generally do not have to do with metaphysics or epistemology. These authors often forget, however, that much of what they do takes for granted metaphysical and epistemological assumptions that go unquestioned and nevertheless affect in important ways the conclusions they reach.

Elsewhere, I have presented an extended argument to the effect that metaphysics consists of the investigation of the most general categories about which we can think, of their interrelations, and of the relation of less general categories to them (Gracia 1999a). The provinces of particular disciplines concern the study of less general categories and their interrelations. Whether we know it or not, insofar as less general categories presuppose more general ones, everything we conclude in specialized fields concerning the former presupposes, and relies on, the latter. Hence, whether we are aware of it or not, all we do in the field of human learning implies a metaphysics, and this makes metaphysics inevitable. Depth in understanding, then, requires that we uncover and critically examine the metaphysical assumptions and commitments presupposed by our more specific views. It also requires that we attempt to put all our knowledge together into a coherent picture that makes sense based on a metaphysical analysis. This is one of the reasons why I have given priority to metaphysics in this book.

To epistemology, I have also given considerable space because the development of the consistent, overall view I have presented requires the critical examination of what we know or think we know. Metaphysics and epistemology go hand in hand, even if their spheres of inquiry are not the same.

Unfortunately, most authors who have dealt with race, ethnicity, and nationality neglect metaphysical and epistemological questions, and some have gone so far as to downplay them or even reject them as useless or illegitimate. We need think only of nineteenth-century positivists, early twentieth-century logical positivists, and recent postmodernists as examples. The results of these attitudes are quite evident in the history of human thought: conceptual confusions of an elementary sort, shoddy thinking, and inferences biased by unexamined assumptions. Indeed, many of the confusions mentioned in chapter 2 of this book are common fare in these discussions.

Have I succeeded in the task I set out to accomplish? I hope to this extent: that I have made clear how the metaphysics and epistemology of race, ethnicity, and nationality are essential to a proper understanding of them and that I have provided a blueprint—however inadequate and incomplete—for future analyses of this sort.

With respect to the value of the views I propose, that is for readers to judge. I shall feel satisfied if I see an increase in the number of discussions of these topics as a result of the publication of this book, for race, ethnicity, and nationality together pose one of the greatest challenges to the twenty-first century. It is essential, then, that we understand them better. In order for humanity to meet this challenge effectively and survive, the notions of race, ethnicity, and nationality must also survive, but they must do so in conceptions that are appropriate to resolve the many problems that they pose and we need to address.

NOTES

1. Copp (1997) has in fact argued that for culturally unified groups to have the right of self-determination, that is, of forming states, is antidemocratic.

2. I discuss this phenomenon in Gracia (forthcoming-a).

3. On November 10, 1975, the United Nations General Assembly voted to adopt resolution 3379, according to which "Zionism is a form of racism and racial discrimination" (see Banton 1983, 1).

4. For the use of the verb "racialize," see Banton (1977, 27–62); Miles (1989, 73–77); and Hudson (1996, 259).

5. For the role of tradition in the identity of groups, including national ones, see Gracia (2003).

6. Eriksen points out that the distinguishing mark of nationalism is the view that "political boundaries should be coterminus with cultural [i.e., ethnic, for him] boundaries" (Eriksen 1997, 35). And Treitschke (1914) argues for the need to unite states under nationality, which he conceives ethnically.

7. Many authors argue that the aim to create a state that represents the nation is essential to nations and a nationalist spirit (Smith 2000, 494). Buchanan has proposed a list of conditions in which ethnic groups seek secession from a state (Buchanan 1991, 152–53). And A. D. Smith (1986) has explored the ethnic origins of nations.

8. The nefarious consequences of these confusions have not escaped some authors. See, for example, Hudson (1996, 258–59).

9. The father of international law is Francisco de Vitoria, who flourished in the sixteenth century. See Reichberg (2003).

10. O'Leary and McGarry (1995) have begun the process of charting and evaluating various ways of managing group conflicts, particularly ethnic ones, within nations.

11. Gooding-Williams has suggested some minimal conditions that do not interfere with democratic ideals (Gooding-Williams 2001b, 250).

12. This attitude is not uncommon. See Modood (2001, 242).

BIBLIOGRAPHY

Abalos, David T. (1986). *Latinos in the United States: The Sacred and the Political*. Notre Dame, IN: University of Notre Dame Press.

Aboud, F. E. (1987). "The Development of Ethnic Self-Identification and Attitudes." In *Children's Ethnic Socialization*, ed. J. S. Phinney and M. J. Rotheram, 32–55. Newbury Park, CA: Sage.

Acosta-Belén, Edna, ed. (1986). *The Puerto Rican Woman: Perspectives on Culture, History, and Society*. 2nd ed. New York: Praeger.

Acosta-Belén, Edna, and Barbara Sjostrom, eds. (1988). *The Hispanic Experience in the United States: Contemporary Issues and Perspectives*. New York: Praeger.

Addams, Jane. (1910). *Twenty Years at Hull-House with Autobiographical Notes*. New York: Macmillan.

Alcoff, Linda Martín. (2005). "Latino vs. Hispanic: The Politics of Ethnic Names." *Philosophy and Social Criticism* 31, 4.

———. (2001). "Toward a Phenomenology of Racial Embodiment." In *Race*, ed. Robert Bernasconi, 267–83. Oxford: Blackwell.

———. (2000a). "Is Latina/o Identity a Racial Identity?" In *Hispanics/Latinos in the United States: Ethnicity, Race, and Rights*, ed. Jorge J. E. Gracia and Pablo De Greiff, 23–44. New York: Routledge.

———. (2000b). "On Judging Epistemic Credibility: Is Social Identity Relevant?" In *Women of Color and Philosophy: A Critical Reader*, ed. Naomi Zack, 255–61. Oxford: Blackwell.

———. (2000c). "Who's Afraid of Identity Politics?" In *Reclaiming Identity: Realist Theory and the Predicament of Postmodernism*, ed. Paula M. L. Moya and Michael R. Hames-García, 312–44. Berkeley: University of California Press.

———. (1999). "Philosophy and Racial Identity." In *Ethnic and Racial Studies Today*, ed. Martin Bulmer and John Solomos, 29–44. London: Routledge.

———. (1995). "*Mestizo* Identity." In *American Mixed Race: The Culture of Microdiversity*, ed. Naomi Zack, 257–58. Lanham, MD: Rowman & Littlefield.

Allen, Anita L. (2000). "Interracial Marriage: Folk Ethics in Contemporary Philosophy." In *Women of Color and Philosophy: A Critical Reader*, ed. Naomi Zack, 182–205. Oxford: Blackwell.

Allen, T. (1994). *The Invention of the White Race: Volume One: Racial Oppression and Social Control*. London: Verso.

Andersen, Margaret, and Patricia Hill Collins, eds. (2001). *Race, Class, and Gender: An Anthology*. Belmont, CA: Wadsworth.

Anderson, Benedict. (1997). "The Nation and the Origins of National Consciousness." In *The Ethnicity Reader: Nationalism, Multiculturalism and Migration*, ed. M. Guibernau and J. Rex, 43–51. Cambridge: Polity.

———. (1990). *Imagined Communities: Reflections on the Origin and Spread of Nationalism*. London: Verso Editions. Original publ. 1983.

Anzaldúa, Gloria. (1987). *Borderlands/La Frontera: The New Mestiza*. San Francisco: Spinsters/Aunt Lute.

Appiah, Kwame Anthony. (2004). *The Ethics of Identity*. Princeton, NJ: Princeton University Press.

———. (2001). "African Identities." In *Race and Racism*, ed. Bernard Boxill, 371–82. Oxford: Oxford University Press.

———. (1996). "Race, Culture, Identity: Misunderstood Connections." In *Color Conscious: The Political Morality of Race*, ed. Kwame Anthony Appiah and Amy Gutmann, 30–105. Princeton, NJ: Princeton University Press.

———. (1992). *In My Father's House: Africa in the Philosophy of Culture*. New York: Oxford University Press.

———. (1990a). "'But Would That Still Be Me?' Notes on Gender, 'Race,' Ethnicity, as Sources of 'Identity.'" *Journal of Philosophy* 87: 493–99.

———. (1990b). "Racisms." In *Anatomy of Racism*, ed. D. T. Goldberg, 3–17. Minneapolis: University of Minnesota Press.

———. (1985). "The Uncompleted Argument: Du Bois and the Illusion of Race." *Critical Inquiry* 12, no. 1: 21–37. Reprinted in Henry Louis Gates Jr., ed. (1986). *Race, Writing and Difference*. Chicago, IL: University of Chicago Press; also in Robert Bernasconi and Tommy L. Lott, eds. (2000). *The Idea of Race*. Indianapolis: Hackett, 118–35.

Appiah, K. Anthony, and Amy Gutmann. (1996). *Color Conscious: The Political Morality of Race*. Princeton, NJ: Princeton University Press.

Archibugi, Daniele, David Held, and Martin Köhler, eds. (1998). *Re-Imagining Political Communities*. Oxford: Polity.

Aristotle. (1984). *The Complete Works of Aristotle*. 2 vols., ed. Jonathan Barnes. Princeton, NJ: Princeton University Press.

Augstein, Hannah F., ed. (1996). *Race: The Origins of an Idea. 1760–1850*. Bristol, England: Thoemmes.

Ayer, A. J. (1936). *Language, Truth and Logic*. New York: Dover.

Babbitt, S. E., and S. Campbell, eds. (1999). *Racism and Philosophy*. Ithaca, NY: Cornell University Press.

Baker, Lee D. (1998). *From Savage to Negro: Anthropology and the Construction of Race, 1896–1954*. Berkeley: University of California Press.

Balibar, Étienne. (1997). "'Class Racism.'" In *The Ethnicity Reader: Nationalism, Multiculturalism and Migration*, ed. M. Guibernau and J. Rex, 318–29. Cambridge: Polity.

Balibar, Étienne, and Immanuel Wallerstein. (1988). *Race, nation, class, les identités ambiguës*. Paris: La Découverte.

Bambrough, R. (1960–61). "Universals and Family Resemblances." *Proceedings of the Aristotelian Society* 61: 207–222.

Banton, Michael. (1998). "Race, Theories of." In *Routledge Encyclopedia of Philosophy*, ed. Edward Craig, vol. 8: 18–21. London: Routledge.

———. (1987a). "The Classification of Races in Europe and North America: 1700–1850." *International Social Science Journal* 39, no. 1: 45–60.

———. (1987b). *Racial Theories*. Cambridge: Cambridge University Press.

———. (1983). *Racial and Ethnic Competition*. Cambridge: Cambridge University Press.

———. (1977). *The Idea of Race*. London: Tavistock.

———. (1970). "The Concept of Racism." In *Race and Racialism*, ed. Sami Zubaida, 17–34. New York: Barnes & Noble.

———. (1967). *Race Relations*. London: Tavistock.

Banton, Michael, and Robert Miles. (1988). "Racism." In *Dictionary of Race and Ethnic Relations*, ed. E. Ellis. 2nd ed. Cashmore. London: Routledge.

Barker, Martin. (1981). *The New Racism*. London: Junction.

Barth, Fredrick, ed. (1969). *Ethnic Groups and Boundaries: The Social Organization of Culture Difference*. Oslo: Universitetsforlaget.

Baumeister, R. (1986). *Identity: Cultural Change and the Struggle for Self*. Oxford: Oxford University Press.

Bell, B., E. R. Grosholz, and J. B. Stewart. (1996). *W. E. B. Du Bois on Race and Culture*. New York: Routledge.

Belliotti, Raymond A. (1995). *Seeking Identity: Individualism versus Community in an Ethnic Context*. Lawrence: University Press of Kansas.

Benn, Stanley I. (1967). "Nationalism." In *The Encyclopedia of Philosophy*, ed. Paul Edwards, vol. 5: 442–45. New York: Macmillan.

Bernal, Martha E., and George P. Knight, eds. (1993). *Ethnic Identity: Formation and Transmission among Hispanics and Other Minorities*. Albany: State University of New York Press.

Bernal, Martin. (1987). *Black Athena*. New Brunswick, NJ: Rutgers University Press.

Bernasconi, Robert. (2002). "Kant as an Unfamiliar Source of Racism." In *Philosophers on Race: Critical Studies*, ed. T. Lott and J. Ward, 161–81. Oxford: Blackwell.

———. (2001a). "The Invisibility of Racial Minorities in the Public Realm of Appearances." In *Race*, ed. Robert Bernasconi, 284–99. Oxford: Blackwell.

———, ed. (2001b). *Race*. Oxford: Blackwell.

———. (2001c). "Who Invented the Concept of Race? Kant's Role in the Enlightenment Construction of Race." In *Race*, ed. Robert Bernasconi, 11–36. Oxford: Blackwell.

Bernasconi, Robert, and Tommy L. Lott, eds. (2000a). *The Idea of Race*. Indianapolis: Hackett.

———. (2000b). "Introduction." In *The Idea of Race*, ed. Robert Bernasconi and Tommy L. Lott, vii–xviii. Indianapolis: Hackett.

Bernier, François. (2000). "A New Dimension of the Earth." From *Journal des Scavans* (April 24, 1684). Trans. T. Bendyshe. In *The Idea of Race*, ed. Robert Bernasconi and Tommy L. Lott, 1–4. Bloomington, IN: Hackett.

Bernstein, Richard. (2001). "Comment on *Hispanic/Latino Identity* by J. J. E. Gracia." *Philosophy and Social Criticism* 27, no. 2: 44–50.

Berreman, G. (1972). "Race, Caste and Other Invidious Distinctions in Social Stratifications." *Race* 13: 385–414.

Bhavnani, Kum-Kum. (1994). "Tracing the Contours: Feminist Research and Feminist Objectivity." In *The Dynamics of 'Race' and Gender: Some Feminist Interventions*, ed. H. Afshar and M. Maynard, 26–40. London: Taylor & Francis.

Bhavnani, Kum-Kum, and Angela Y. Davis. (2000). "Women in Prison: Researching Race in Three National Contexts." In *Racing Research, Researching Race: Methodological Dilemmas in Critical Race Studies*, ed. France Winddance Twine and Jonathan W. Warren, 227–45. New York: New York University Press.

Block, Ned. (2001). "How Heritability Misleads about Race." In *Race and Racism*, ed. Bernard Boxill, 114–15. Oxford: Oxford University Press.

Block, N. D., and G. Dworkin. (1976). *The IQ Controversy*. New York: Pantheon.

Blum, L. (2002). *"I'm Not Racist, But. . . ."* Ithaca, NY: Cornell University Press.

———. (1999). "Ethnicity, Identity, and Community." In *Justice and Caring: The Search for Common Ground*, 127–45. New York: Teachers College.

Blumenbach, Johann Friedrich. (2000). *On the Natural Variety of Mankind*. Trans. Thomas Bendyshe. In *The Idea of Race*, ed. Robert Bernasconi and Tommy L. Lott, 27–37. Bloomington, IN: Hackett.

Boas, Franz. (2000). "Instability of Human Types." In *The Idea of Race*, ed. Robert Bernasconi and Tommy Lott, 84–88. Indianapolis, IN: Hackett.

Boethius. (1968). *The Theological Tractates*. Cambridge, MA: Harvard University Press.

Bonnett, Alastair. (1999). "Construction of 'Race,' Place and Discipline: Geographies of 'Racial' Identity and Racism." In *Ethnic and Racial Studies Today*, ed. Martin Bulmer and John Solomos, 136–51. London: Routledge.

Bougainville, Louis de. (1967). *A Voyage Round the World*. Ridgewood, NJ: Gregg.

Boxill, Bernard. (2001a). "Introduction." In *Race and Racism*, ed. Bernard Boxill, 1–42. Oxford: Oxford University Press.

———, ed. (2001b). *Race and Racism*. Oxford: Oxford University Press.

Boyd, W. C. (1963). "Genetics and the Human Race." *Science* 140: 1057.

Bracken, H. M. (1978). "Philosophy on Racism." *Philosophia* 8, no. 2–3: 241–60.

———. (1973). "Essence, Accident, and Race." *Hermathema* 116: 81–95.

Brennan, Andrew. (1988). *Conditions of Identity: A Study of Identity and Survival*. Oxford: Clarendon.

Brentano, Franz. (1981). *The Theory of Categories*. Trans. R. M. Chisholm and N. Gutterman. The Hague: Nijhoff.

Breton, Albert, Gianluigi Galeotti, Pierre Salmon, and Ronald Wintrobe, eds. (1995). *Nationalism and Rationality*. Cambridge: Cambridge University Press.

Brewer, Robert E., and Marilyn Brewer. (1971). "Expressed Evaluation toward a Social Object as a Function of Label." *Journal of Social Psychology* 84: 257–60.

Brown, Jennifer I. (2002). "Power Struggle Between Two Seminole Indian Chiefs Centers on Race." *Buffalo News*, May 11, A-6.

Brown, Michael E. (1997). "Causes and Implications of Ethnic Conflict." In *The Ethnicity Reader: Nationalism, Multiculturalism and Migration*, ed. M. Guibernau and J. Rex, 80–99. Cambridge: Polity.

Buchanan, Allen. (1995). "The Morality of Secession." In *The Rights of Minority Cultures*, ed. Will Kymlicka, 350–74. Oxford: Oxford University Press.

———. (1991). *Secession: The Morality of Political Divorce from Fort Sumter to Lithuania and Quebec*. Boulder, CO: Westview.

Bulmer, Martin, and John Solomos, eds. (1999). *Ethnic and Racial Studies Today*. London: Routledge.

Butler, Judith. (2001). "Conversational Break: A Reply to Robert Gooding-Williams." In *Race*, Robert Bernasconi, 260–64. Oxford: Blackwell.

———. (1990). *Gender Trouble: Feminism and the Subversion of Identity*. London: Routledge.

Butler, R. E. (1986). *On Creating a Hispanic America: A Nation within a Nation?* Special Report, Washington, DC: Council for Inter-American Security.

Cafferty, Pastora San Juan, and William C. McCready, eds. (1985). *Hispanics in the United States: A New Social Agenda*. New Brunswick, NJ: Transaction.

Calderón, F. (1995). "Latin American Identity and Mixed Temporalities; or, How to Be Postmodern and Indian at the Same Time." In *The Postmodernism Debate in Latin America*, ed. J. Beverly, J. Oviedo, and M. Aronna, 55–64. Durham, NC: Duke University Press.

Card, C. (1995). "On Race, Racism, and Ethnicity." In *Overcoming Racism and Sexism*, ed. L. A. Bell and D. Blumenfeld, 141–52. Lanham, MD: Rowman & Littlefield.

Carter, Bob. (2000). *Realism and Racism: Concepts of Race in Sociological Research*. London: Routledge.

Cashmore, E. (1988). *Dictionary of Race and Ethnic Relations*. London: Routledge.

Cashmore, E., and B. Troyna. (1990). *Introduction to Race Relations*. Basingstoke: Farmer.

Castoriadis, Cornelius. (1992). "Reflections on Racism." *Thesis Eleven* 32: 1–12.

Cavalli-Sforza, L. L. (1977). *Elements of Human Genetics*. Menlo Park, CA: Benjamin.

Cavalli-Sforza, L. Luka, et al. (1994). *The History and Geography of Human Genes*. Princeton, NJ: Princeton University Press.

Chapman, Malcolm, Maryon McDonald, and Elizabeth Tonkin. (1989). "Introduction: History and Social Anthropology." In *History and Ethnicity*, ed. Elizabeth Tonkin, Maryon McDonald, and Malcolm Chapman, 1–21. London: Routledge.

Cohen, Roger. (2001). "How Open to Immigrants Should Germany Be? An Uneasy Country's Debate Deepens." *New York Times International*, May 13.

Cohen, Phil. (1999a). "Through a Glass Darkly: Intellectuals on Race." In *New Ethnicities, Old Racism?* ed. Phil Cohen, 1–17. London: Zed.

———, ed. (1999b). *New Ethnicities, Old Racism?* London: Zed.

Collins, F. (1997). *Social Reality.* New York: Routledge.

Collins, Patricia Hill. (1991). *Black Feminist Thought: Knowledge, Consciousness, and the Politics of Empowerment.* New York: Routledge.

Connolly, William. (1991). *Identity/Difference: Democratic Negotiations of Political Paradox.* Ithaca, NY: Cornell University Press.

Connor, Walker. (1992). "The Nation and Its Myth." In *Ethnicity and Nationalism*, ed. Anthony D. Smith, 48–57. Leiden, Netherlands: Brill.

Coon, C. S. (1965). *The Living Races of Man.* New York: Knopf.

———. (1962). *The Origin of Races.* New York: Knopf.

Copp, David. (1997). "Democracy and Communal Self-Determination." In *The Morality of Nationalism*, ed. Robert McKim and Jeff McMahan, 277–300. Oxford: Oxford University Press.

Corlett, J. Angelo. (2003). *Race, Racism, and Reparations.* Ithaca, NY: Cornell University Press.

———. (2001). "Latino/a Identity." *APA Newsletter on Hispanic/Latino Issues in Philosophy* (Fall): 97–104.

———. (2000). "Latino Identity and Affirmative Action." In *Hispanics/Latinos in the United States: Ethnicity, Race, and Rights*, ed. Jorge J. E. Gracia and Pablo De Greiff, 223–34. New York: Routledge.

———. (1999). "Latino Identity." *Public Affairs Quarterly* 13, no. 3: 273–95.

———. (1998). "Analyzing Racism." *Public Affairs Quarterly* 12, no. 1: 23–50.

———. (1997). "Parallels of Ethnicity and Gender." In *Race/Sex: Their Sameness, Difference and Interplay*, ed. Naomi Zack, 83–93. New York: Routledge.

Count, Earl W., ed. (1950). *This Is Race: An Anthology Selected from the International Literature on the Races of Man.* New York: Henry Shuman.

Cox, Oliver C. (1970). *Caste, Class, and Race: A Study in Social Dynamics.* New York: Modern Reader.

Dane, Leila, F. (1997). "Ethnic Identity and Conflict Transformation." *Peace Review* 9, no. 4: 503–7.

Darwin, Charles. (1874). "On the Races of Man." In *The Descent of Man, and Selection in Relation to Sex*, 189–233. New York: A. L. Burt Co.

Davis, F. J. (1991). *Who Is Black? One Nation's Definition.* University Park: Pennsylvania State University Press.

Davis, C., et al. (1988). "U.S. Hispanics: Changing the Face of America." In *The Hispanic Experience in the United States: Contemporary Issues and Perspectives*, ed. E. Acosta-Belén and B. R. Sojstrom, 3–78. New York: Praeger.

Davis, M. (1983). "Race as Merit." *Mind* 92: 347–67.

Dawkins, Richard. (1982). *The Extended Phenotype.* San Francisco: Freeman.

———. (1976). *The Selfish Gene*. Oxford: Oxford University Press.

De Greiff, Pablo. (2000). "Deliberation and Hispanic Representation." In *Hispanics/Latinos in the United States: Ethnicity, Race, and Rights*, ed. Jorge J. E. Gracia and Pablo De Greiff, 235–52. New York: Routledge.

Delgado, Richard, and Jean Stefancic, eds. (1995). *Critical Race Theory: The Cutting Edge*. Philadelphia: Temple University Press.

Deloria, Vine, and Clifford Lytle. (1984). *Two Nations Within*. New York: Pantheon.

Deutsch, K. W. (1966). *Nationalism and Social Communication*. Cambridge, MA: MIT Press.

Diamond, Jared. (1994). "Race without Color." *Discover* 15, no. 11 (November): 82–89.

Dikötter, Frank. (2002). "Race in China." In *A Companion to Race and Ethnicity*, ed. D. T. Goldberg and J. Solomos, 495–510. Oxford: Blackwell.

Dinnerstein, Leonard, and David M. Reimers. (1975). *Ethnic Americans: A History of Immigration and Assimilation*. New York: Dodd, Mead & Co.

Donald, James, and Ali Rattansi, eds. (1992). *"Race," Culture and Difference*. London: Sage/Open University Press.

D'Souza, D. (1995). "Is Racism a Western Idea?" *American Scholar* (Autumn): 517–39.

Du Bois, W. E. B. (1976). *The World and Africa*. Millwood, NY: Kraus-Thomas Organization.

———. (1970). "The Conservation of Races." In *W. E. B. Du Bois Speaks: Speeches and Addresses 1890–1919*, ed. Philip S. Foner, 73–85. New York: Pathfinders.

———. (1968). *The Health and Physique of the Negro American. Report of a Social Study Made under the Direction of Atlanta University; Together with the Proceedings of the Eleventh Conference for the Study of the Negro Problems, Held at Atlanta University, on May the 29th, 1906*. Reprinted in *Atlanta University Publications (Numbers 7–11–1902–1906)*, vol. II. New York: Octagon.

———. (1940). *Dusk of Dawn: An Essay toward an Autobiography of a Race Concept*. New York: Harcourt Brace. Reprinted in 1975 by Kraus-Thomson, Millwood, NY.

———. (1897). *The Conservation of Races*. American Negro Academy Occasional Papers, no. 2. Washington, DC: American Negro Academy, 5–15. Reprinted in *Race*, ed. Robert Bernasconi, 84–92. Oxford: Blackwell.

Dummett, Ann. (1984). *A Portrait of English Racism*. Manchester: CARAF.

Dumont, Louis. (2001). "Caste, Racism and 'Stratification': Reflections of a Social Anthropologist." In *Race*, ed. Robert Bernasconi, 218–34. Oxford: Blackwell.

Dunn, L. C. (1975). "Race and Biology." In *Race, Science, and Society*, ed. L. Kuper, 31–67. Paris: UNESCO Press; New York: Columbia University Press.

Durkheim, É. (1987). *Émile Durkheim: Selected Writings*, ed. A. Giddens. Cambridge: Cambridge University Press.

———. (1986). "A Debate on Nationalism and Patriotism." Trans. W. D. Halls. In *Durkheim on Politics and the State*, ed. A. Giddens, 205–211. Stanford, CA: Stanford University Press.

Dyer, Richard. (1997). *White*. New York: Routledge.

Elshtein, Jean Bethke. (1995). *Democracy on Trial*. New York: Basic.

Engels, F. (1952). "Hungary and Panslavism." In K. Marx and F. Engels, *The Russian Menace to Europe*, ed. P. Blackstock and B. Hoselitz. Glencoe, IL: Free Press.

Epstein, Steven. (1987). "Gay Politics, Ethnic Identity: The Limits of Social Constructionism." *Socialists Review* 17: 54.

Eriksen, Thomas Hylland. (1997). "Ethnicity, Race, and Nation." In *The Ethnicity Reader: Nationalism, Multiculturalism and Migration*, ed. M. Guibernau and J. Rex, 33–42. Cambridge: Polity.

———. (1993). *Ethnicity and Nationalism: Anthropological Perspectives*. London: Pluto.

Eze, Emmanuel, ed. (1997). *Race and the Enlightenment: A Reader*. Oxford: Blackwell.

———. (1995). "The Color of Reason: The Idea of 'Race' in Kant's Anthropology." In *Anthropology and the German Enlightenment: Perspectives on Humanity*, ed. Katherine M. Faull. Lewisburg, PA: Bucknell University Press.

Ezorsky, Gertrude. (1991). *Racism and Justice*. Ithaca, NY: Cornell University Press.

Fairchild, H. H., and J. A. Cozens. (1981). "Chicano, Hispanic or Mexican American: What's in a Name?" *Hispanic Journal of Behavioral Sciences* 3: 191–98.

Fanon, Frantz. (2001). "The Lived Experience of the Black." In *Race*, ed. Robert Bernasconi, 184–202. Oxford: Blackwell.

———. (1967). *Black Skin, White Masks*. New York: Grove.

Fernández, Carlos A. (1992). "*La Raza* and the Melting Pot: A Comparative Look at Multiethnicity." In *Racially Mixed People in America*, ed. Maria P. P. Root, 126–43. Newbury Park, CA: Sage.

Fichte, J. G. (1979). *Addresses to the German Nation*. Westport, CT: Greenwood.

Flynn, J. R. (1987a). "Massive I.Q. Gains in 14 Nations: What I.Q. Tests Really Measure." *Psychological Bulletin* 101, no. 2: 171–91.

———. (1987b). "Race and IQ: Jensen's Case Refuted." In *Arthur Jensen: Consensus and Controversy*, ed. S. Modgil and C. Modgil, 221–32. London: Falmer International.

Fox, Geoffrey. (1996). *Hispanic Culture, Politics, and the Constructing of Identity*. New York: Carol.

Francis, E. K. (1976). *Interethnic Relations*. New York: Elsevier.

Frankenberg, Ruth. (1993). *White Women, Race Matters: The Social Construction of Whiteness*. Minneapolis: University of Minnesota Press.

Fraser, S. (1995). *The Bell Curve Wars*. New York: Basic.

Fuss, Diana. (1980). *Essentially Speaking: Feminism, Nature and Difference*. New York: Routledge.

Galton, Francis. (2000). "Eugenics: Its Definition, Scope, and Aims." In *Essays in Eugenics. Read Before the Sociological Society at a Meeting in the School of Economics and Political Science of London University, on May 16th, 1904*. Reprinted in *The Idea of Race*, ed. R. Bernasconi and T. L. Lott, 79–83. Indianapolis: Hackett.

García, Jorge. (forthcoming). "Racism in Social Behavior, Judgment, and Vice." In *Racism, Philosophy, and Mind*, ed. Michael Levine and Tamas Pataki. Ithaca, NY: Cornell University Press.

———. (2001a). "Is Being Hispanic an Identity? Reflections on J. J. E. Gracia's Account." *Philosophy and Social Criticism* 27, no. 2: 29–43.

———. (2001b). "Concepts of Racism." In *Encyclopedia of Ethics*, ed. Lawrence Becker and Charlotte Becker, vol. 3: 1437–40. New York: Routledge.

———. (2001c). "Racism and Racial Discourse." *Philosophical Forum* 32, no. 2: 125–45.

———. (1999a). "Philosophical Analysis and the Moral Concept of Racism." *Philosophy and Social Criticism* 25, no. 5: 1–32.

———. (1999b). "Racism." In *Cambridge Dictionary of Philosophy*, ed. Robert Audi, 769. 2nd ed. Cambridge: Cambridge University Press.

———. (1997a). "Current Conceptions of Racism: A Critical Examination of Some Recent Social Philosophy." *Journal of Social Philosophy* 28, no. 2: 5–42.

———. (1997b). "Racism as Model for Understanding Sexism." In *Race/Sex: Their Sameness, Difference and Interplay*, ed. Naomi Zack, 45–59. New York: Routledge.

———. (1996). "The Heart of Racism." *Journal of Social Philosophy* 27, no. 1: 5–45.

———. (1992). "African-American Perspectives, Cultural Relativism, and Normative Issues: Some Conceptual Questions." In *African-American Perspectives in Biomedical Ethics*, ed. Harley E. Flack and Edmund D. Pellegrino, 44–54. Washington, DC: Georgetown University Press.

Garn, Stanley M. (1993). "Modern Human Populations." In *The New Encyclopedia Britannica*, vol. 18: 844–54. Chicago: Encyclopedia Britannica.

———. (1971). *Human Races*. Springfield, IL: Charles C. Thomas.

Geertz, Clifford. (1973). *The Interpretation of Cultures*. New York: Basic.

Gellner, Ernest. (1997). "Nationalism as a Product of Industrial Society." In *The Ethnicity Reader: Nationalism, Multiculturalism and Migration*, ed. M. Guibernau and J. Rex, 52–69. Cambridge: Polity.

———. (1983). *Nations and Nationalism*. Oxford: Blackwell.

George, David. (1996). "National Identity and Self-Determination." In *National Rights, International Obligations*, ed. Simon Caney, David George, and Peter Jones, 13–33. Boulder, CO: Westview.

Giddens, A. (1985). *The Nation-State and Violence*. Cambridge: Polity.

Gilroy, Paul. (1993). *The Black Atlantic: Modernity and Double Consciousness*. Cambridge, MA: Harvard University Press.

Gil-White, Francisco J. (2001a). "Sorting Is Not Categorization: A Critique of the Claim that Brazilians Have Fuzzy Racial Categories." *Cognition and Culture* 1, no. 3: 1–23.

———. (2001b). "Are Ethnic Groups Biological 'Species' to the Human Brain? Essentialism in Our Cognition of Some Social Categories." *Current Anthropology* 42, no. 4: 515–54.

———. (1999). "How Thick Is Blood? The Plot Thickens . . . : If Ethnic Actors Are Primordialists, What Remains of the Circumstantialist/Primordialist Controversy?" *Ethnic and Racial Studies* 22, no 5: 789–820.

Giménez, Martha. (1989). "'Latino?/Hispanic'—Who Needs a Name? The Case against a Standardized Terminology." *International Journal of Health Services* 19, no. 3: 557–71.

Glavanis, Pandeli. (2002). "The Salience of Ethnoreligious Identities in the Middle East: An Interpretation." In *A Companion to Race and Ethnicity*, ed. D. T. Goldberg and J. Solomos, 521–37. Oxford: Blackwell.

Glazer, Nathan. (1996). "The Hard Questions: Race for the Cure." *New Republic* (October 7): 29.

———. (1995). "Individual Rights against Group Rights." In *The Rights of Minority Cultures*, ed. Will Kymlicka, 123–38. Oxford: Oxford University Press.

———. (1982). "Government and the American Ethnic Pattern." In *Ethnicity and Public Policy*, ed. Winston A. Van Horne, 24–41. Milwaukee: University of Wisconsin.

Glazer, Nathan, and Daniel P. Moynihan. (1963). *Beyond the Melting Pot: The Negroes, Puerto Ricans, Jews, Italians, and Irish of New York City.* Cambridge, MA: MIT. Press.

———, eds. (1975). *Ethnicity: Theory and Experience.* Cambridge, MA: Harvard University Press.

Gleason, P. (1992). "Identifying Identity: A Semantic History." In *Speaking of Diversity: Language and Ethnicity in Twentieth-Century America*, 123–49. Baltimore, MD: Johns Hopkins University Press.

Gleditsch, Nils Petter, Peter Wallensteen, Mikael Eriksson, Margareta Sollenberg, and Håvard Strand. (2002). "Armed Conflict 1946–2001: A New Dataset." *Journal of Peace Research* 39, no. 5: 615–37.

Gobineau, Comte Arthur de. (2000). *The Inequality of Human Races, [1853–55].* Trans. Collins Adrian. In *The Idea of Race*, ed. Robert Bernasconi and Tommy L. Lott, 45–53. Bloomington, IN: Hackett.

Goldberg, David T. (1999). "Racism and Rationality: The Need for a New Critique." In *Racism*, ed. Leonard Harris, 369–97. Amherst, NY: Humanities Press.

———. (1994). "Racial Exclusions," *Philosophical Forum* 26: 21–32.

———. (1993). *Racist Culture: Philosophy and the Politics of Meaning.* Oxford: Blackwell.

———. (1992). "The Semantics of Race." *Ethnic and Racial Studies* 15: 543–69.

Goldberg, David T., and John Solomos, eds. (2002). *A Companion to Racial and Ethnic Studies.* Oxford: Blackwell.

Gomberg, Paul. (1990). "Patriotism Is Like Racism," *Ethics* 101: 144–50.

González, Justo L. (1992). "Hispanics in the United States." *Listening: Journal of Religion and Culture* 27, no. 1: 7–16.

Gooding-Williams, Robert. (2001a). "Comment on J. J. E. Gracia's *Hispanic/Latino Identity.*" *Philosophy and Social Criticism* 27, no. 2: 3–10.

———. (2001b). "Race, Multiculturalism and Democracy." In *Race*, ed. Robert Bernasconi, 237–59. Oxford: Blackwell.

Gordon, L. (1995). *Bad Faith and Antiblack Racism.* Atlantic Highlands, NJ: Humanities Press.

Gordon, Milton. (1988). *The Scope of Sociology.* New York: Oxford University Press.

———. (1964). *Assimilation in American Life.* New York: Oxford University Press.

Gossett, Thomas F. (1997). *Race: The History of an Idea in America*. Dallas, TX: Southern Methodist University Press.

Gould, Stephen Jay. (1994). "The Geometer of Race." *Discover* 15, no 11 (November): 65–69.

Gracia, Jorge J. E. (forthcoming-a). "The Oreo Phenomenon: Puzzles Posed by Race and Ethnicity." In Carey Nederman and Manuel Martín-Rodríguez, eds. *Sites of Identity: Configurations of Space, Community, and Self*.

———. (forthcoming-b). "Can Racial and Ethnic Groups Be Effectively Individuated? The Problems of Circularity and Demarcation." In *Black Ethnicity, Latino Race?* ed. Jorge J. E. Gracia.

———. (2005). "A Political Argument in Favor of Ethnic Names." *Philosophy and Social Criticism* 31, 4: 409–417.

———. (2004). "Language Priority in the Education of Children: Pogge's Argument in Favor of English-First for Hispanics." *Journal of Social Philosophy* 35, 3: 420–31.

———. (2003). *¿Qué son las categorías?* Madrid: Editorial Encuentros.

———. (2002). "Globalization, Philosophy, and Latin America." In *Latin American Perspectives on Globalization: Ethics, Politics, and Alternative Visions*, ed. Mario Sáenz, 123–31. Lanham, MD: Rowman & Littlefield.

———. (2001). "Response to My Critics: *Tahafut Al-Tahafut*." *Philosophy and Social Criticism* 27, 2: 51–75.

———. (2000a). "Affirmative Action for Hispanics/Latinos? Yes and No." In *Hispanics/Latinos in the United States: Ethnicity, Race, and Rights*, ed. Jorge J. E. Gracia and Pablo De Greiff, 201–21. New York: Routledge.

———. (2000b). *Hispanic/Latino Identity: A Philosophical Perspective*. Oxford: Blackwell.

———. (2000c). "Hispanic/Latino Identity: Homogeneity and Stereotypes." *Ventana Abierta* 2, 8: 17–25.

———. (1999a). *Metaphysics and Its Task: The Search for the Categorial Foundation of Knowledge*. Albany: State University of New York Press.

———. (1999b). "The Nature of Ethnicity with Special Reference to Hispanic/Latino Identity." *Public Affairs Quarterly* 13, no. 1: 25–42.

———. (1998). *Filosofía hispánica: Concepto, origen y foco historiográfico*. Pamplona: Universidad de Navarra.

———. (1994). "Christian Wolff on Individuation." In *Individuation and Identification in Early Modern Philosophy*, ed. K. Barber and Jorge J. E. Gracia, 219–43. Albany, NY: State University of New York Press.

———. (1993). "Hispanic Philosophy: Its Beginning and Golden Age." *Review of Metaphysics* 46, no. 3: 475–502. Reprinted in K. White, ed. (1997). *Hispanic Philosophy in the Age of Discovery*, 3–27. Washington, DC: Catholic University of America Press.

———. (1992a). *Philosophy and Its History: Issues in Philosophical Historiography*. Albany, NY: State University of New York Press.

———. (1992b). "Suárez and the Transcendentals." *Topoi* 11: 11–23.

———. (1988). *Individuality: An Essay on the Foundations of Metaphysics*. Albany, NY: State University of New York Press.

————, ed. (1986). *Latin American Philosophy in the Twentieth Century: Man, Values, and the Search for Philosophical Identity.* Buffalo, NY: Prometheus.

Gracia, Jorge J. E., and Iván Jaksić, eds. (1988). *Filosofía e identidad cultural en América Latina.* Caracas: Monte Avila.

Gracia, Jorge J. E., and Iván Jaksić. (1984). "The Problem of Philosophical Identity in Latin America: History and Approaches." *Inter-American Review of Bibliography* 34: 53–71.

Graham, Gordon. (1997). *Ethics and International Relations.* Oxford: Blackwell.

Graham, Richard, ed. (1990). *The Idea of Race in Latin America, 1870–1940.* Austin: University of Texas Press.

Greeley, Andrew M. (1974). *Ethnicity in the United States: A Preliminary Reconnaissance.* New York: Wiley.

Greenfeld, L. (1992). *Nationalism: Five Roads to Modernity.* Cambridge, MA: Harvard University Press.

Grier, William H., and Price M. Cobb. (1968). *Black Rage.* New York: Basic.

Grosfoguel, Ramón, and Chloé S. Georas. (1996). "The Racialization of Latino Caribbean Migrants in the New York Metropolitan Area." *CENTRO Journal of the Center for Puerto Rican Studies* 8, no. 1–2: 190–201.

Guibernau, M. (1999). *Nations without States: Political Communities in a Global Age.* Cambridge: Polity.

————. (1997). "Nations without States: Catalonia, a Case Study." In *The Ethnicity Reader: Nationalism, Multiculturalism and Migration*, ed. M. Guibernau and J. Rex, 133–53. Cambridge: Polity.

————. (1996). *Nationalisms: The Nation-State and Nationalism in the Twentieth Century.* Cambridge: Polity.

Guibernau, M., and John Rex. (1997a). "Introduction." In *The Ethnicity Reader: Nationalism, Multiculturalism and Migration*, ed. M. Guibernau and J. Rex, 1–12. Cambridge: Polity.

————, eds. (1997b). *The Ethnicity Reader: Nationalism, Multiculturalism and Migration.* Cambridge: Polity.

Gurr, Ted Robert. (2000). "Ethnic Warfare on the Wane." *Foreign Affairs* 79, no. 3: 52–64.

————. (1993). *Minorities at Risk: A Global View of Ethnopolitical Conflict.* Washington, DC: U.S. Institute of Peace Press.

Gurr, Ted Robert, and Barbara Harff. (1994). *Ethnic Conflicts in World Politics.* Boulder, CO: Westview.

Gurr, Ted Robert, Monty Marshall, and Deepa Khosla. (2000). *Peace and Conflict 2000: A Global Survey of Armed Conflicts, Self-Determination Movements, and Democracy.* College Park, MD: Center for International Development and Conflict Management, University of Maryland.

Gutmann, Amy. (1996). "Responding to Racial Injustice." In *Color Conscious: The Political Morality of Race*, ed. K. Anthony Appiah and Amy Gutmann, 106–178. Princeton, NJ: Princeton University Press.

Habermas, J. (1992–93). "Citizenship and National Identity: Some Reflections on the Future of Europe." *Praxis International* 12: 1–19.

Hacker, Andrew. (1992). *Two Nations: Black and White, Separate, Hostile, Unequal.* New York: Scribner's.

Hacking, Ian. (2002). *Historical Ontology.* Cambridge, MA: Harvard University Press.

———. (1999). *The Social Construction of What?* Cambridge, MA: Harvard University Press.

———. (1986). "Making Up People." In *Reconstructing Individualism: Autonomy, Individuality and the Self in Western Thought*, ed. Thomas C. Heller et al., 222–36. Stanford, CA: Stanford University Press.

Hall, Barbara. (2000). "The Libertarian Role Model and the Burden of Uplifting the Race." In *Women of Color and Philosophy: A Critical Reader*, ed. Naomi Zack, 168–205. Oxford: Blackwell.

Hall, Stuart. (1994). "Ethnicity," W. E. B. Du Bois Lecture. Cambridge, MA: Harvard University.

———. (1980). "Race, Articulation, and Societies Structured in Dominance." In *Sociological Minorities: Race and Colonialism*, 11–31. Paris: UNESCO.

Hames-García, Michael R. (2000). "'Who Are Our Own People?': Challenges for a Theory of Social Identity." In *Reclaiming Identity: Realist Theory and the Predicament of Postmodernism*, ed. Paula M. L. Moya and Michael R. Hames-García, 102–132. Berkeley: University of California Press.

Hammar, T. (1990). *Democracy and the Nation State.* Aldershot, England: Avebury.

Hanchard, Michael G. (2000). "Racism, Eroticism, and the Paradoxes of a U.S. Black Researcher in Brazil." In *Racing Research, Researching Race: Methodological Dilemmas in Critical Race Studies*, ed. France Winddance Twine and Jonathan W. Warren, 165–86. New York: New York University Press.

———. (1994). "Black Cinderella: Race and the Public Sphere in Brazil." *Public Culture* 7, no. 1: 165–85.

Haney López, Ian F. (1996). *White by Law: The Legal Constructions of Race.* New York: New York University Press.

Hannaford, Ivan. (1996). *Race. The History of an Idea in the West.* Washington, DC: Woodrow Wilson Center Press; Baltimore: Johns Hopkins University Press.

Harding, S., ed. (1993). *The Racial Economy of Science: Toward a Democratic Future.* Bloomington: Indiana University Press.

Hargreaves, A. G., and J. Leaman, eds. (1995). *Racism, Ethnicity, and Politics in Contemporary Europe.* Aldershot, England: Elgar.

Harris, Leonard, ed. (1999a). *Racism.* Amherst, NY: Humanities Press.

———. (1999b). "What, Then, Is Racism?" In *Racism*, ed. Leonard Harris, 437–50. Amherst, NY: Humanities Press.

Haslanger, S. (2000). "Gender and Race: (What) Are They? (What) Do We Want Them to Be?" *Nous* 34, no. 1: 31–55.

Hayes-Bautista, David E. (1983). "On Comparing Studies of Different *Raza* Populations." *American Journal of Public Health* 73: 274–76.

————. (1980). "Identifying 'Hispanic' Populations: The Influence of Research Methodology upon Public Policy." *American Journal of Public Health* 70: 353–56.

Hayes-Bautista, David E., and Jorge Chapa. (1987). "Latino Terminology: Conceptual Bases for Standardized Terminology." *American Journal of Public Health* 77: 61–68.

Haymes, Stephan Nathan. (1995). *Race, Culture, and the City: A Pedagogy for Black Urban Struggle.* Albany: State University of New York Press.

Heckman, S. (1994). "The Feminist Critique of Rationality." In *The Polity Reader in Gender Studies*, ed. S. Heckman, 50–61. Cambridge: Polity.

Hegel, G. W. F. (2000). "Anthropology." In *Encyclopaedia of the Philosophical Sciences*, trans. A. V. Miller, in *Philosophy of Mind*. Oxford: Oxford University Press. Reprinted in *The Idea of Race*, ed. Robert Bernasconi and Tommy L. Lott, 38–44. Indianapolis: Hackett.

Helg, Aline. (1990). "Race in Argentina and Cuba, 1880–1930: Theory, Policies, and Popular Reaction." In *The Idea of Race in Latin America, 1870–1940*, ed. Richard Graham, 36–69. Austin: University of Texas Press.

Henwood, Karen, and Ann Phoenix. (1999). "'Race' in Psychology: Teaching the Subject." In *Ethnic and Racial Studies Today*, ed. Martin Bulmer and John Solomos, 98–114. London: Routledge.

Herder, Johann Gottfried von. (2000). "Ideas on the Philosophy of History of Humankind." In *The Idea of Race*, ed. Robert Bernasconi and Tommy L. Lott, 23–26. Bloomington, IN: Hackett.

————. (1969). *Herder on Social and Political Culture.* Ed. F. M. Barnard. Cambridge: Cambridge University Press.

————. (1968). *Reflections on the Philosophy of the History of Mankind.* Abridged. Chicago: University of Chicago Press.

————. (1966). *Outlines of a Philosophy of the History of Man.* Trans. T. Churchill. New York: Bergman.

Heredia, Antonio. (1994). "Hispanismo filosófico." In *Identidades culturales en el cambio de siglo*, ed. José Abellán, 133–42. Madrid: Trotta.

————. (1987). "Espacio, tiempo y lenguaje en la filosofía hispánica." In *Filosofía de Hispanoamérica: Aproximación al panorama actual*, ed. Eulalio Forment, 43–59. Madrid: PPU.

Hernández, Ramona, and Silvio Torres-Saillant. (1992). "Marginality and Schooling: Editor's Foreword." *Punto 7 Review: A Journal of Marginal Discourse* 2: 1–7.

Herrenstein, R. J., and C. Murray. (1994). *The Bell Curve.* New York: Simon and Schuster.

Hintzen, Percy C. (2002). "The Caribbean: Race and Creole Ethnicity." In *A Companion to Race and Ethnicity*, ed. D. T. Goldberg and J. Solomos, 475–94. Oxford: Blackwell.

Hirschfeld, Lawrence A. (1996). *Race in the Making: Cognition, Culture, and the Child's Construction of Human Kinds.* Cambridge, MA: MIT Press.

Hirschfeld, Magnus. (1938). *Racism.* London: Victor Gollancz.

Hobsbawm, Eric. (1997). "An Anti-Nationalist Account of Nationalism Since 1989." In *The Ethnicity Reader: Nationalism, Multiculturalism and Migration*, ed. M. Guibernau and J. Rex, 69–79. Cambridge: Polity.

———. (1992a). "Ethnicity and Nationalism in Europe Today." *Anthropology Today* 8, no. 1: 3–8.

———. (1992b). *Nations and Nationalism since 1780: Programme, Myth, Reality*. Cambridge: Cambridge University Press.

Hobsbawm, Eric, and Terence Ranger, eds. (1983). *The Invention of Tradition*. Cambridge: Cambridge University Press.

Hoffman, Paul. (1994). "The Science of Race." *Discover* 15, no. 11 (November): 4.

Hooks, Bell. (1990). *Yearning: Race, Gender, and Cultural Politics*. Boston: South End.

Horowitz, Donald L. (1985). *Ethnic Groups in Conflict*. Berkeley: University of California Press.

———. (1975). "Ethnic Identity." In *Ethnicity: Theory and Experience*, ed. N. Glazer and D. P. Moynihan, 111–40. Cambridge, MA: Harvard University Press.

Hudson, Nicholas. (1996). "From 'Nation' to 'Race': The Origin of Racial Classification in Eighteenth-Century Thought." *Eighteenth-Century Studies* 29, no. 3: 247–64.

Hume, David. (1987). "Of National Characters." In *Essays: Moral, Political, and Literary*, ed. Eugene F. Miller, 197–201. Indianapolis: Liberty Classics.

Hughes, Everett C. (1994). *On Work, Race and the Sociological Imagination*, ed. L. A. Coser. Chicago: University of Chicago Press.

Hutchinson, John. (1992). "Moral Innovators and the Politics of Regeneration: The Distinctive Role of Cultural Nationalists in Nation-Building." In *Ethnicity and Nationalism*, ed. Anthony D. Smith, 101–117. Leiden, Netherlands: Brill.

Hutchinson, J., and A. D. Smith, eds. (1996). *Ethnicity*. Oxford: Oxford University Press.

Ignatiev, Noel. (1935). *How the Irish Became White*. New York: Routledge.

Ingle, Dwight J. (1978). "Fallacies in Arguments on Human Differences." In *Human Variation: The Biopsychology of Age, Race, and Sex*, ed. R. Travis Osborne et al., 5–27. New York: Academic.

Isaacs, Harold R. (1975). "Basic Group Identity." In *Ethnicity: Theory and Experience*, ed. Nathan Glazer and Daniel P. Moynihan, 29–52. Cambridge, MA.: Harvard University Press.

Jackson, P., ed. (1987). *Race and Racism: Essays in Social Geography*. London: Allen and Unwin.

Jacobson, Matthew Fry. (1998). *Whiteness of a Different Color*. Cambridge, MA: Harvard University Press.

Jaffe, A. J., et al. (1980). *The Changing Demography of Spanish Americans*. New York: Academic.

Jenkins, Richard. (1999). "Ethnicity Etcetera: Social Anthropological Points of View." In *Ethnic and Racial Studies Today*, ed. Martin Bulmer and John Solomos, 85–97. London: Routledge.

———. (1997). *Rethinking Ethnicity: Arguments and Explorations.* London: Sage.

———. (1996). *Social Identity.* London: Routledge.

———. (1994). "Rethinking Ethnicity: Identity, Categorization and Power." *Ethnic and Racial Studies* 17: 196–223.

Jensen, Arthur R. (1978). "Genetic and Behavioral Effects of Nonrandom Mating." In *Human Variation: The Biopsychology of Age, Race, and Sex*, ed. R. Travis Osborne et al., 51–105. New York: Academic.

———. (1969). "How Much Can We Boost IQ and Scholastic Achievement?" *Harvard Education Review* 39: 1–123.

Jones, Siân. (1999). "Peopling the Past: Approaches to 'Race' and Ethnicity in Archeology." In *Ethnic and Racial Studies Today*, ed. Martin Bulmer and John Solomos, 152–66. London: Routledge.

Jordan, Terry G., and Lester Rowntree. (1997). *The Human Mosaic: A Thematic Introduction to Cultural Geography.* 7th ed. New York: Longman.

Jordan, Winthrop D. (1968). *White over Black: American Attitudes toward the Negro, 1550–1812.* Chapel Hill: University of North Carolina Press.

Kaldor, Mary. (1999). *New and Old Wars: Organized Violence in a Global Era.* Stanford, CA: Stanford University Press.

Kant, Immanuel. (2001). "On the Use of Teleological Principles in Philosophy (1788)." In *Race*, ed. Robert Bernasconi, 37–56. Oxford: Blackwell.

———. (1991). *Observations on the Feeling of the Beautiful and Sublime.* Trans. John T. Goldthwait. Berkeley: University of California Press.

———. (1963). *Critique of Pure Reason.* Trans. Norman Kemp Smith. New York: Macmillan.

Katz, Judy H. (1978). *White Awareness: Handbook for Anti-Racism Training.* Norman: University of Oklahoma Press.

Kedourie, E. (1961). *Nationalism.* New York: Praeger.

Keen, David. (1998). "The Economic Functions of Violence in Civil War." *Adelphi Paper 320.* Oxford: Oxford University Press.

Kellas, James. (1991). *The Politics of Ethnicity and Nationalism.* New York: St. Martin's.

Kendall, Ann. (1973). *Everyday Life of the Incas.* New York: Dorset.

Kennedy, Kenneth K. R. (1973). "Race and Culture." In *Main Currents in Cultural Anthropology*, ed. Raoul Naroll and Frada Naroll. New York: Appleton-Century-Crofts.

Keyes, Charles F. (1981). *Ethnic Change.* Seattle: University of Washington Press.

King, James C. (1981). *The Biology Race.* Berkeley: University of California Press.

Knight, Alan. (1990). "Racism, Revolution, and *Indigenismo*: Mexico, 1910–1940." In *The Idea of Race in Latin America, 1870–1940*, ed. Richard Graham, 71–113. Austin: University of Texas Press.

Knowles, C. (1992). *Race, Discourse and Labourism.* London: Routledge.

Kohn, H. (1946). *The Idea of Nationalism.* New York: Macmillan.

Kymlicka, Will. (1997). "Ethnicity in the USA." In *The Ethnicity Reader: Nationalism, Multiculturalism and Migration*, ed. M. Guibernau and J. Rex, 229–47. Cambridge: Polity.

———. (1995a). *Multicultural Citizenship.* Oxford: Oxford University Press.

———, ed. (1995b). *The Rights of Minority Cultures.* Oxford: Oxford University Press.

Ladd, John. (1997). "Philosophical Reflections on Race and Racism." *American Behavioral Scientist* 41, no. 2: 212–22.

Las Casas, Bartolomé de. (1992). *In Defense of the Indians: The Defense of the Most Reverend Lord, Don Fray Bartolomé de las Casas, of the Order of Preachers, Late Bishop of Chiapa, against the Persecutors and Slanderers of the Peoples of the New World Discovered Across the Seas.* Trans., ed. Stafford Poole. DeKalb: Northern Illinois University Press.

Lasch-Quinn, Elisabeth. (2001). *Race Experts: How Racial Etiquette, Sensitivity Training, and New Age Therapy Hijacked the Civil Rights Revolution.* New York: Norton.

Lauret, Maria. (1999). "'The Approval of Headquarters': Race and Ethnicity in English Studies." In *Ethnic and Racial Studies Today*, ed. Martin Bulmer and John Solomos, 124–35. London: Routledge.

Lentz, C. (1995). "'Tribalism' and 'Ethnicity' in Africa: A Review of Four Decades of Anglophone Research." *Cahiers des Sciences Humanes* 31: 303–328.

Levin, Michael. (1997). *Why Race Matters: Race Differences and What They Mean.* Westport, CT: Praeger.

———. (1994). "Race, Biology and Justice." *Public Affairs Quarterly* 8, no. 3: 267–85.

Levinson, Daniel J. (1950). "The Study of Ethnocentric Ideology." In *The Authoritarian Personality*, ed. Theodor Adorno et al., 102–115. New York: Norton.

Lewis, B. (1998). "The Historical Roots of Racism." *American Scholar* (Winter): 17–25.

———. (1990). *Race and Slavery in the Middle East.* New York: Oxford University Press.

Lewontin, R. C. (1998). "Race." In *Encyclopedia Americana*, vol. 23: 116–22. Danbury, CT: Grolier.

———. (1972). "The Apportionment of Human Diversity." *Evolutionary Biology* 6: 381.

Lichtenberg, Judith. (1997). "Nationalism, For and (Mainly) Against." In *The Morality of Nationalism*, ed. Robert McKim and Jeff McMahan, 158–75. Oxford: Oxford University Press.

Lionnett, Françoise. (1989). *Autobiographical Voices: Race, Gender, Self-Portraiture.* Ithaca, NY: Cornell University Press.

Lissak, Rivka Shpak. (1989). *Pluralism and Progressives: Hull-House and the New Immigrants, 1890–1919.* Chicago: University of Chicago Press.

Litt, E. (1970). *Ethnic Politics in America: Beyond Pluralism.* Glenview, IL: Scott, Foresman.

Livingstone, Frank B. (1993). "On the Nonexistence of Human Races." In *The Racial Economy of Science: Toward a Democratic Future*, ed. Sandra Harding, 133–41. Bloomington: Indiana University Press.

Llobera, J. (1994). *The God of Modernity: The Development of Nationalism in Western Europe.* Oxford: Berg.

Locke, Alain LeRoy. (1992). *Race Contacts and Interracial Relations: Lectures on the Theory and Practice of Race*, ed. Jeffrey C. Stewart. Washington, DC: Howard University Press.

———. (1924). "The Concept of Race as Applied to Social Culture." *Howard Review* 1: 290–99.

Lott, Tommy. (2001). "Du Bois's Anthropological Notion of Race." In *Race*, ed. Robert Bernasconi, 59–83. Oxford: Blackwell.

———. (1999). *The Invention of Race: Black Culture and the Politics of Representation*. Oxford: Blackwell.

Lowry, I. S. (1982). "The Science and Politics of Ethnic Enumeration." In *Ethnicity and Public Policy*, ed. W. A. Van Horne, 42–61. Milwaukee: University of Wisconsin System, American Ethnic Studies Coordinating Committee/Urban Corridor Consortium.

Lynn, Richard. (1978). "Ethnic and Racial Differences in Intelligence: International Comparisons." In *Human Variation: The Biopsychology of Age, Race, and Sex*, ed. R. Travis Osborne et al., 261–86. New York: Academic.

MacCormick, N. (1982). "Nation and Nationalism." In *Legal Right and Social Democracy*, 247–68. Oxford: Clarendon.

MacFarquhar, Neil. (2001). "Beware of Hidden Enemies and Their Wolves and Foxes." *New York Times*, December 9, 7.

MacIntyre, A. (1995). "Is Patriotism a Virtue?" In *Theorizing Citizenship*, ed. R. Beiner. Albany: State University of New York Press.

Malcomson, Scott L. (2000). *One Drop of Blood: The American Misadventure of Race*. New York: Farrar, Straus and Giroux.

Mandt, A. J. (1989). "The Inevitability of Pluralism: Philosophical Practice and Philosophical Excellence." In *The Institution of Philosophy: A Discipline in Crisis?* ed. Avner Cohen and Marcelo Dascal, 71–101. La Salle, IL: Open Court.

Martiniello, Marco. (2002). "Citizenship." In *A Companion to Race and Ethnicity*, ed. D. T. Goldberg and J. Solomos, 114–23. Oxford: Blackwell.

Margalit, Avishai, and Joseph Raz. (1995). "National Self-Determination." In *The Rights of Minority Cultures*, ed. Will Kymlicka, 79–92. Oxford: Oxford University Press.

Marín, G. (1984). "Stereotyping Hispanics: The Differential Effect of Research Method, Label and Degree of Contact." *International Journal of International Relations* 8: 17–27.

Marín, G., and B. VanOss Marín. (1991). *Research with Hispanic Populations*. Newbury Park, CA: Sage.

Marshall, T. H. (1992). "Citizenship and Social Class." In *Citizenship and Social Class*, ed. T. H. Marshall and T. Bottomore, 6–20. London: Pluto.

Marshall, T. H., and T. Bottomore, eds. (1992). *Citizenship and Social Class*. London: Pluto.

Martí, José. (1946). "La verdad sobre los Estados Unidos." In *Obras completas*, vol. 1: 2035–38. Havana: Editorial Lex.

Martínez, Elizabeth. (2001). "Seeing More Than Black and White: Latinos, Racism, and the Cultural Divides." In *Race, Class, and Gender: An Anthology*, ed. Margaret Andersen and Patricia Hill Collins, 108–114. Belmont, CA: Wadsworth.

Martínez-Echazábal, Lourdes. (1998). "*Mestizaje* and the Discourse of National/Cultural Identity in Latin America, 1845–1959." *Latin American Perspectives* 25: 21–42.

Marx, Karl. (1978). *The German Ideology*. Ed. C. J. Arthur. New York: New York International.

Marx, Karl, and Friedrich Engels. (1976). *Basic Writings on Politics and Philosophy*, ed. L. S. Feuer. Glasgow: Fontana Library.

———. (1975). *Collected Works*. London: Lawrence & Wishart.

———. (1968). *Manifesto of the Communist Party*. Peking: Foreign Language Press.

Mason, David. (1999). "The Continuing Significance of Race? Teaching Ethnic and Racial Studies in Sociology." In *Ethnic and Racial Studies Today*, ed. Martin Bulmer and John Solomos, 13–28. London: Routledge.

———. (1994). "On the Dangers of Disconnecting Race and Racism." *Sociology* 28, no. 4: 845–58.

Mattson, Mark T. (1992). *Atlas of the Census.* New York: Macmillan.

McGarry, J., and B. O'Leary, eds. (1993). *The Politics of Ethnic Conflict Regulation.* London: Routledge.

McGary, H. (1999). *Race and Social Justice.* Oxford: Blackwell.

McKee, Jesse O., ed. (2000). *Ethnicity in Contemporary America: A Geographical Appraisal.* 2nd ed. Lanham, MD: Rowman & Littlefield.

McKim, Robert, and Jeff McMahan, eds. (1997). *The Morality of Nationalism.* Oxford: Oxford University Press.

McLemore, S. D. (1994). *Race and Ethnicity in America*, 4th ed. Boston: Allyn and Bacon.

Medina, José. (2004). "Pragmatism and Ethnicity: Critique, Reconstruction, and the New Hispanic." *Metaphilosophy* 35, 1–2: 115–46.

Mendieta, Eduardo. (2002). "Review of Leonard Harris's *Racism*." *Continental Philosophy Review* 35, no. 1: 108–115.

———. (2001). "The 'Second *Reconquista*,' or Why Should a 'Hispanic' Become a Philosopher." *Philosophy and Social Criticism* 27, no. 2: 11–19.

———. (2000). "The Making of New Peoples: Hispanizing Race." In *Hispanics/Latinos in the United States: Ethnicity, Race, and Rights*, ed. Jorge J. E. Gracia and Pablo De Greiff, 45–59. New York: Routledge.

Michaels, Walter Benn. (1997). "Identity and Liberation." *Peace Review* 9, no. 4: 494–502.

———. (1994). "The No-Drop Rule." *Critical Inquiry* 20: 767–68.

———. (1992). "Race and Culture: A Critical Genealogy of Cultural Identity." *Critical Inquiry* 18, no. 4: 655–85.

Midgley, Mary. (1999). "Towards an Ethic of Global Responsibility." In *Human Rights in Global Politics*, ed. Tim Dunne and Nicholas J. Wheeler, 195–213. Cambridge: Cambridge University Press.

Miles, Robert. (1989). *Racism*. New York: Routledge.

Mill, John Stuart. (1972). *Considerations on Representative Government*. In *Utilitarianism, On Liberty, Considerations on Representative Government*, ed. H. B. Acton. London: J. M. Dent and Sons.

Miller, David. (1998). "Nation and Nationalism." In *Routledge Encyclopedia of Philosophy*, ed. Edward Craig, vol. 6: 657–62. London: Routledge.

———. (1995). *On Nationality*. Oxford: Clarendon.

———. (1993). "In Defense of Nationality." *Journal of Applied Philosophy* 10, no. 1: 3–16.

Miller, Robin L. (1992). "The Human Ecology of Multiracial Identity." In *Racially Mixed People in America*, ed. Maria P. P. Root, 24–36. Newbury Park, CA: Sage.

Mills, Charles. (1998). "But What Are You Really?" In *Blackness Visible: Essays on Philosophy and Race*, 41–66. Ithaca, NY: Cornell University Press.

———. (1997). *The Racial Contract*. Ithaca, NY: Cornell University Press.

Mindel, Charles H., et al., eds. (1988). *Ethnic Families in America: Patterns and Variations*. Englewood Cliffs, NJ: Prentice Hall.

Minogue, K. (1967). *Nationalism*. London: Batsford.

Minow, Martha. (1990). *Making All the Difference: Inclusion, Exclusion and American Law*. Ithaca, NY: Cornell University Press.

Modood, Tariq. (2001). "'Difference,' Cultural Racism and Anti-Racism." In *Race and Racism*, ed. Bernard Boxill, 238–56. Oxford: Oxford University Press.

Mohanty, Satya P. (2000). "The Epistemic Status of Cultural Identity: On *Beloved* and the Postcolonial Condition." In *Reclaiming Identity: Realist Theory and the Predicament of Postmodernism*, ed. Paula M. L. Moya and Michael R. Hames-García, 29–66. Berkeley: University of California Press.

Montagu, M. F. Ashley, ed. (1964). *The Concept of Race*. London: Collier-Macmillan.

———. (1945). *Man's Most Dangerous Myth: The Fallacy of Race*. New York: Columbia University Press.

———. (1941). "The Concept of Race in the Human Species in the Light of Genetics." *Journal of Heredity* 32: 243–47.

Montville, Joseph, ed. (1990). *Conflict and Peacemaking in Multiethnic Societies*. Washington, DC: Lexington.

Moore, Joan, and Harry Pachón. (1985). *Hispanics in the United States*. Englewood Cliffs, NJ: Prentice-Hall.

———. (1976). *Mexican-Americans*. 2nd ed. Englewood Cliffs, NJ: Prentice Hall.

Mörner, Magnus. (1967). *Race Mixture in the History of Latin America*. Boston: Little, Brown.

Mosley, Albert. (1997). "Are Racial Categories Racist?" *Research in African Literatures* 284: 101–111.

Moya, Paula M. L. (2002). *Learning from Experience: Minority Identities, Multicultural Struggles*. Berkeley: University of California Press.

———. (2001). "Why I Am Not Hispanic: An Argument with Jorge Gracia." *American Philosophical Association Newsletter on Hispanic/Latino Issues in Philosophy* 2 (Spring): 100–105.

———. (2000a). "Introduction: Reclaiming Identity." In *Reclaiming Identity: Realist Theory and the Predicament of Postmodernism*, ed. Paula M. L. Moya and Michael R. Hames-García, 1–26. Berkeley: University of California Press.

———. (2000b). "Postmodernism, 'Realism,' and the Politics of Identity: Cherríe Moraga and Chicana Feminism." In *Reclaiming Identity: Realist Theory and the Predicament of Postmodernism*, ed. Paula M. L. Moya and Michael R. Hames-García, 67–101. Berkeley: University of California Press.

Moya, Paula M. L. and Michael R. Hames-García, eds. (2000). *Reclaiming Identity: Realist Theory and the Predicament of Postmodernism*. Berkeley: University of California Press.

Mueller, John. (2001). "The Remnants of War: Thugs as Residual Combatants." Paper presented at Uppsala University, 8–9 June. Available at www.pcr.uu.se.

———. (1989). *Retreat from Doomsday: The Obsolescence of Major Wars*. New York: Basic.

Murguia, Edward. (1991). "On Latino/Hispanic Ethnic Identity." *Latino Studies Journal* 2: 8–18.

Nagel, Thomas. (1991). *Equality and Partiality*. New York: Oxford University Press.

Nairn, T. (1993). "Demonising Nationalism." *London Review of Books*, 25 February.

———. (1977). *The Break-Up of Britain*. London: New Left.

Nardal, Paulette. (2001). "The Awakening of Race Consciousness." In *Race*, ed. Robert Bernasconi, 107–111. Oxford: Blackwell.

Nascimento, Amós. (1997). "Identities in Conflict? Latin (African) American." *Peace Review* 9, no. 4: 489–95.

Nathanson, Stephen. (1992). "Is Patriotism Like Racism?" *APA Newsletter on Philosophy and the Black Experience* 91: 9–11.

Nei, Masatoshi. (1978). "The Theory of Genetic Distance and Evolution of Human Races." *Japanese Journal of Human Genetics* 23: 341–69.

Nei, Masatoshi, and A. K. Roychoudhury. (1982). "Genetic Relationship and Evolution of Human Races." *Evolutionary Biology* 14: 1–59.

———. (1974). "Genetic Variation within and between the Three Major Races of Man, Caucasoids, Negroids, and Mongoloids." *American Journal of Human Genetics* 26: 421–43.

———. (1972). "Gene Differences between Caucasian, Negro, and Japanese Populations." *Science* 177: 434–35.

Nelson, C., and Marta Tienda. (1985). "The Structuring of Hispanic Identity: Historical and Contemporary Perspectives." *Ethnic and Racial Studies* 8, no. 1: 49–74.

Nimni, Ephraim. (1995). "Marx, Engels, and the National Question." In *The Rights of Minority Cultures*, ed. Will Kymlicka, 57–75. Oxford: Oxford University Press.

Noble, Clyde E. (1978). "Age, Race, and Sex in the Learning and Performance of Psychomotor Skills." In *Human Variations: The Biopsychology of Age, Race, and Sex*, ed. R. Travis Osborne et al., 278–87. New York: Academic.

Nuccetelli, Susana. (2001). "'Latinos,' 'Hispanics,' and 'Iberoamericans': Naming or Describing?" *Philosophical Forum* 32, no. 2: 175–88.

Oboler, Suzanne. (1995). *Ethnic Labels, Latino Lives: Identity and the Politics of (Re)Presentation in the United States*. Minneapolis: University of Minnesota Press.

O'Leary, Brendan, and John McGarry. (1995). "Regulating Nations and Ethnic Communities." In *Nationalism and Rationality*, ed. Albert Breton et al., 245–89. Cambridge: Cambridge University Press.

Olson, Steve. (2001). "The Genetic Archeology of Race." *Atlantic Monthly* (April): 1–7.

Omi, Michael, and Howard Winant. (1994). *Racial Formation in the United States: From the 1960s to the 1990s*. 2nd ed. New York: Routledge.

Osborne, R. Travis. (1978). "Race and Sex Differences in Heritability of Mental Test Performance: A Study of Negroid and Caucasoid Twins." In *Human Variation: The Biopsychology of Age, Race, and Sex*, ed. R. Travis Osborne et al., 137–69. New York: Academic.

Osborne, R. Travis, et al., eds. (1978). *Human Variation: The Biopsychology of Age, Race, and Sex*. New York: Academic.

Outlaw, Lucius T., Jr. (2001). "Toward a Critical Theory of 'Race.'" In *Race and Racism*, ed. Bernard Boxill, 58–82. Oxford: Oxford University Press.

———. (1996). *On Race and Philosophy*. New York: Routledge.

———. (1987). "On Race and Class: or, On the Prospects of 'Rainbow Socialism.'" In *The Year Left 2: An American Socialist Yearbook*, ed. Mike Davis et al., 106–121. London: Verso.

———. (1983). "Race and Class in the Theory and Practice of Emancipatory Social Transformation." In *Philosophy Born in Struggle: Anthology of Afro-American Philosophy from 1917*, ed. Leonard Harris, 117–29. Dubuque, IA: Kendal/Hunt.

Padilla, Félix. (1985). *Latino Ethnic Consciousness: The Case of Mexican Americans and Puerto Ricans in Chicago*. Notre Dame, IN: University of Notre Dame Press.

Parsons, Talcott. (1975). "Some Theoretical Considerations on the Nature and Trends of Change of Ethnicity." In *Ethnicity: Theory and Experience*, ed. N. Glazer and D. P. Moynihan, 53–83. Cambridge, MA: Harvard University Press.

París Pombo, M. D. (1990). *Crisis e identidades colectivas en América Latina*. Mexico City: Plaza y Valdés.

Patterson, Orlando. (2000). "America's Worst Idea." *New York Times Review of Books*, October 22, 15–16.

Paz, Octavio. (1961). *El laberinto de la soledad*. Mexico City: Cuadernos Americanos.

Peterson, William. (1982). "Concepts of Ethnicity." In *Concepts and Ethnicity*, ed. William Peterson, Michael Novak, and Philip Gleason, 1–26. Cambridge, MA: Harvard University Press.

Piper, Adrian. (1992). "Passing for White, Passing for Black." *Transition* 58: 4–58.

Plamenatz, John. (1976). "Two Types of Nationalism." In *Nationalism: The Nature and Evolution of an Idea*, ed. Eugene Kamenda, 23–36. London: Edward Arnold.

Pogge, Thomas W. (2000). "Accommodation Rights for Hispanics in the United States." In *Hispanics/Latinos in the United States: Ethnicity, Race, and Rights*, ed. Jorge J. E. Gracia and Pablo De Greiff, 181–200. New York: Routledge.

Poliakov, Léon. (1974). *The Aryan Myth: A History of Racist and Nationalist Ideas in Europe*, trans. Edmund Howard. New York: Basic.

Popkin, Richard. (1980). "The Philosophical Bases of Modern Racism." In *The High Road to Pyrrhonism*, ed. Richard A. Watson and James E. Force, 79–102. San Diego: Austin Hill.

Puzzo, Dante. (1964). "Racism and the Western Tradition." *Journal of the History of Ideas* 25, no. 4: 579–86.

Ramos, Samuel. (1963). *El perfil del hombre y la cultura en México*. Mexico City: Universidad Nacional Autónoma de México.

Reed, T. E. (1969). "Caucasian Genes in American Negroes." *Science* 165: 762–68.

Reichberg, Gregory. (2003). "Francisco de Vitoria: *De Indis*." In *The Classics of Western Philosophy*, ed. Jorge J. E. Gracia et al., 197–203. Oxford: Blackwell.

Renan, Ernest. (1996). *Qu'est-ce qu'une nation? What Is a Nation?* Toronto: Tapir.

Rex, J. (1986). *Race and Ethnicity*. Milton Keynes, England: Open University Press.

———. (1967). *Race, Community and Conflict*. Oxford: Oxford University Press.

Rex, J., and D. Mason, eds. (1986). *Theories of Race and Ethnic Relations*. Cambridge: Cambridge University Press.

Ringer, Benjamin B., and Elinor R. Lawless. (1989). *Race-Ethnicity and Society*. London: Routledge.

Ripley, W. Z. (1899). *The Races of Europe*. New York: Appleton.

Robinson, Richard. (1954). *Definition*. Oxford: Clarendon.

Root, Maria P. P., ed. (1992). *Racially Mixed People in America*. Newbury Park, CA: Sage.

Rorty, Richard, ed. (1967). *The Linguistic Turn: Recent Essays in Philosophical Method*. Chicago: Chicago University Press.

Rose, Harold M. (2000). "The Evolving Spatial Pattern of Black America: 1910–1990 and Beyond." In *Ethnicity in Contemporary America: A Geographical Appraisal*, ed. Jesse O. McKee, 81–109. 2nd ed. Lanham, MD: Rowman & Littlefield.

Rothenberg, Paula. (1988). *Racism and Sexism: An Integrated Study*. New York: St. Martin's.

Rothschild, Joseph. (1981). *Ethnopolitics*. New York: Columbia University Press.

Roychoudhury, A. K. (1976). "Genetic Distance and Gene Diversity among Linguistically Different Tribes of Mexican Indians." *American Journal of Physical Anthropology* 42: 449–54.

Roychoudhury, A. K., and Matoshi Nei. (1988). *Human Polymorphic Genes: World Distribution*. New York: Oxford University Press.

Rushton, J. P. (1990). "Race Differences, R/K Theory, and a Reply to J. R. Flynn." *Psychologist* 3, no. 5: 195–98.

Sartre, Jean-Paul. (2001). "Black Orpheus." In *Race*, ed. Robert Bernasconi, 115–42. Oxford: Blackwell.

Schaefer, Richard. (1990). *Racial and Ethnic Groups*. 4th ed. Glenview, IL: Scott, Foresman.

Schermerhorn, R. A. (1970). *Comparative Ethnic Relations: A Framework for Theory and Research*. New York: Random House.

Schlesinger, Arthur M., Jr. (1998). *The Disuniting of America: Reflections on a Multicultural Society.* New York: Norton.

Schmid, W. T. (1996). "The Definition of Racism." *Journal of Applied Philosophy* 13, no. 1: 31–40.

Schutte, Ofelia. (2000). "Negotiating Latina Identities." In *Hispanics in the United States: Ethnicity, Race, and Rights,* ed. Jorge J. E. Gracia and Pablo De Greiff, 61–75. New York: Routledge.

———. (1993). *Cultural Identity and Social Liberation in Latin American Thought.* Albany: State University of New York Press.

———. (1987). "Toward an Understanding of Latin-American Philosophy: Reflections on the Foundations of Cultural Identity." *Philosophy Today* 31: 21–34.

Searle, John. (1995). *The Construction of Social Reality.* New York: Free Press.

Sedillo López, Antoinette. (1995). *Historical Themes and Identity: Mestizaje and Labels.* "Latinos in the United States: History, Law and Perspective Series." Vol. 1. New York: Garland.

Segal, L. (1990). *Slow Motion: Changing Men, Changing Masculinities.* London: Virago.

Sen, A. (2002). "Civilizational Imprisonments." *New Republic* (June 10): 28–33.

———. (2001). "Being and Being of Mixed Race." *Social Theory and Practice* 27: 285–307.

———. (1999). *Reason before Identity.* Oxford: Oxford University Press.

Senghor, Leopold. (2001). "Negritude and Modernity or Negritude as a Humanism for the Twentieth Century." In *Race,* ed. Robert Bernasconi, 143–66. Oxford: Blackwell.

———. (1961). "What Is Negritude?" *West Africa* (November 4): 1211.

Sengupta, Somini. (2000). "Removing a Relic of the Old South." *New York Times,* "Week in Review," November 5, 5.

Seton-Watson, Hugh. (1977). *Nations and States.* London: Methuen.

Sharpley-Whiting, T. Denean. (2001). "Paulette Nardal, Race Consciousness and Antillean Letters." In *Race,* ed. Robert Bernasconi, 95–106. Oxford: Blackwell.

Shibutani, R., and K. M. Kwan. (1965). *Ethnic Stratification.* New York: Macmillan.

Shreve, James. (1994). "Terms of Estrangement." *Discover* 15, no. 11 (November): 57–63.

Singer, M. G. (1978). "Some Thoughts on Race and Racism." *Philosophia* 8, no. 2–3: 153–83.

Singer, P. (1978). "Is Racial Discrimination Arbitrary?" *Philosophia* 8, no. 2–3: 185–203.

Skillen, Anthony. (1993). "Racism: Flew's Three Concepts of Racism." *Journal of Applied Philosophy* 10: 73–89.

Small, Stephen. (2002). "Racisms and Racialized Hostility at the Start of the New Millennium." In *A Companion to Race and Ethnicity,* ed. D. T. Goldberg and J. Solomos, 258–81. Oxford: Blackwell.

Smedley, Audrey. (1993). *Race in North America: Origin and Evolution of a Worldview.* Boulder, CO: Westview.

Smith, Anthony D. (1997). "Structure and Persistence of *Ethnie.*" In *The Ethnicity Reader: Nationalism, Multiculturalism and Migration,* ed. M. Guibernau and J. Rex, 27–33. Cambridge: Polity.

———. (1994). "The Problem of National Identity: Ancient, Medieval and Modern?" *Ethnic and Racial Studies* 17: 375–99.

———, ed. (1992). *Ethnicity and Nationalism.* Leiden, Netherlands: Brill.

———. (1991). *National Identity.* Reno: University of Nevada Press.

———. (1986). *The Ethnic Origins of Nations.* Oxford: Blackwell.

———. (1981). *The Ethnic Revival.* Cambridge: Cambridge University Press.

Smith, Dan. (2000). "Ethical Uncertainties of Nationalism." *Journal of Peace Research* 37, no. 4: 489–502.

Smith, Dan, and Øyvind Østerud. (1995). *Nation-State, Nationalism and Political Identity.* Oslo: Advance Research on the Europeanisation of the Nation-State, University of Oslo.

Smith, M. G. (1986). "Pluralism, Race and Ethnicity in Selected African Countries." In *Theories of Race and Ethnic Relations,* ed. J. Rex and D. Mason, 177–208. Cambridge: Cambridge University Press.

Smith, J., and A. Kornberg. (1969). "Some Considerations Bearing Upon Comparative Research in Canada and the United States." *Sociology* 3: 341–57.

Smith, S. (1989). "Race and Racism." *Urban Geography* 10, no. 10: 593–606.

Snowden, F. M., Jr. (1983). *Before Color Prejudice: The Ancient View of Blacks.* Cambridge, MA: Harvard University Press.

———. (1970). *Blacks in Antiquity: Ethiopians in the Greco-Roman Experience.* Cambridge, MA: Harvard University Press.

Sollors, Werner. (2002). "Ethnicity and Race." In *A Companion to Race and Ethnicity,* ed. D. T. Goldberg and J. Solomos, 97–104. Oxford: Blackwell.

———, ed. (1997). *Theories of Ethnicity: A Classical Reader.* Basingstoke, England: Macmillan.

Solomos, J., and L. Back. (1994). "Conceptualizing Racisms: Social Theory, Politics and Research." *Sociology* 28, no. 1: 142–61.

Sowell, Thomas. (1994). *Race and Culture: A World View.* New York: Basic.

Spinner, J. (1994). *The Boundaries of Citizenship: Race, Ethnicity, and Nationality in the Liberal State.* Baltimore: Johns Hopkins University Press.

Spoonley, P. (1993). *Racism and Ethnicity.* Oxford: Oxford University Press.

Stepan, Nancy. (1982). *The Idea of Race in Science: Great Britain 1800–1960.* Hamden, CT: Archon.

Stephan, Cookie White. (1992). "Mixed-Heritage Individuals: Ethnic Identity and Trait Characteristics." In *Racially Mixed People in America,* ed. Maria P. P. Root, 50–63. Newbury Park, CA: Sage.

Stocke, Verena. (1994). "Invaded Women: Gender, Race, and Class in the Formation of Colonial Society." In *Women, "Race," and Writing in the Early Modern Period,* ed. Mango Hendricks and Patricia Parker, 272–86. London: Routledge.

Stojanović, Svetozar. (2002). *Democratic Revolution in Serbia in the International Context*. Amherst, NY: Prometheus.

Stolberg, Sheryl Gay. (2001). "Shouldn't a Pill Be Color Blind?" *New York Times*, section 4, 1 and 3.

Strawson, P. F. (1959). *Individuals*. London: Methuen.

Stubblefield, A. (1995). "Race Identity and Non-Essentialism about Race." *Social Theory and Practice* 21, no. 3: 341–68.

Sweet, James. (1997). "The Iberian Roots of American Racist Thought." *William and Mary Quarterly* 54, no. 1: 143–66.

Szalay, Lorand B., and Rogelio Díaz-Guerrero. (1985). "Similarities and Differences between Subjective Cultures: A Comparison of Latin, Hispanic, and Anglo Americans." In *Cross-Cultural and National Studies in Social Psychology: Proceedings of the XXIII International Congress of Psychology of the International Union of Psychological Science (IUPsyS), Acapulco, Mexico, September 2–7, 1984: Selected/Revised Papers*, ed. Rogelio Díaz-Guerrero, vol. 2: 105–132. Amsterdam: Elsevier Science.

Takaki, Ronald. (2002). "The Twenty-First Century: We Will All Be Minorities." In *Debating Diversity: Clashing Perspectives on Race and Ethnicity in America*, ed. Ronald Takaki, 1–4. New York: Oxford University Press.

———. (1993). *A Different Mirror: A History of Multicultural America*. Boston: Little Brown.

———. (1982). "Reflections on Racial Patterns in America: An Historical Perspective." In *Ethnicity and Public Policy*, ed. Winston A. Van Horne, 1–23. Milwaukee: University of Wisconsin.

Tamir, Yael. (1993). *Liberal Nationalism*. Princeton, NJ: Princeton University Press.

Tatum, Daniel. (1997). *Why Are All the Black Kids Sitting Together in the Cafeteria? and Other Conversations about Race*. New York: Basic.

Taylor, Charles. (1993). "The Politics of Recognition." In *Multiculturalism and the "Politics of Recognition,"* ed. Amy Gutmann, 25–74. Princeton, NJ: Princeton University Press.

Taylor, P. (2000). "Appiah's Uncompleted Argument: W. E. B. Du Bois and the Reality of Race." *Social Theory and Practice* 26: 103–128.

Taylor, Rupert. (1999)."Political Science Encounters 'Race' and 'Ethnicity.'" In *Ethnic and Racial Studies Today*, ed. Martin Bulmer and John Solomos, 115–23. London: Routledge.

Thernstrom, Stephan. (1982). "Ethnic Groups in American History." In *Ethnic Relations in America*, ed. Lance Liebman, 3–27. Englewood Cliffs, NJ: Prentice Hall.

Thomas, Laurence. (2001a). "Group Autonomy and Narrative Identity: Blacks and Jews." In *Race and Racism*, ed. Bernard Boxill, 357–70. Oxford: Oxford University Press.

———. (2001b). "Sexism and Racism: Some Conceptual Differences." In *Race and Racism*, ed. Bernard Boxill, 344–56. Oxford: Oxford University Press.

Thompson, E. P. (1963). *The Making of the English Working Class*. New York: Pantheon.

Tienda, M., and V. Ortíz. (1986). "'Hispanicity' and the 1980 Census." *Social Sciences Quarterly* 67: 3–20.

Todorov, Tzvetan. (1986). "'Race,' Writing and Culture." In *Race, Writing, and Difference*, ed. Henry L. Gates Jr., 370–80. Chicago: University of Chicago Press.

Treitschke, H. von. (1914). *Selections from Treitschke's Lectures on Politics*. London: Gowan and Gray.

Treviño, Fernando. (1987). "Standardized Terminology for Hispanic Populations." *American Journal of Public Health* 77: 69–72.

Triandis, Harry C., et al. (1984). "*Simpatía* as a Cultural Script of Hispanics." *Journal of Personality and Social Psychology* 47: 1363–75.

Twine, France Winddance, and Jonathan W. Warren, eds. (2000). *Racing Research, Researching Race: Methodological Dilemmas in Critical Race Studies*. New York: New York University Press.

van den Berghe, Pierre L. (2001). "Does Race Matter?" In *Race and Racism*, ed. Bernard Boxill, 101–113. Oxford: Oxford University Press.

———. (1981). *The Ethnic Phenomenon*. New York: Elsevier.

———. (1967). *Race and Racism: A Comparative Perspective*. New York: Wiley.

van der Walt, B. I. (1997). *Afrocentric or Eurocentric: Our Task in Multicultural South Africa*. Potchefstroom, South Africa: Potchefstroomse Universiteit.

Van Dijk, Teun A. (2002). "Discourse and Racism." In *A Companion to Race and Ethnicity*, ed. D. T. Goldberg and J. Solomos, 145–59. Oxford: Blackwell.

———. (1987). *Communicating Racism: Ethnic Prejudice in Thought and Talk*. Newbury Park, CA: Sage.

Van Dyke, Vernon. (1995). "The Individual, the State, and Ethnic Communities in Political Theory." In *The Rights of Minority Cultures*, ed. Will Kymlicka, 31–56. Oxford: Oxford University Press.

Van Horne, Winston A., ed. (1982). *Ethnicity and Public Policy*. Vol. 1. Milwaukee: University of Wisconsin.

Vincent, Joan. (1974). "The Structuring of Ethnicity." *Human Organization* 33, no. 4: 375–79.

Visweswaran, Kamala. (2001). "Is There a Structuralist Analysis of Racism? On Louis Dumont's Philosophy of Hierarchy." In *Race*, ed. Robert Bernasconi, 205–218. Oxford: Blackwell.

Vobejda, Barbara. (1998). "Hispanic Children Are Leading Edge of the U.S. Demographic Wave." *Washington Post*. Reprinted in *Buffalo News*, July 15, A-6.

Voegelin, Eric. (1940). "The Growth of the Race Idea." *Review of Politics* 2: 283–317.

Voltaire, François Marie Arouet de. (1965). *The Philosophy of History*. New York: Citadel.

Wagley, C., and M. Harris. (1958). *Minorities in the New World*. New York: Columbia University Press.

Wallman, S. (1986). "Ethnicity and the Boundary Process in Context." In *Theories of Race and Ethnic Relations*, ed. J. Rex and D. Mason, 296–313. Cambridge: Cambridge University Press.

————. (1978). "The Boundaries of Race: Processes of Ethnicity in England." *Man* 13: 200–217.

Walzer, Michael. (1997). "The Politics of Difference: Statehood and Toleration in a Multicultural World." In *The Morality of Nationalism*, ed. Robert McKim and Jeff McMahan, 245–57. Oxford: Oxford University Press.

————. (1995). "Pluralism: A Political Perspective." In *The Rights of Minority Cultures*, ed. Will Kymlicka, 139–54. Oxford: Oxford University Press.

————. (1993). "Comment." In *Multiculturalism and the "Politics of Recognition,"* ed. Amy Gutmann, 100–101. Princeton, NJ: Princeton University Press.

————. (1992). *What It Means to Be an American*. New York: Marsilio.

————. (1970). "The Obligations of Oppressed Minorities." In *Obligations: Essays on Disobedience, War, and Citizenship*, 46–73. Cambridge, MA: Harvard University Press.

Warren, Jonathan W., and F. W. Twine. (2002). "Critical Race Studies in Latin America: Recent Advances, Recurrent Weaknesses." In *A Companion to Race and Ethnicity*, ed. D. T. Goldberg and J. Solomos, 538–60. Oxford: Blackwell.

Wasserstrom, Richard A. (2001). "Racism and Sexism." In *Race and Racism*, ed. Bernard Boxill, 307–344. Oxford: Oxford University Press.

Waters, Mary C. (1990). *Ethnic Options: Choosing Identities in America*. Berkeley: University of California Press.

Weber, Max. (1997). "What Is an Ethnic Group?" In *The Ethnicity Reader: Nationalism, Multiculturalism and Migration*, ed. M. Guibernau and J. Rex, 15–26. Cambridge: Polity.

————. (1991). *From Max Weber: Essays in Sociology*. Ed. H. Gerth and Mills Wright. London: Routledge.

————. (1978). *Economy and Society*. Ed. G. Roth and C. Wittich. Berkeley: University of California Press.

————. (1969). *Methodological Essays*. New York: Free Press.

Weinberg, Julius. (1965). "The Concept of Relation." In *Abstraction, Relation, and Induction: Three Essays in the History of Thought*, 61–119. Madison: University of Wisconsin Press.

Weissman, David. (2000). *A Social Ontology*. New Haven: Yale University Press.

West, Cornel. (1993). *Race Matters*. Boston: Beacon.

————. (1982). *Prophecy Deliverance! An Afro-American Revolutionary Christianity*. Philadelphia: Westminster.

Weyr, Thomas. (1988). *Hispanic U.S.A.: Breaking the Melting Pot*. New York: Harper and Row.

Wieseltier, L. (1996). *Against Identity*. New York: William Drenttel.

Wieviorka, Michel. (2002). "The Development of Racism in Europe." In *A Companion to Race and Ethnicity*, ed. D. T. Goldberg and J. Solomos, 460–74. Oxford: Blackwell.

————. (1997). "Racism in Europe: Unity and Diversity." In *The Ethnicity Reader: Nationalism, Multiculturalism and Migration*, ed. M. Guibernau and J. Rex, 291–302. Cambridge: Polity.

Wilkins, David B. (1996). "Introduction: The Context of Race." In *Color Conscious: The Political Morality of Race*, ed. K. Anthony Appiah and Amy Gutmann, 3–29. Princeton, NJ: Princeton University Press.

———. (1993). "Two Paths to the Mountaintop? The Role of Legal Education in Shaping the Values of Black Corporate Lawyers." *Stanford Law Review* 45, no. 6 (July): 1981–2026.

Williams, Patricia J. (2001). "Of Race and Risk." In *Race, Class, and Gender: An Anthology*, ed. Margaret Andersen and Patricia Hill Collins, 106–108. Belmont, CA: Wadsworth.

Wills, Christopher. (1994). "The Skin We're In." *Discover* 15, no. 11 (November): 76–81.

Wilmer, Franke. (1997). "First Nations in the USA." In *The Ethnicity Reader: Nationalism, Multiculturalism and Migration*, ed. M. Guibernau and J. Rex, 185–201. Cambridge: Polity.

Wilson, William J. (1978). *The Declining Significance of Race*. Chicago: University of Chicago Press.

Wilterlink, N. (1993). "An Examination of European and National Identity." *Archives Européennes de Sociologie* 34: 119–36.

Wittgenstein, Ludwig. (1981). *Tractatus logico-philosophicus*. Trans. D. F. Pears and B. F. McGuinness. London: Routledge and Kegan Paul.

———. (1965). *Philosophical Investigations*. Trans. G. E. M. Anscombe. New York: Macmillan.

Wright, Crispin. (1993). *Realism, Meaning, and Truth*. 2nd ed. Oxford: Blackwell.

Wu, Frank. (2002). *Yellow: Race in America beyond Black and White*. New York: Basic.

Yamato, Gloria. (2001). "Something about the Subject Makes It Hard to Name." In *Race, Class, and Gender: An Anthology*, ed. Margaret Andersen and Patricia Hill Collins, 90–94. Belmont, CA: Wadsworth.

Young, C. (1983). "The Temple of Ethnicity." *World Politics* 35, no. 4: 652–62.

Young, Iris Marion. (2001). "Social Movements and the Politics of Difference." In *Race and Racism*, ed. Bernard Boxill, 383–421. Oxford: Oxford University Press.

———. (2000). "Structure, Difference, and Hispanic/Latino Claims of Justice." In *Hispanics/Latinos in the United States: Ethnicity, Race, and Rights*, ed. Jorge J. E. Gracia and Pablo De Greiff, 147–66. New York: Routledge.

———. (1997). "Asymmetrical Reciprocity: On Moral Respect, Wonder, and Enlarged Thought." In *Intersecting Voices: Dilemmas of Gender, Political Philosophy, and Policy*. Princeton, NJ: Princeton University Press.

———. (1995). "Together in Difference: Transforming the Logic of Group Political Conflict." In *The Rights of Minority Cultures*, ed. Will Kymlicka, 155–76. Oxford: Oxford University Press, 1995.

———. (1990). *Justice and the Politics of Difference*. Princeton, NJ: Princeton University Press.

Young, Robert J. C. (1995). *Colonial Desire: Hybridity in Theory, Culture and Race*. London: New York: Routledge.

Zack, Naomi. (2002). *Philosophy of Science and Race.* New York: Routledge.

———. (2001). "Race and Philosophic Meaning." In *Race and Racism*, ed. Bernard Boxill, 43–57. Oxford: Oxford University Press.

———. (1998). *Thinking about Race.* Belmont, CA: Wadsworth.

———, ed. (1997). *Race/Sex: Their Sameness, Difference, and Interplay.* New York: Routledge.

———. (1996). *Bachelors of Science: Seventeenth Century Identity Then and Now.* Philadelphia: Temple University Press.

———, ed. (1995). *American Mixed Race: The Culture of Microdiversity.* Lanham, MD: Rowman & Littlefield.

———. (1993). *Race and Mixed Race.* Philadelphia: Temple University Press.

Zaibert, Leonardo, and Elizabeth Millán-Zaibert. (2000). "Universalism, Particularism, and Group Rights: The Case of Hispanics." In *Hispanics/Latinos in the United States: Ethnicity, Race, and Rights*, ed. Jorge J. E. Gracia and Pablo De Greiff, 167–80. New York: Routledge.

INDEX